U0723507

藏源·藏缘

藏地行者手卷

TIBETAN SOURCES
& PREDESTINATION
WITH TIBET

A POCKET BOOK
FOR TRAVELERS IN
TIBETAN-INHABITED REGIONS

向红笳 著

朝華出版社
BLOSSOM PRESS

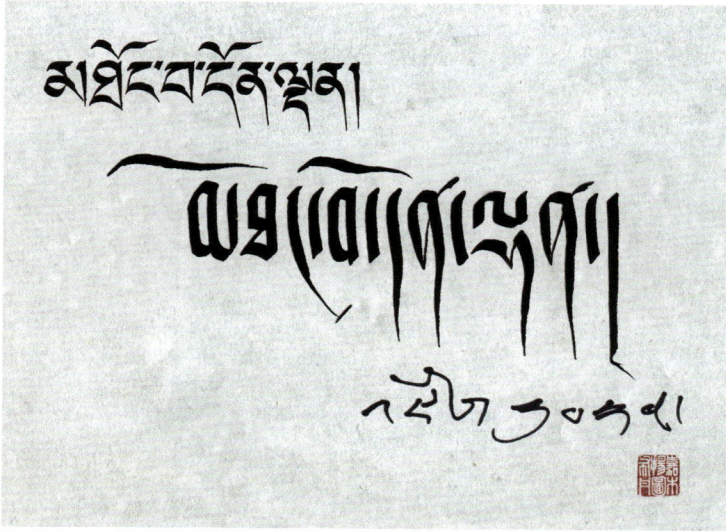

见即获益（藏文）

雍和宫嘉木样·图布丹大活佛题

Reading for Intelligence

Inscribed by Byams-dbyangs Thub-btsan Rin-po-che from Yonghe Lamasery.

藏源·藏缘

书名题签：韩书力

Title of the book inscribed by Han Shuli.

　　与"大家小书"相比，我认为这部小书应算是"小家小书"吧。我希望它能成为身体和灵魂乐游于广袤藏地的中外行者随身携带的"口袋书"，或是当今"闪读"一族的"随身读"。与我本人翻译并出版过的藏学学术专著相比，它更为浅显、易读、易懂，抓人眼球，因为，它以图文并茂的形式回答了一些既令人困惑又令人颇感兴趣的有关藏族、藏族文化和藏传佛教的问题。我深信，汉英对照的文本不仅能使外国读者，也能使从事藏学翻译的中国读者受益。我的初衷是让它成为一本大众读物，但我清楚地知道，我精选的任何一个条目都可能成为专家学者的学术论文和专著所论述的主题，因此，在条目的选择上，我采取了十分审慎的态度。我真诚地希望，准备踏上或已经踏上藏地之旅的人们在行前或途中可以不时地翻阅，以答疑解惑，真正做到一书在手，知彼知行。我更希望人们在藏地旅程中利用短暂的休憩之机或在繁忙的工作之余能心无旁骛地、静心惬意地享受这一读史、读神、读人的过程。

　　30余年从事藏学汉英互译的经验和实践给了我编写和翻译这样一本小书的信心和勇气，也使我能在条目选择和译文的精准把握上略有优势。实际上，编写和翻译这样一部贴近大众、满足大众需求的小书是我由来已久的愿望，特别是看到有人把"空行母"译成"空心母"，把"佛本生经"写成"佛本身经"，甚至把多闻天王手捧的"吐宝鼠鼬"译成"正在呕吐的大老鼠"等时，我的这一愿望就变得格外强烈。由于中外行者对藏地文化的兴趣与日俱增，我认为这样一本小书的出版恰逢其时。它以碎片化方式采集了260个条目，可粗略地分为神佛与器物、宗教与寺院、自然与地理、民俗与习惯、人文与人物五大部分，涉及藏地文化、历史、宗教、民俗、自然地理和人物等诸多方面。每一部分的具体条目均参照汉语拼音字母顺序和词条内容进行编排。在此，必须指出的是，由于篇幅所限，条目的选择更多是出于对知识性、趣味性和可读性的考量，因此无法做到面面俱到，难免有以偏概全、挂一漏万之处。

本书在编辑翻译过程中得到了一些朋友和家人的帮助及鼓励。中国国际出版集团朝华出版社对这一选题给予了极大的肯定和关注，出版社的编辑人员也为此付出了艰辛的努力。我的儿子沈晋在图文编辑方面助我一臂之力，南加博士在百忙之中抽出时间通读了全文并提出了一些中肯的意见和建议，严钟义先生等友人为本书提供了精美的照片。在洪涛先生的牵线搭桥下，我有幸得到了著名美术家韩书力先生特赐的墨宝。最值得一提的是北京雍和宫嘉木样·图布丹大活佛特为本书题了词。我衷心地希望读者如题词所言能在阅读中"见即获益"。

敬奉三宝，愿得吉祥！

向红笳

2016 年 5 月 28 日

In comparison with "little books written by great masters", I think, this book should be considered as "a little book written by a nobody". It is my hope that it will serve as a portable "pocketbook" for Chinese and foreign travelers to go on pleasant trips with their bodies and souls in a vast expanse of Tibet, or for present-day "Flashing read family" to read it at any time. It is more simple, readable, digestible and eye-catching than already published academic works on Tibetan studies that I have translated. For this book, by illustrating with vivid photos and words, answers some confusing and interesting questions related to Tibetan, Tibetan culture and Tibetan Buddhism. I am deeply convinced that both foreign travelers and Chinese readers engaged in Tibetological translation work will enjoy the benefit of such a Chinese-English version. I know clearly that each carefully chosen entry can be viewed as a subject by experts or scholars in their treatises or monographs. So, I did it in a very cautious way. My original intention is to make it a popular literature. I sincerely hope that those who get ready for their trips or already stay in Tibet can read it before or during their trips so as to find answers to their doubts. In that case, they will have a better understanding of the conditions there and their own doings. I hope that people can make full use of short rests during their trips in Tibet or their leisure time after work to enjoy the process of comprehending history, divinities and human beings single-mindedly and pleasantly.

I have been doing Chinese-English translation work on Tibetan studies for over thirty years and accumulated rich experience, which gave me not only confidence and encouragement in making such a book, but also an advantage in precise choice of entries and accurate translation. In fact, it is my cherished desire to do so. In particular, whenever I see some wrong translations, for example, "Hollow Goddess" for "Dakini", "Buddha's Own Texts" for "Jatakas", even "disgorging rat" for "jewel-disgoring mongoose" held by the Heavenly King of the North (Vaisramana), my desire will become much stronger. Nowadays, Chinese and foreign travelers' interest in Tibetan culture is increasing rapidly, so I believe that its publication is at the right time. This book contains 260 entries collected in a fragmented way, roughly divided into five parts (Deities and Attributes; Religions and Monasteries; Nature and Geography; Customs and Habits; Society and Humans). They involve Tibetan culture, history, religions, folk customs, nature, geography, personages and other aspects. It must be pointed out that due to space constraints, only informative, interesting and readable entries are under my consideration. Therefore, I cannot reach every aspect of a matter and avoid for one thing cited.

During this process, some friends and my family helped and encouraged me a lot. The Blossom Press of China International Publishing Group showed its great affirmation and concern for this selected topic, and its editors also made a hard effort for it. My son Shen Jin lent me a helping hand in editing illustrations and characters. Mr. Yan Zhongyi and other friends offered their beautiful photos. Dr. rNam-rgyal made a thorough reading of the full text in his busy time and proposed some pertinent ideas and suggestions. With the help of Mr. Hong Tao, I am fortunate to have received an exquisite calligraphy for its title written by Mr. Han Shuli, a well-known artist. It is worth mentioning that Byams-dbyangs Thub-btsan Rin-po-che from Yonghe Lamasery personally wrote an inscription for this book. It is earnestly hoped that as the inscription goes, readers can "read for intelligence" in their reading.

Worship the Three Jewels, willing to have good luck.

Xiang Hongjia
May 28, 2016

目录

Part 2 皈依之旅：宗教与寺院
Religions and Monasteries

Part 3　发现之旅：自然与地理
Nature and Geography

Part 4 | 徜徉之旅：民俗与习惯
Customs and Habits

Part 5 | 追寻之旅：人文与人物
Society and Humans

Part 1

朝圣之旅：神佛与器物
Deities and Attributes

布袋和尚

布袋和尚（？～916），名契比，五代后梁人。传说常以杖背一布袋入市，见物即乞，出语无定，随处寝卧，形如疯癫。他死前曾说一偈："弥勒真弥勒，化身千百亿，时时示时人，时人自不认。"在佛教寺院中常有他的形象，俗称"大肚子弥勒"。其坐像两侧常配有一副楹联，楹联上写道："大肚能容容天下难容之事，开口常笑笑世上可笑之人。"尽管身穿汉式僧袍，但在一些藏传佛教寺院中，他的造像也很常见，如在北京雍和宫大殿中就供奉着这样的一尊塑像。

Cloth-bag Monk

Cloth-bag Monk (? ~ 916) also named Qi Bi, was born in the Later Liang (907 ~ 923 A.D.). Tradition has it that he always carried a staff with a cloth bag suspended on it and went begging for everything. Just like an insane man, he spoke indefinitely and lay down freely, sleeping everywhere. Prior to his death, he left a Buddhist hymn. It says: "Maitreya, true Maitreya. Reborn innumerable times. From time to time manifested to men. The men of the age do not recognize you." His images often appear in Buddhist monasteries, popularly called "Big-bellied Maitreya". His seated statue is flanked by a couplet with the following inscriptions: "The big belly is capable to contain—it contains the things under Heaven which are difficult to contain. The broad face is inclined to laugh—to laugh at the laughable men on Earth." Though in Han-style monk's robe, he is often seen in some Tibetan monasteries, for example a statue of Cloth-bag Monk enshrined in a hall in Yonghe Lamasery in Beijing.

擦擦与擦擦模具

擦擦（藏文发音：Tsha-tsha）是一种刻有佛像或佛塔的小型脱模泥塑。根据制作者的不同亦可分为普通擦擦、懂擦（藏文：gDung-tsha）、骨擦（藏文：Rus-tsha）和恰擦（藏文：Phyag-tsha）等。高僧大德和活佛圆寂后，将其真身进行脱水处理并涂以香料，用脱出来的水泡制出的胶泥刻制的擦擦为"懂擦"。骨擦是用掺有人骨灰的胶泥制作的擦擦，而"恰擦"指的是佛教名家或高僧活佛亲手制作的擦擦。在制作过程中，常使用木质和铜质模具。

Tsha-tshas and Tsha-tsha Molds

Tsha-tsha in Tibetan refers to a kind of small-sized molded clay sculpture with engraved Buddha images or pagodas. According to different makers, they can be classified as follows: ordinary clay Tsha-tshas, body Tsha-tshas (Tib. gDung-tsha), bone Tsha-tshas (Tib. Rus-tsha) and hand Tsha-tshas (Tib. Phyag-tsha), etc. After eminent monks or Rin-po-ches passed away, their corpses should be dehydrated and then coated with spices. Afterwards, clay mixed with water from dehydrated corpses is used to make body Tsha-tshas. Bone Tsha-tshas are made of clay mixed with human bone ashes while hand Tsha-tshas are made by some famous Buddhist masters or eminent monks themselves. Wooden or copper molds are often used in the making process.

❑ 二十四塔擦擦
Tsha-tsha

大白伞盖佛母

　　大白伞盖佛母（都噶，藏文：gDugs-dkar），亦称"千头千手佛母"，是佛教密宗本尊之一。她有多种化相，有千手的、十臂的、六臂的及二臂的形像。常见的塑像色白，有三层或五层头，其身体四周无数的手臂形成一个很大的同心圆。同心圆的最外缘是一圈火焰，每只小臂又生一眼。大白伞盖佛母手持钩、剑、弓箭、金刚杵等法器。她的主臂左手持金刚杵，右手持一柄白伞盖。她脚下踩着的人、飞禽走兽及鱼鳖代表着受她庇佑的芸芸众生。

White Umbrella Goddess

　　White Umbrella Goddess (Tib. gDugs-dkar), also known as "One-thousand Headed and One thousand-handed Goddess", is one of the Yidams of Tantric Buddhism. She has many manifestations, including 1,000-handed statues and ten-, six- or two-armed ones. Usually, she is in white, and has three or five layers of heads. Numerous arms around her body form a large concentric circle. A circle of flames circles the outer ring, and each arm has an eye on it. She holds a hook, a sword, a bow, an arrow, a Vajra club and other ritual implements with her hands. She holds a Vajra club and a white umbrella with her left and right hands on her principal arms. Human beings, fowls and beasts, fish and turtles beneath her feet represent all sentient beings under her protection.

大黑天神

大黑天神（玛哈噶拉，梵文：Mahakala）原是婆罗门教湿婆（梵文：Shiva）的化身，也是古印度的一位战神。他最初仅是寺庙的护法神，后成为整个藏地的守护神。大黑天神像多为蓝身，多臂，面呈愤怒相。其主臂的左手持嘎巴拉碗，右手持金刚钺刀，双手交叉于胸前，代表智慧与慈悲的结合。

Great Black Deva

Great Black Deva (Skt. Mahakala) used to be an incarnation of Shiva of Brahmanism and also a war god in ancient India. At first, he was only a protective deity to guard monasteries and temples, and later on, he became a protective deity to defend the whole Tibetan-inhabited regions. He has a blue body and many arms, showing a very wrathful facial expression. He holds a skull-cup and a curved knife in his right and left hands on his principal arms, crossing his both hands in front of his chest, which implies the union of intelligence and compassion.

大红司命主

大红司命主亦称"姊妹护法"或"披铠甲护法"。司命神指的是掌管人类寿命的神。大红司命主又被视为大红大黑天神或战神。战神是藏传佛教中特有的五守舍神（乡土神、父族神、母族神、战神和生命神）之一，位于人的右肩之上，主要职能是佑护敬拜者不受外敌伤害。

□ 大红司命主
Red Master of Life

Red Master of Life

Red Master of Life are also known as "Sisters Protector" or "Dharmapala with a Suit of Armor". Deities of Life refer to deities who can control human's lifespan. Red Master of Life is also regarded as Red Mahakala or War god. War god is one of the unique Five Kinds of Deities (local deity, paternal deity, maternal deity, war god and life god) in Tibetan Buddhism. He stands on a person's right shoulder, and his duty is to bless and protect worshippers from injuries caused by foreign enemies.

大势至菩萨

大势至菩萨（梵文：Mahasthamaprapta）是西方极乐世界无上尊佛阿弥陀佛的右胁侍，他与阿弥陀佛及其左胁侍观音菩萨合称为"西方三圣"。在中国民间信仰中，大势至菩萨的影响远不如观音菩萨，也几乎没有单独供奉的。其法相和装饰与观音菩萨相同，差异在于大势至菩萨的肉髻（梵文：Usnisa）似红莲花，肉髻上有一宝冠，而观音菩萨头上宝冠有一化佛。

Powerful Vajrapani

Powerful Vajrapani (Skt. Mahasthamaprapta) is the Incomparable Buddha Amitabha's right attendant in the Western Paradise. Amitabha, Mahasthamaprapta and Avalokiteshvara (left attendant) are jointly known as "Trinity in the West". In Chinese folk beliefs, Mahasthamaprapta is far less influential than Avalokiteshvara, and its statue is almost not enshrined alone. Its image and adornments are identical with Avalokiteshvara's. The difference lies in the fact that Mahasthamaprapta has a red lotus-shaped topknot (Skt. Usnisa) with a crown on it while Avalokiteshvara Bodhisattva has a crown on his head with a statue of emanation Buddha on it.

大威德金刚

大威德金刚（阎魔德迦，梵文：Yamantaka）亦称"怖畏金刚"，格鲁派密宗所修本尊之一，因其能降伏恶魔，故称大威。又因其有护善之功，故又称大德。其塑像身青黑色，九面、三十四臂、十六足，以凶暴威猛之姿慑服一切障魔。

Great Dignity and Virtue

Great Dignity and Virtue (Skt. Yamantaka) is also known as "The Lord of Great Dignity and Virtue". He is one of the Yidams of dGe-lugs-pa Sect of Tantric Buddhism. He was given this title "great dignity and virtue" not only for his ability to subdue evil demons, but also for his protection of virtuous deeds. His sculpture has a dark blue body, nine faces, thirty-four arms and sixteen feet. He uses a powerful and ferocious posture to shock and subdue all obstructive demons.

□ 八瓣莲花大威德金刚镏金铜像
Great Dignity and Virtue in Gilt Bronze

地藏菩萨

地藏菩萨（梵文：Kshitigarbha）是中国佛教四大菩萨之一。他受释迦牟尼嘱托，在释迦牟尼寂灭后、未来佛弥勒诞生前的这段时间承担起超度众生的重任，让他们脱离苦海，不下地狱。地藏菩萨曾发过大愿："众生度尽，方证菩提；地狱未空，誓不成佛。"地藏菩萨多为身披袈裟的光头僧人形象。他一手持锡杖，一手持莲花或幡幢、宝珠等，并以狮状怪兽为其坐骑。安徽九华山是他的道场。

Bodhisattva Kshitigarbha

Bodhisattva Kshitigarbha is one of the four major Bodhisattvas in Chinese Buddhism. Exhorted by Sakyamuni, Bodhisattva Kshitigarbha took on heavy responsibilities to release souls of sentient beings from the hell in the period after Sakyamuni's death and before Maitreya's birth. In that case, they were able to get rid of this troublesome life and avoid going to hell. He once made a great vow: "Buddhahood is unable to be verified until all sentient beings get enlightened, I am not able to become a Buddha until the hell is empty". Normally, in an image of a bareheaded monk, he drapes a cassock, holds a Tantric staff and a lotus in both his hands and takes a lion-shaped monster as his mount. Mount Jiuhua in Anhui Province is his meditation site.

独髻佛母

独髻佛母（梵文：Ekajati）是班登拉姆（藏文：dPal-ldan-lha-mo）护法女神的化身，也是藏传佛教万神殿中的首席女护法神。她有多种形相，常见的塑像为青黑色身，一面二臂，三目双足。她体粗腹大，面带怒笑，以虎皮为裙。她的头发直竖，右手持钺刀，左手持盈血颅器。她的一面表示一切法聚慧体于一身，二臂代表二谛，怒笑的表情表示降伏鬼魔，钺刀表示斩断烦恼之根，盈血颅器表示舍离四分别。修持独髻佛母可增智慧，并能救度一切受苦受难之人。

Ekajati

As a female protective goddess, Ekajati is not only Goddess dPal-ldan-lha-mo's manifestation, but also the chief female Dharmapala in the pantheon of Tibetan Buddhism. She has many manifestations. Usually, she has a black body, one face, two arms, three eyes and two feet. With a sturdy body and a big belly, she has a bitter smile on her face and straight hair and wears a tiger-skin apron around her waist. She holds a curved knife and a skull-cup filled with blood with her right and left hands. One face indicates that Dharma and wisdom are in one body; two arms imply Two Truths; her bitter smile shows subduing evil spirits and demons; the curved knife embodies that it is able to cut off root of troubles and the skull-cup filled with blood represents the renunciation of Fourfold Illusion. Meditation on Ekajati enables people to increase wisdom and enlighten all people in sufferings.

度母女神

　　度母女神（卓玛，藏文：sGrol-ma）是藏传佛教中最重要的女性本尊神（梵文：Yidam），因救济诸难并将遇难之人送至彼岸得救度而得名。依身色、标帜、姿态不同分为二十一度母。在密宗佛教中，流传最广的是白度母（藏文：sGrol-dkar）和绿度母（藏文：sGrol-ljang）。而无量寿佛、白度母和尊胜佛母并称为"长寿三尊"。白度母身色雪白，一面、二臂、三眼，面相端庄祥和，手心和足心各有一眼，端坐于莲台上。绿度母传为观音菩萨的化身，身色翠绿，右手持乌巴拉花（梵文：Upala）结施愿印，象征施予众生无畏和慈悲。根据功能，救八难度母分指能救狮、象、火、蛇、贼、镣铐、水、非人所致八种灾难的救度度母。

Tara Goddess

　　Tara (Tib. sGrol-ma)is the most important feminine tutelary deity (Skt. Yidam) in Tibetan Buddhism. She is given such a name for her ability to protect people from dangers and send them to the other shore. In terms of bodily colors, hand-attributes and postures, Tara goddesses can be classified into Twenty-one Taras. White Tara (Tib. sGrol-dkar) and Green Tara (Tib. sGrol-ljang) are the most popular ones in Tantric Buddhism. Moreover, Amitayus, White Tara and Goddess of Dignity are jointly called "Trinity of Longevity". White Tara has a snow white body, one face, two arms, three eyes and an elegant and peaceful facial appearance. With eyes on both her palms and soles, she sits on a lotuspedestal. Green Tara is seen as Avalokiteshvara Bodhisattva's manifestation. With a bluish green body, Green Tara holds a blue lotus (Skt. Upala) in her right hand, giving a vow-fulfilling gesture, which symbolizes her ability to give fearlessness and compassion to all sentient beings. In light of their functions, Taras Protecting from Eight Dangers show their abilities to protect people from dangers caused by lions, elephants, fire, snakes, thieves, fetters, water and non-human beings.

□ 度母像壁画
Tara Goddess Mural

阿弥陀佛

阿弥陀佛（梵文：Amitabha）亦称"无量光佛"或"无量光如来"，因能接引芸芸众生往生"西方净土"，故亦称"接引佛"。在过去久远劫时，他曾立大愿，建立西方净土，广度无边众生，成就庄严功德，因而受到大乘佛教广大信众的崇敬。在造像艺术中，他右手下垂，掌心向前结施愿印，左手持莲花，结施予印。在密教中，阿弥陀佛象征大日如来的妙观察智，名为"甘露王"。阿弥陀佛共有13个名号，"无量寿佛"就是其中一个名号。

Amitabha

Amitabha is also known as "Lord of Boundless Light" or "Buddha of Unlimited Light". He can lead all sentient beings to be reborn in the Pure Land, so he is also called "Leading Buddha". In the past aeons (Skt. Kalpa), he made great vows to establish the Pure Land, make great efforts to enlighten all sentient beings and achieve solemn merits and virtues. Therefore, he is broadly adored by adherents of the Greater Vehicle of Buddhism. In sculptural art, he hangs down his right hand with his palm forwards, giving a vow-fulfilling gesture, and in the meanwhile, he holds a lotus with his left hand, also giving a boon-granting gesture. In Tantric Buddhism, Amitabha symbolizes Vairocana's discrimination wisdom, so he is also called "Dew King". He enjoys thirteen titles, and Amitayus is one of them.

法轮

　　法轮意指佛教的真理之轮。释迦年尼成道后，到鹿野苑首次说法，宣讲四谛、八正道等原始佛教的基本教义。他的第一次说法被称作"初转法轮"。法轮转起可使众生得以解脱。法轮也被视为一种法器，象征佛法永生不灭。轮上的八条轮辐，代表着佛陀的"八正道"。

Wheel of Dharma

　　Wheel of Dharma (Skt. Dharmachakra) refers to the wheel of truth in Buddhism. After Sakyamuni's enlightenment, he gave his first sermon in the Deer Park, expounding Four Truths, Eightfold Noble Path and other basic primitive Buddhist doctrines. His first sermon is called "setting in motion of Wheel of Dharma". The turning of Wheel of Dharma enables all sentient beings to get liberated. Wheel of Dharma is also regarded as a ritual implement, symbolizing the eternality of Dharma. Eight spokes on it represent Buddha's "Eightfold Noble Path".

佛龛

佛龛亦称"莲龛",是专门供奉佛像、神位等的小阁子,除用紫檀木、楠木等珍稀木材外,还有用金、银等金属制成,有些龛上还镶嵌着红蓝宝石、绿松石、珊瑚和蜜蜡等装饰物。龛的式样可分为宫殿式、楼阁式、亭式和各种塔式。在现今各大佛教遗迹中,中国河南的龙门石窟、山西的云冈石窟等就是神龛式。佛龛的装饰题材除了常见的龙外,还有藏传佛教的"八宝"及各种

□ 镏金铜佛龛
Niches in Gilt Bronze

传统祥瑞之物,如大象、蝙蝠、桃子、葫芦、缠枝牡丹,寓意为吉祥、多福、长寿、福禄、富贵。装饰性花纹包括八宝、卷云、如意云、流云、花卉等。

Niches

Niches, also known as "lotus-shaped niches", are a kind of check especially used to enshrine Buddha statues and memorial tablets. In addition to rosewood, purple Nanmu and other rare wood niches, some niches are made of gold, silver and other metals, and some are inlaid with red sapphire, turquoise, coral, beeswax and other decorations. They can be classified into palace, building and pavilion styles as well as pagoda styles of all sorts. For example, in today's major Buddhist sites, grottos in Longmen in Henan and Yungang in Shanxi of China are all in niche style. Apart from dragon patterns, there are other decorative thematic patterns on them, including Tibetan Buddhist Eight Auspicious Signs and other traditional auspicious items (elephant, bat, peach, gourd, peony with entwined branches), which imply auspiciousness, happiness, longevity, wealth and honor. Decorative patterns include Eight Auspicious Signs, rolled clouds, wishful clouds, floating clouds and flowers.

佛旗

　　佛教旗帜分为六色，是佛陀圣体之光。佛陀于公元前 588 年在印度菩提迦耶菩提树下修成正等正觉时，圣体即放光明，而后，在其一生随意大放光明，以六色光体化导众生。六色分为蓝、黄、红、白、橙及以上五色合为的一色，即第六色。

Buddhist Flag

　　Buddhist flag has six colors, which represent lights of Buddha's holy body. At a time when Buddha attained full enlightenment under a Bodhi tree in Bodhgaya of India in 588 B.C., his holy body immediately emitted lights. Henceforth, he optionally gave out lights in the rest of his life and made use of six colored illuminating bodies to enlighten all sentient beings. Six colors include blue, yellow, red, white, orange and the color mixed with the five colors mentioned above.

佛舍利

佛舍利（梵文：Sarira），亦称"舍利子"，意为尸体或身骨。最初是指释迦牟尼遗体火化后出现的结晶状珠体，后来也指德行比较高的僧人死后烧剩的骨头。据说分为白色骨舍利、黑色发舍利和赤色肉舍利三种。又有全身舍利（全身埋葬的遗骨）和碎身舍利（火葬的遗骨）的区别，以及佛指、佛牙、佛发等舍利的说法。

Buddhist Relics

Buddhist relics (Skt. Sarira), also known as "holy relics", refer to corpses or bodily bones. Originally, they were crystallized beads which appeared after Sakyamuni's body was cremated. Later on, they also included bones of monks with great virtues after cremation. It is said that Buddhist relics can be classified into white bone relics, black hair relics and red flesh relics. There is a difference between "whole body relics" (osseous remains from whole body buried) and "broken body relics" (osseous remains after cremation). There are also some sayings about Buddha's fingers, teeth, hair relics and others.

佛祖释迦牟尼

佛祖释迦牟尼（梵文：Sakyamuni）原名乔达摩·悉达多（梵文：Siddhārtha Gautama）。"释迦牟尼"原意为释迦族出身的圣者，他是古印度著名的思想家和佛教创始人。释迦牟尼出生在今尼泊尔南部的蓝毗尼。幼年时他曾接受过传统的婆罗门教育，后有感于人生之生、老、病、死带来的各种痛苦，舍弃王族身份，出家修道，被后世尊为"佛陀"（Buddha，意为"觉者"）。根据佛经的说法，释迦牟尼像应有三十二大相和八十种好。

Buddha Sakyamuni

Buddha Sakyamuni was originally called "Siddhārtha Gautama". "Sakyamuni" originally meant "sage from Sakya Family". He is a well-known ancient Indian thinker and founder of Buddhism. He was born in current Lumbini in south of Nepal. In his childhood, he received traditional Brahman education, and later on, he felt various sufferings of life caused by birth, old age, sickness and death. As a result, he abandoned his royal family and became a monk. He was revered as "Buddha" ("The Awakened"). According to Buddhist texts, Buddha Sakyamuni statue should have thirty-two signs and eighty major marks.

嘎巴拉碗

　　嘎巴拉碗（梵文：Kapala）亦称"内供颅器"，是密宗佛教中常用的一种法器，意为"护乐"，是大悲和空性的象征。它是根据高僧大德生前遗嘱从其遗体上取下的头盖骨制成。人们认为带有六条纹路的颅骨十分异常，只能在某些神秘仪式上使用。嘎巴拉碗是众多金刚乘神灵的供器、碗具或祭祀用碗。瑜伽师、大成就者、空行母、本尊神和护法神的左手都持有嘎巴拉碗，碗内盛有甘露、酒、多玛供品等。神灵通常用"智慧"左手将嘎巴拉碗捧至胸前，与之相配的"方法"右手持有金刚杵或钺刀之类的器物。许多怒相护法神和本尊神都握有一把钺刀，置于胸前嘎巴拉碗上方，象征着他们的"方法"和"智慧"的结合。作为温相神或略带怒相之神的器物，嘎巴拉碗也可被看作一个"大海螺"，内盈甘露、水果、药品、食物、珠宝，或一个盈满甘露的长寿瓶。

　　嘎巴拉碗
　　Skull-cup

Skull-cups

Skull-cup (Skt. Kapala), also known as "inner offering skull-cup", is a ritual implement used in Tantric Buddhism. With a meaning of "preservation of bliss", it is a symbol of great compassion and emptiness. They are made of eminent monks or virtuous men's skulls according to their testaments left prior to their deaths. It is believed that skulls with six fissures are very unique, so they can only be used in certain mysterious rites. Skull-cups serve as offering, eating or libation bowls for a large number of Vajrayana deities. Yogis, Siddhas, Dakinis, Yidams and protective deities usually hold skull-cups with their left hands. A skull-cup usually contains the following substances: vital nectar, alcohol, ritual cakes (Tib. gTor-ma), etc. Usually, a deity holds a skull-cup with his left "wisdom" hand frequently against his chest, probably paired with a Vajra club or a curved knife in his right "method" hand. Many wrathful protective deities and Yidams hold curved knives above skull-cups against their chests, symbolizing the union of "method" and "wisdom". As peaceful or slightly wrathful deities' attributes, skull-cups are probably identical with large conches full of nectar, fruit, medicines, food and jewels or nectar-filled longevity vases.

观音菩萨

　　佛教徒把观音菩萨（梵文：Avalokiteshvara）视为救苦救难之神。通常，观音菩萨既可呈男相亦可呈女相。唐代以前以男相居多，后来的观音像越来越趋向于女性化，其相貌端庄慈祥，经常手持净瓶杨柳。她具有无量的智慧和神通，大慈大悲，普救人间灾难。观音菩萨有三十三种化身，其中包括杨柳观音、白衣观音、鱼篮观音、水月观音、马郎妇观音和洒水观音等，民间常见的有千手千眼观音、送子观音、四臂观音和十一面观音等。值得注意的是，供奉观音像的神桌应正对大门，而且不应将观音像与祖先牌位平排摆放。

Avalokiteshvara Bodhisattva

　　Buddhist adherents view Goddess of Mercy (Skt. Avalokiteshvara Bodhisattva) as a deity who can help people in sufferings and disasters. Usually, Avalokiteshvara Bodhisattva takes on both masculine and feminine appearance. Before the Tang Dynasty, masculine appearance was in great majority. Afterwards, statues of Avalokiteshvara Bodhisattva gradually tended to take on feminine appearance. With a dignified and kind facial expression, she frequently holds a bottle of pure water with a willow wand in it. With immeasurable wisdom, supernatural power and great compassion, she is able to save all people from disasters on earth. She has thirty-three manifestations, including Avalokiteshvara Carrying a Willow Wand, White-robed Avalokiteshvara, Avalokiteshvara Carrying a Fish-creel, Avalokiteshvara Gazing at the Moon over the Water, Avalokiteshvara in the Form of an Ordinary Woman and Avalokiteshvara Pouring Water from a Bottle of Pure Water, etc. In civil, Thousand-armed and Thousand-eyed Avalokiteshvara, Baby-giving Avalokiteshvara, Four-armed Avalokiteshvara and Eleven-faced Avalokiteshvara are very common. It is worth noting that Avalokiteshvara statue's pedestal is expected to face the main entrance, and the statue is not allowed to line up with ancestors' tablets.

□ 白檀香木观音菩萨像
Avalokiteshvara Bodhisattva in White Sandalwood

哼哈二将

哼哈二将是佛教寺院门神的俗称，是执金刚神的一种，常立于寺庙的内门。在明代小说《封神演义》中，哼哈二将形象威武凶猛，一位是鼻哼白气制敌的郑伦，另一位是能口哈黄气擒将的陈奇。他们呈金刚力士状，双眼圆睁，鼓鼻，裸露上身，体魄强健，手持兵器，神态威严，怒视凡间。

Two Wrathful Gigantic Guardians

Two Wrathful Gigantic Guardians are popular names of door-gods in Buddhist monasteries. As a kind of Vajra-holding deities, they often stand in interior doors of a monastery. In *General Summaries of Investiture of the Gods*, a novel of the Ming Dynasty, they are mighty and ferocious in image. One is Zheng Lun who can subdue the enemy by blowing out white vapor from his nostrils. The other is Chen Qi who can arrest generals by breathing out yellow vapor from his mouth. Just like Vajra warriors, they have open-wide eyes, protruding noses and exposed upper bodies, looking physically strong. They hold weapons with their hands and angrily look down the earth with awful facial expressions.

三世佛

佛教中的三世佛指的是过去佛、现在佛、未来佛。三世佛常有横三世佛和竖三世佛之分。所谓"横三世佛"是以空间为排列顺序，而"竖三世佛"则是以时间为排列顺序。横三世佛有多种排列形式：一种是释迦牟尼居中，两侧为文殊菩萨（右）和普贤菩萨（左）；一种是西方极乐世界的阿弥陀佛居中，两侧为观音菩萨和大势至菩萨；还有一种是东方净琉璃世界的药师佛居中，两侧为月光菩萨和日光菩萨。竖三世佛为释迦牟尼佛居中，两侧为燃灯佛（左）和弥勒佛（右）。藏传佛教寺院中专门供奉三世佛的殿堂称作三佛殿。

Trinity of Buddhas

Trinity of Buddhas refers to the Past, the Present and the Future Buddhas. It can be classified into Horizontal Trinity of Buddhas and Vertical Trinity of Buddhas which are sorted respectively in light of space and time. Horizontal Trinity of Buddhas has many groups. Group One: Sakyamuni (central) with Manjusri Bodhisattva (right) and Samantabhadra Bodhisattva (left); Group Two: Amitabha from the Paradise (central) with Avalokiteshvara Bodhisattva and Mahasthamaprapta Bodhisattva on both his sides. Group Three: Medicine Buddha Bhaisajyaguru from the Eastern Lapis Lazuli World (central) with Moonlight Bodhisattva and Sunlight Bodhisattva. Vertical Trinity of Buddhas is arranged as follows: Sakyamuni (central) with Buddha of Fixed Light (left) and Maitreya (right). In Tibetan Buddhist monasteries, grand halls dedicated to enshrine statues of Trinity of Buddhas are called Halls of Trinity of Buddhas.

未来佛赤金像
Buddha Maitreya in Pure Gold

护身佛盒

护身佛盒（嘎乌，藏文：Gavu）指的是盛放护身佛像的盒子。盒内有小型佛像、印有经文的绸布片、舍利或甘露丸，还有高僧念经加持过的药丸与活佛的头发及衣服碎片等。男子多用方形护身佛盒，女子多用圆形护身佛盒，外出时护身佛盒常挂在颈上，垂于胸前。置于家中时，须将其供奉于神龛上。护身佛盒分有金、铜、银三种，银制护身佛盒最为常见。

Amulet Boxes

Amulet boxes (Tib. Gavu) refer to small boxes used to lay aside statues of protective deities. Boxes contain small-sized Buddha statues, silk films with printed Buddhist texts, relics or nectar pills, medicine pills empowered by eminent monks through chanting texts as well as Rin-po-ches' hair and pieces of clothes. Men and women respectively wear square and round amulet boxes. When going out, people usually hang amulet boxes around their necks in their chests, and when at home, they should place them over niches. There are gold, silver and copper amulet boxes, and silver ones are very common.

吉祥天母与五大神器

　　吉祥天母（班登拉姆，藏文：dPal-ldan-lha-mo）是八佛母之一，也是众神之首和众佛之母。据说她能给人以智慧和幸福。她也是密教的护法神，怒相吉祥天母像结火焰状发髻，中间饰有半月，头戴骷髅冠，怒目圆睁，口衔活人，貌相凶神恶煞，令人生畏。她右手持金刚杵，左手托着嘎巴拉碗，骑跨在一头四眼骡的背上，骡脚下是一片火海。吉祥天母有五种神器，分别是疾病种子袋、红咒语包、黑白骰子、魔线球和拘鬼牌。前四种挂在其装饰在骡鞍上的小毒蛇身上，后一种别在其腰部的蛇皮带上。

Auspicious Goddess and Five Magical Weapons

Auspicious Goddess (Tib. dPal-ldan-lha-mo) is not only one of the eight mothers of Buddha, but also the chief of deities and the mother of Buddhas. It is said that she can bring people wisdom and happiness. As a protective deity in Tantric Buddhism, wrathful dPal-ldan-lha-mo statue has a flame-like topknot with a half-moon-shaped adornment decorated on it. With a skull-crown on her head, she angrily opens her eyes wide and holds a living person in the mouth, looking very malicious and forbidding. With a Vajra club and a skull-cup in her right and left hands, she rides a four-eyed mule with a sea of flame under its feet. She has five magical weapons, including bag of diseases, bundle of red curses, white and black spotted dice, ball of thread and demon cross-stick. The first four magical weapons are hung on small poisonous serpents that adorn the saddle of her mule, while the fifth is tucked into the serpent girdle around her waist.

金翅鸟和琼鸟

金翅鸟（格鲁达，梵文：Garuda）亦称"大鹏鸟"或"妙翅鸟"，其形象经常出现在佛像背屏上。其形象常为长有喷焰双角的鸟，双角间有一块如意宝。其喙叼着一条蛇，象征着对龙众（梵文：Naga）的辖制。或者身为红色，三只眼，上身如人，下身似鸟，双翅锋利如钢剑，其手上扬结期克印（梵文：Tarjani），立于白狮之上。藏族神话中经常提到的琼鸟（藏文：Khyung）类似于金翅鸟，是鹰一样的神圣化身，象征着对不同非人生灵消极活动的控制。

Garuda and Khyung Birds

Garuda is known as "mythological bird" or "gold feathered sun-bird". Its image often appears on a back rest behind a Buddha statue. Its image is often represented with two flaming horns with a wish-fulfilling gem between them. It holds a snake with its beak, which symbolizes the dominion over Naga; or it is in red, and has three eyes and a human body (upper part) and a bird body (lower part). Its two wings are as sharp as swords. It raises its hand, giving a threatening gesture (Skt. Tarjani) and standing on a white lion. Khyung bird often mentioned in Tibetan myths is similar to it. As the holy embodiment of an eagle, it symbolizes the control over negative activities conducted by all sorts of non-human beings.

金刚杵

金刚杵（梵文：Vajra）是古代印度的一种武器，坚固无比，能打碎任何东西，故冠以金刚之名。在密教中，它象征摧破烦恼的菩提心（梵文：Bodhicitta）。金刚杵是金刚乘佛教坚不可摧的典型象征。"金刚"二字既是金刚杵的名称，也是一群以金刚冠名的神灵、器物和力士的称号或前缀。佛教的金刚杵象征着绝对现实的难以捉摸、不会毁灭、不可撼动、不可改变、无形和坚不可摧毁的状态，即佛性的圆满。善相神右手持金色金刚杵，其五股股叉并拢，象征着神灵的方法或"方便"。怒相神右手所持的金刚杵经常画成铁的深蓝色，其股叉如对称的三股叉那样张开。金刚杵股叉数量不同代表着不同的含义。

Vajra Club

As a kind of extremely solid weapon in ancient India, Vajra clubs are able to break everything, so named "diamond club". In Tantric Buddhism, it symbolizes mind of enlightenment (Skt. Bodhicitta), which is able to smash emotional troubles. As a typical sign, it displays a typical feature of indestructible nature of Vajrayana Buddhism. "Vajra" not only serves as a Vajra club's title, but also refers to a group of deities' titles or prefixes as well as attributes or warriors in the name of Vajra. In Buddhism, it also symbolizes the impenetrable, imperishable, immovable, immutable, indivisible and indestructible state of absolute reality, that is, the enlightenment of Buddhahood. Peaceful deities hold golden five-pointed prong-closed Vajra clubs in their right hands, which symbolizes the perfection of deities' method. Vajra club held by a wrathful deity with his right hand is often painted the dark blue of iron and its prongs symmetrically open, just like pairs of tridents. Vajra clubs with different prongs mean differently.

金刚亥母

金刚亥母（梵文：Vajravarahi）是藏传佛教密宗的本尊神之一，也是噶举派修密宗时的主要本尊。其塑像分单身像和双身像两类。金刚亥母像宛如 16 岁妙龄女，一面两臂，头现猪形，全身发出红光。她右手持金刚钺刀，左手持盈血嘎巴拉碗，左肩斜倚着一根天杖。她头戴五骷髅冠，三目圆睁，獠牙紧咬下唇，颈部挂有一串五十人头骨饰项链，项链上装饰着小铃铛

□ 金刚亥母壁画
Thunderbolt Sow Mural

和花朵。她的右足悬空，左足踩在莲花座上的一具人尸上，身后有般若烈焰。作为胜乐金刚的明妃，其塑像常为与胜乐金刚呈相拥之状。

Thunderbolt Sow

Thunderbolt Sow (Skt. Vajravarahi) is not only one of the Yidams in Tantric Buddhism, but also the principal goddess of bKav-brgyud-pa Sect in religious practices. Her sculptures can be classified into single form or in a sexual form. Just like a sixteen-year-old maiden, she has one face and two arms. Her head is shaped like a sow head and her whole body emits red light. She holds a curved knife and a skull-cup full of blood with her right and left hands. Her left shoulder leans against a monk's staff. She wears a crown with five skulls, opens wide her three eyes and tightly grips her lower lip with her tusks. She wears a fifty-skull necklace adorned with small bells and flowers around her neck. She suspends her right leg in midair and places her left one on a corpse lying on the lotus-pedeotal. Behind her are roaring flames of wisdom. As Samvara's consort, she is often sculpted to be embraced by Samvara in a sexual form.

金刚橛

三棱金刚橛（梵文：Kila）主要象征怒相神金刚橛神（梵文：Vajrakilaya）强力无比的佛性。作为礼器的金刚橛通常是铁制的，但在某些仪式中也使用特殊的木料或骨料制成的金刚橛。铁制金刚橛的深蓝色象征着陨铁般无坚不摧的金刚特质。金刚橛顶部通常有三个怒相神头作为头饰，要分别画成白、蓝、红三色，象征着贪、嗔、痴三毒。作为手持器物，由于体积相对小巧，在藏族绘画作品中，金刚橛的形式更为简洁。在彩绘木制金刚橛组结上或八角形橛杆的杆面上常绘制金翅鸟、老虎和狮子这样的"图腾动物"和金刚杵、法轮这样的武器。金刚橛是藏传佛教宁玛派传承大师或伏藏师常用的器物。

Ritual Dagger

The triple-bladed ritual dagger (Skt. Kila) essentially symbolizes the powerful Buddha-nature of wrathful deity Vajrakilaya. As ritual daggers, they are usually made of iron, but those made of special woods or bones are also used in certain rituals. The color of iron ritual dagger is a symbol of its meteoric or indestructible Vajra-nature. It is usually topped with heads of three wrathful deities, and their colors of white, blue and red represent destruction of lust, hatred and delusion. As hand-attributes, they are often depicted in Tibetan paintings in a more simplified form because of their small size. Painted wooden ritual daggers are often depicted with such "totem animals" as Garudas, tigers and lions as well as Vajra clubs, chakras (wheel) and other weapons on their knots and shaft's octagonal faces. Lineage masters or treasure-finders of rNying-ma-pa Sect often hold such ritual daggers with their hands.

□ 镏金铜金刚橛
Ritual Dagger
in Gilt Bronze

金刚铃 / 杵

金刚杵和金刚铃是密教的常用法器，分别代表方便和智慧。通常，瑜伽师左手持铃，右手持杵，瑜伽母右手持铃，左手持杵。摇动金刚铃有督励众生精进修持、召集金刚众神之意。金刚杵表示破除愚痴妄想与外道魔障。金刚铃 / 杵既不能任意使用，也不能随意悬挂和摆放。

Vajra Bells and Clubs

As common ritual implements in Tantric Buddhism, Vajra bells and clubs are respectively representative of method and wisdom. Usually, Yogi holds a Vajra bell and a Vajra club with his left and right hands while Yogini has a Vajra bell and a Vajra club in her right and left ones. Shaking Vajra bells means to encourage all sentient beings to make diligent efforts in Buddhist practices and to call together Vajra deities. Vajra clubs signify to get rid of ignorance, illusion, non-Buddhists and evil spirits. Vajra bells and Vajra clubs are neither used arbitrarily, nor suspended or placed casually.

□ 金刚铃 / 杵
Vajra Bell and Club

金刚手菩萨

金刚手菩萨（梵文：Vajrapani）是一位威力无比的神，因手持金刚杵，故而又称为"执金刚神"（梵文：Vajradhara），因其身、口、意速疾，隐秘难知，因此又名"密迹金刚"（梵文：Guhyapādavajra）。密迹金刚只有一位，但在寺院三门殿内的两侧常常各有一尊金刚像。他们头戴宝冠，袒露上身，手持金刚杵，呈愤怒相。

Vajrapani Bodhisattva

Vajrapani is an extremely powerful deity. He holds a Vajra club with his hand, so he is also known as "Vajra club-holder" (Skt. Vajradhara). He moves and speaks very quickly and has a nimble mind, so he is given the name of "Secret Vajra Deity" (Skt. Guhyapādavajra). There is only one Vajrapani, however, his two statues stand on both sides of the hall with three-doors in a monastery. They wear crowns on their heads, expose their chests and hold Vajra clubs with their hands, looking wrathfully.

空行与空行母

空行分为业力空行和智慧空行。男性称作"空行勇士",女性称作"空行母"(堪卓玛,藏文:mKhav-vgro-ma;梵文:Dakini)。空行母十分常见,如狮面、虎面或熊面空行母。有的造型十分独特:单腿直立,脚下踩着外道徒,头戴五骷髅冠,手持嘎巴拉碗和钺刀。在藏传佛教中,她是代表智慧和力量的飞行女神。

Sky-goers and Female Sky-goers

Sky-goers can be classified into Karma and wisdom sky-goers. Male and female sky-goers are respectively called "celestial warriors" and "female celestial goers" (Tib. mKhav-vgro-ma;Skt. Dakini). Female sky-goers are very common, such as lion-faced, tiger-faced or bear-faced female sky-goers. In a very unique modeling, she stands with her single leg and tramples a few non-Buddhists under her feet. She wears a crown with five skulls, holding a skull-cup and a curved knife in her both hands. In Tibetan Buddhism, she is a flying goddess representative of wisdom and strength.

空行母合金像
Female Sky-goer in Alloy

莲花座与师子座

　　佛座指的是安放佛像和佛教高僧说法时所坐的台座，最为尊贵的宝座由八头狮子昇举。据传释迦牟尼和观音菩萨均喜爱莲花，并以莲花为座，因此，所有寺院里的佛像都是以莲花为宝座，称为莲花座。莲花座的莲瓣分有四层，每个莲瓣的边缘均用白、红、白三条曲线勾勒。莲花座一般呈六角形，下部为呈束腰状的须弥座，莲花部分分仰莲式与俯莲式两种。师子座亦称"狮子座"或"狮子宝座"，原指释迦牟尼的座席，后泛指寺院中摆放佛像和菩萨像的台座。

Lotus Throne and Buddha's Seat

　　Buddhist thrones refer to Buddha statues' pedestals or Buddhist eminent monks' thrones used in preaching Buddhist doctrines. The most honorable throne is lifted up by eight lions. As it is said, Sakyamuni and Avalokiteshvara Bodhisattva were very fond of lotuses and took them as their seats. Such a lotus throne has four layers, and each lotus petal is edged with white, red and white curves. Usually it is shaped like a hexagon, and a funnel-shaped Sumeru seat is its lower part. Lotus petals are respectively upward-lotus style and downward-lotus style. "Buddha's Seat", also known as "Lion Throne", originally referred to Sakyamuni's throne, and later on, it means in general pedestals dedicated to arrange statues of Buddhas and Bodhisattvas.

六灵捧座与六异座

人们常常可以在佛像的木雕或铜铸背屏上看到由祥云卷草和六种动物组成的精美"六灵捧座"图。六灵为金翅鸟、龙女、神鲸、孩童、祥麟、巨象，分别象征着慈悲、护佑、救度、资福、自在和善施。六异座是供奉佛像的宝座，座基上有狮子、大象、宝马、孔雀、共命鸟和力士，被称作"异座六力"。

Six Spirit Decorative Patterns and Throne with Six Creatures

People often see exquisite "Six Spirit Decorative Patterns" on wooden or copper backrests of Buddha statues. It is composed of auspicious clouds, rolled grass and six creatures, including Garuda, Dragon King's daughter, divine whale, child, kylin, and giant elephant. They respectively symbolize compassion, blessing, salvation, merit accumulation, relaxation and virtuous beneficence. "Throne with Six Creatures" refers to a kind of throne for people to lay out Buddha statues. Its base has a lion, an elephant, an excellent horse, a peacock, a jivam-jivaka bird and an athlete, who are called "Six Creatures on Throne".

六牙白象

　　六牙白象亦称"六肢白象"，象征释迦牟尼入胎。据说，释迦牟尼的母亲摩耶夫人梦见六牙白象入其胎中，因而怀孕，产下释迦牟尼。除了六牙白象外，还有四牙白象，据说它是普贤菩萨的坐骑。

Six-toothed White Elephant

　　Six-toothed White Elephant, also known as "Six-trunked White Elephant", symbolizes Sakyamuni's entry into a womb. It is said that his mother Mahamaya saw a six-toothed white elephant entering her womb in her dream. As a result, she got pregnant and gave birth to Sakyamuni. In addition to six-toothed white elephants, there are four-toothed ones. Allegedly, it is Bodhisattva Samantabhadra's mount.

嘛呢轮和转经筒

嘛呢轮和转经筒指的是一种带有纵轴的圆筒，根据体积大小分而称之。它们的表面刻有六字真言"唵、嘛、呢、叭、咪、吽"及其他图案，圆筒内常常存有经文。每转动一次嘛呢轮或转经筒就相当于诵念经文一次。嘛呢轮分为手摇和指捻两类。转经筒分为风力、手动和水转等类，它们通常矗立在寺院广场上、转经路上、水边或回廊里。

Mani Wheels and Prayer-wheels

Mani wheel or prayer-wheel refers to a kind of cylinder with a vertical axis inside. According to different sizes, they are given different names. Six Sacred Words (Om Mani Padme Hum) and other patterns are inscribed on their surfaces, and some Buddhist texts are kept in their interiors. Turning Mani wheel or prayer-wheel once resembles chanting Buddhist texts once. Mani wheels can be classified into two kinds: whirled by hand and twisted by fingers. And prayer-wheels have three kinds: whirled by wind, by hand or by water. Usually, they are erected on squares in front of monasteries or on circumambulation roads and riversides or in winding corridors.

□ 转经筒
Prayer-wheel

马头观音

　　马头观音（梵文：Hayagrivaavalokiteshvara）是六观音之一，因以马头置于头顶而得名。马头观音是六道畜生道中的护法明王。马头观音相貌愤怒威猛，通体赤红，三面八臂，三目圆睁，獠牙外露，头发和胡须直立，呈红黄两色。马头观音的三面表示空灵悟性，八臂表示智悲双运，圆睁的三目表示降伏三界恶魔，外露的獠牙表示震慑障魔。

Horse-headed Avalokiteshvara

As one of the Six Avalokiteshvara Bodhisattvas, Horse-headed Avalokiteshvara (Skt. Hayagrivaavalokiteshvara) is given the name because a there is horse head on the top of his head. He is a protective Diamond-king in the Realm of Animals, one of the Six Kinds of Existence. With a wrathful and powerful facial expression, he has a crimson body, three faces, eight arms, three wide open eyes, protruding buckteeth as well as red and yellow straight hair and beard. Three faces imply flexible and unpredictable insight. Eight arms symbolize the union of wisdom and compassion. Three open-wide eyes embody subduing demons on the Three Realms while protruding buckteeth demonstrate his ability to shock and awe evils.

马头金刚

马头金刚（藏文：rTa-mgrin；梵文：Hayagriva）是藏传佛教密宗九尊马头明王之一。藏密认为马头金刚是观音菩萨的愤怒相之一，也是藏传佛教上下密院护法神之一。其造型分有单身和双身。单身为二臂、四臂或三面六臂，双身则多为三头六臂。根据不同的教派，分为带翅和不带翅的两种塑像。常见的马头金刚颈挂骷髅项链，腰围虎皮围腰，三眼圆睁，膝、手、腕、颈处均被蛇缠绕。他的手中分持嘎巴拉碗、绳索、骷髅杖等，红色鬃毛里的一个或三个绿色小马头是其最显著的标志。

Horse-headed Vajra Deity

Horse-headed Vajra Deity (Tib. rTa-mgrin; Skt. Hayagriva) is one of nine Horse-headed Diamond-kings in Tantric Tibetan Buddhism. It is believed that he is not only one of the furious-looking manifestations of Avalokiteshvara Bodhisattva, but also one of Dharmapalas who protect the Upper and Lower Tantric Colleges of Tibetan Buddhism. His sculptures can be classified into a single form and a sexual union, the former has two arms, four arms or three faces and six arms while the latter usually has three heads and six arms. There are winged sculptures and no-winged sculptures in light of different religious sects. A common sculpture of Horse-headed Vajra Deity wears a skull necklace around his neck and a tiger apron around his waist. He opens wide his three eyes, and has snakes twined around his knees, hands, wrists and neck. He holds a skull-cup, a rope noose, a skull-decorated staff and other items with his several hands. One or three small green horse heads in the midst of red horsehair are his most outstanding sign.

弥勒佛

　　在藏传佛教中，未来佛弥勒（梵文：Maitreya）被称作"强巴佛"（藏文：Byams-pa）。他出生于婆罗门家庭，与释迦牟尼为同时代人。后随释迦牟尼出家，成为佛弟子，是大乘佛教（梵文：Mahayana）八大菩萨之一。佛教传说认为，他是根据释迦牟尼的预言将继承佛位、成为未来佛的一位菩萨。常见的弥勒佛造像身着菩萨装，呈坐姿，左腿下垂，右腿屈曲，右手托着脸颊，描绘了他在兜率天（梵文：Tusita）等待降世的情景。

Buddha Maitreya

　　In Tibetan Buddhism, the Future Buddha Maitreya is also known as Byams-pa. As a contemporary of Sakyamuni, he was born from a Brahman family. Later on, he followed Sakyamuni and became his disciple and one of the eight major Bodhisattvas in the Greater Vehicle of Buddhism (Skt. Mahayana). According to Buddhist legends, he was a Bodhisattva who was going to succeed the state of Buddhahood and become a future Buddha in the light of predications left by Buddha Sakyamuni. In Bodhisattva's costume, the statue of Maitreya usually sits cross-legged with his left leg drooped and right one bended and props up his check with his right hand, which depicts a scene: Maitreya was waiting to descend onto earth from the Tusita Palace.

念珠

　　念珠是佛教徒诵经时用来计算次数的成串珠子，一般由 108 颗尺寸划一的珠粒制成。念珠通常握在神灵或世系大师的右手中，象征着通过背诵咒语、供奉和慈悲觉识体现出其语之纯净。108 颗念珠表示断除 108 种烦恼，从而使身心达到一种寂静的状态。水晶、珍珠、白莲籽、白珊瑚、螺壳或象牙念珠用于怀柔仪式；菩提子、莲籽、黄金、白银或青铜念珠用于增财或增长仪式；红珊瑚、红珍珠、红玛瑙、红檀香木或发出藏红花香味的红木念珠用于召唤、吸引或息灭仪式；诃子、铁、铅、人骨或兽骨念珠用于诛灭仪式。念珠的珠数因仪式不同各异：108 颗珠粒的念珠用于怀柔和增长仪式，25 颗珠粒的念珠用于息灭仪式，60 颗珠粒的念珠用于恐怖仪式。108 颗珠粒用三股或九股捻线穿成，象征着"三宝"、执金刚菩萨（梵文：Vajradhara）和八大菩萨。

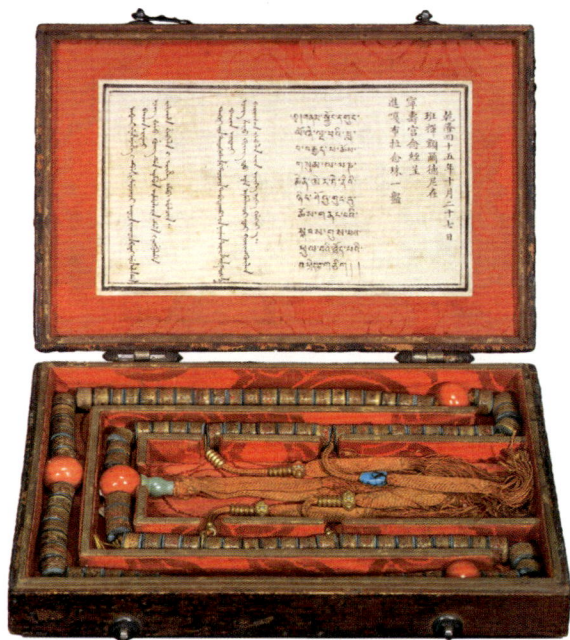

□ 念珠
Rosaries

Rosaries

Rosaries refer to stringed beads used by Buddhist adherents to count the times of their chanting Buddhist scriptures. They are made of 108 beads in the same size. Rosaries are usually held in the right hands of deities or successive masters, which symbolize the purity of their speech through chanting incantations, worships and merciful consciousness. 108 beads manifest cutting off 108 kinds of troubles so that body and mind can reach a calm and peaceful state. Crystal, pearl, white lotus seed, white coral, conch shell or ivory rosaries are often used in subjugating rites. Grape-fruit, lotus seed, gold, silver or bronze rosaries are used in wealth-increasing or enriching rites. Red coral, red pearl, red agate, red sandalwood or saffron fragrant rosewood rosaries are used in summoning, attracting and pacifying rites. Chebula, iron, lead, human bone or beast bone rosaries are used in destroying rites. Numbers of beads vary in different rites. Rosaries of 108 beads are usually used in subjugating and enriching rites. Rosaries of twenty-five and sixty beads are respectively used in pacifying rites and terrifying rites. Three or nine packthreads are used to string 108 beads together, symbolizing Three Jewels as well as Vajradhara and other eight major Bodhisattvas.

怒相神与善相神

在密宗体系中，有许多各不相同的怒相神和善相神。怒相神亦称"凶相神"或"恶相神"，善相神亦称"温和相神"。怒相神和善相神都是藏传佛教的传统造像，是以面相、服饰等特征进行的分类。修习者要根据自身目的——是想要从轮回之苦中解救芸芸众生，还是想获得佛门的最高成就——来选择修善相神还是怒相神。班登拉姆怒相像是常见的怒相神之一。

Wrathful and Peaceful Deities

In the system of Tantric Buddhism, there are many different wrathful and peaceful deities. Wrathful deities are also known as "furious-looking deities" or "vicious-looking deities" while peaceful deities are also called "warm-looking deities". Both of them are traditional Tibetan Buddhist statues, classified in terms of their facial expressions and costumes. Conducting mediations on peaceful or wrathful deities depends on a meditator's own purpose of liberating all sentient beings from sufferings of the cycle of rebirth or gaining the highest achievements. Furious-looking Goddess dPal-ldan-lha-mo is one of the wrathful deities.

□ 怒相神
Wrathful Deity

菩提树

　　菩提一词是梵文"Bodhi"的音译，其意为觉悟、智慧，指人们大彻大悟，达到超凡脱俗的境界。据传，佛祖释迦牟尼在无花果树下成道，而在当时无花果树亦称"菩提树"或"道树"。唐代高僧神秀和慧能用对话形式以物表意、借物论道，有两首著名的偈诗流传，前一首是："身是菩提树，心如明镜台。时时勤拂拭，勿使惹尘埃。"后一首是："菩提本无树，明镜亦非台。本来无一物，何处惹尘埃。"诗作的流传使菩提树更加声名远扬。

Bodhi Tree

　　As a Sanskrit transliteration, Bodhi has meanings of enlightenment and wisdom and refers to one's profound and complete realization and extraordinary refined mind. Tradition has it that Buddha Sakyamuni got enlightened under a fig tree. At that time, fig trees were also called Bodhi trees or trees of enlightenment. A pair of senior fellow apprentices named Shen Xiu and Hui Neng wrote Zan poems in dialogues in the Tang Dynasty. They employed things to express and discuss their ideas. The former is: "Like a Bodhi tree is my body. Like a bright mirror stand is my heart. They need cleaning from time to time. No dust is allowed to fall there." The latter is: "Bodhi is not a tree at all. Bright mirror has not a stand. Nothing is actually there. Dust falls nowhere." Bodhi tree's fame spreads far and wide because of the circulation of these two poems.

普贤菩萨

　　普贤菩萨（梵文：Samantabhadra）是中国佛教四大菩萨之一。他是释迦牟尼佛的右胁侍，专司"理"，与专司"智慧"的左胁侍文殊菩萨并称，其塑像多骑六牙白象。相传其显灵说法的道场在四川峨眉山，峨眉山山顶有一尊普贤骑象铜像。普贤菩萨像神态庄重，头戴五佛金冠，身披袈裟，手执如意，端坐在大象背上，呈跏趺坐姿（梵文：Vajraparyanka）。大象造型栩栩如生，四肢健壮，粗鼻下垂。整座铜像工艺精湛，制作精良，实属罕见。

Samantabhadra Bodhisattva

Samantabhadra Bodhisattva is one of the four major Bodhisattvas in Chinese Buddhism. As Buddha Sakyamuni's right attendant, he is responsible for "rations", and is often mentioned together with Manjusri, Sakyamuni's left attendant in charge of "wisdom". He often rides a white six-toothed elephant. Tradition has it that Mount Emei is his meditation site, where he manifests himself and explains Buddhist doctrines. On the top of Mount Emei stands a copper statue of Samantabhadra sitting on elephant's back. Samantabhadra wears a crown with Five Dhyani-Buddhas, drapes a cassock and holds a S-shaped ornamental scepter. He sits leg-crossed on the back of an elephant, looking dignified. This lifelike elephant has strong limbs and hangs down its big and thick trunk. The entire copper statue is rare, exquisite in craftsmanship and fine in making.

□ 普贤菩萨赤金像
Samantabhadra Bodhisattva
in Pure Gold

驱魔灵器

驱魔灵器（垛，藏文：mDos）亦称"灵器""供施替代品"或"十字网纹灵器"。它是藏传佛教仪轨中使用的一种法器。与制作朵玛一样，在举行仪式时也要经常制作"垛"来充当神灵的临时住所。灵器的基本形状是用两根细木棍捆成的十字。要用彩线在十字上缠出蜘蛛网状菱形彩色图案或更为复杂的几何图形，还要根据即将举行的仪式安排彩线的顺序。彩线共有黑、白、黄、红、绿、蓝六种颜色。仪式结束后，要将附有邪魔的灵器毁掉、捣碎或焚烧，并在十字路口或偏僻之处进行抛撒。用彩线绕成的"垛"（藏文：rGyal-mdos）是献给世间天神的，以祈福禳灾。

Thread-cross

Thread-cross (Tib. mDos) is a kind of ritual implements used in Tibetan Buddhist rites. Just like making a gTor-ma, thread-cross is often made to function as a temporary abode for a deity in a ritual. Its basic shape is a cross made of two thin wooden sticks bound together. Colored threads are used to twine webbed, diamond-shaped patterns or more complicated geometric forms. How to arrange the sequence of colored threads depends upon the ritual to be performed. Colors of threads include black, white, yellow, red, green and blue. After rituals, thread-crosses entangled with evil spirits are destroyed, pounded to pieces, burnt or cast away at a crossroad or a lonely place. Another kind of colored thread-cross (Tib. rGyal-mdos) is dedicated to heavenly deities to pay for blessings and eliminate calamities.

燃灯佛

　　燃灯佛（梵文：Dipamkara）亦称"过去燃灯佛"。释迦牟尼的前世是一位虔诚敬佛的善慧童子。他曾花重金买了一枝十分罕见的五茎莲花来供养燃灯佛，燃灯佛对此深为喜悦，故给其授记，预言该童子将在九十一劫（梵文：Kalpa）之后的贤劫时成佛，授释迦牟尼佛。许多供奉"竖三世佛"的寺庙，一般在大雄宝殿中供奉的三世佛的排列是释迦牟尼佛居中，两侧为燃灯佛（左）和弥勒佛（右），代表过去、现在、未来。

Buddha of Fixed Light

　　Buddha of Fixed Light (Skt. Dipamkara) is also known as "Buddha of Fixed Light of the Past". A boy named Shanhui in devout worship of Buddha was Sakyamuni's previous incarnation. He spent much money on a five-stemmed lotus to worship Buddha of Fixed Light, who was very pleased about it. As a result, he left a prediction, foretelling that this boy would become a Buddha in this aeon after ninety-one aeons (Skt. Kalpa) and calling him Sakyamuni Buddha. Many monasteries enshrine statues of Vertical Trinity of Buddhas in their Majesty Halls as follows: Dipamkara (left), Sakyamuni (middle) and Maitreya (right), respectively representing the past, the present and the future.

如意宝、如意树与如意瓶

如意宝亦称"称心末尼"，是传说中能随意增长财宝的如意珠之一，也是最为珍稀的宝物。据说，它能消除百病，带来好运。藏俗认为如意宝的图形象征财运昌隆，常用于壁画或绒毯上。如意树指的是传说中能随意生出财物的宝树。根据神话传说，如意树结出的果实可以食用，树叶可做衣服。如意瓶指的是能随意满足各种需要的理想妙瓶，在佛像和菩萨像手中常可见到它们。

Wish-fulfilling Gems, Wish-fulfilling Trees and Talismanic Vases

Wish-fulfilling gems, also known as "fabulous gems", are not only legendary wish-fulfilling gems which can increase wealth, but also the most valuable ones. As it is said, they can eliminate various diseases and bring good lucks. According to Tibetan customs, wish-fulfilling gem patterns, a symbol of wealth growth, are often used on murals and cotton carpets. Precious wish-fulfilling trees can increase wealth at any time. According to legends, their fruits are edible and leaves are used to make clothes. Talismanic vases refer to perfect vases which can meet all the needs at any moment. They are often seen in the hands of Buddha and Bodhisattva statues.

□ 如意宝、如意树与如意瓶
Wish-fulfilling Gems, Wish-fulfilling Trees and Talismanic Vases

胜乐金刚

胜乐金刚（登确，藏文：bDe-mchog；梵文：Samvara）亦称"上乐金刚"（梵文：Cakrasamvara）。他是藏密无上瑜伽部母续的本尊。其艺术形象十分复杂，常为立姿，头戴五骷髅冠，足下有莲花座。胜乐金刚有白、黄、红、蓝四面，每面有三目。在他的十二臂中，主臂的左手持金刚铃，右手持金刚杵，双手拥抱明妃金刚亥母（藏文：Vajravarahi）。其余各臂向两侧平伸，手中持有斧、钺刀、金刚索等法器。金刚亥母一面呈红色，双臂，三目，戴骷髅冠，右手持钺刀，左手持盈血嘎巴拉碗。有的双腿姿势十分奇特，左腿伸开，与主尊右腿并拢，右腿盘在主尊腰间。

□ 胜乐金刚合金像
Samvara in Alloy

Samvara

Samvara (Tib. bDe-mchog), also known as "Cakrasamvara", is a Yidam in Mother Tantra of the Highest Yoga Tantra of Tibetan Buddhism. He is very complicated in artistic image. Usually, he wears a five-skull crown and stands on a lotus pedestal. He has white, yellow, red and blue faces, and each face has three eyes. He holds a Vajra bell and a Vajra club with his left and right hands respectively of all his twelve principal arms, embracing his consort Sakti Vajravarahi with both his hands. He horizontally stretches his other arms, and holds an axe, a curved knife, a snooze and other ritual implements with his hands. Vajravarahi has one red face, two arms and three eyes. She wears a skull-crown on her head, holding a curved knife and a skull-cup full of blood with her right and left hands. In a peculiar posture, she stretches her left leg and puts it and the major statue's right leg together while she coils her right leg around his waist.

十二丹玛

丹玛（藏文：brTan-ma）指的是分布在西藏各地的女性土地神，分静、怒两种形相。她们原是西藏的十二位魔女，能造成灾荒和瘟疫。在被莲花生大师收服后，她们立誓永远保佑藏土，成为守护菩萨。十二丹玛又名"永宁地母"或"地母金刚"。十二尊女神形象大同小异，坐骑为金翅鸟、狮子、龙、马等。

Twelve brTan-ma Goddesses

"brTan-ma" in Tibetan refers to peaceful and wrathful female earth deities in different parts of Tibet. As twelve she-demons in Tibet, they were able to cause famines and pestilences. After they were subdued by Padmasambhava, they vowed to defend Tibet forever. As a result, they became protective Bodhisattvas. Twelve brTan-ma Goddesses are also known as "Goddess-defenders of Buddhism" or "Vajra Earth Goddesses". Their images are largely identical with minor differences, and they take Garuda, lion, dragon, horse and others as their mounts.

时轮金刚与时轮坛城

　　时轮金刚密法于 12 世纪从古印度传入西藏，时轮金刚是该密法之尊。时轮金刚形象多种多样，其塑像一般上身为蓝色，四面二十四臂，右腿呈红色，左腿呈白色。其上身佩戴璎珞臂钏和腕镯，下身穿虎豹皮裙，与佛母相拥，呈站姿。其手持各种法器，脚下踩人，表示降妖伏魔。时轮坛城多用于佛教密宗，是时轮金刚及其眷神的宫殿。布达拉宫所藏的时轮坛城唐卡长 96 厘米，宽 83 厘米，绘有密迹金刚、喜金刚和胜乐金刚等本尊像。

Time-wheel Vajra Deity and Time-wheel Vajra Mandala

The Time-wheel Vajra Tantric Teaching was introduced into Tibet from ancient India in the twelfth century. As its Yidam, Time-wheel Vajra deity is varied in image. His sculpture usually has a blue upper body, four faces, twenty-four arms, a red right leg and a white left leg. His upper body is adorned with a pearl and jade necklace, armlets and wrist bracelets while his lower body is wrapped with a tiger-leopard skin apron. In a standing posture, he embraces his consort, holds various ritual implements with his hands and treads on human figures, which shows his subduing demons and evil spirits. Time-wheel Mandala is often used in Tantric Buddhism as a palace inhabited by Time-wheel Vajra deity and his retinues. Images of Guhyap davajra, Hevajra, Samvara and other Yidams are painted on Thang-ka Depicting Time-wheel Mandala kept in the Potala Palace. It is ninety-six centimeters long and eighty-three centimeters wide.

□ 时轮金刚
Time-wheel Vajra Deity

四大天王

　　四大天王亦称"四金刚"或"护世四天王"。根据印度佛教传说的说法，有一座山位于须弥山山腰中，山有四峰，各有一天王居住，各护一天下，分别是持国天王（梵文：Dhrtarastra）、增长天王（梵文：Virudhaka）、广目天王（梵文：Virupaksa）和多闻天王（梵文：Vaisramana）。他们是专门守护皈依佛法之人的护法神。持国天王位居东方，身白色，持琵琶。增长天王位居南方，身青色，持宝剑。广目天王位居西方，身红色，手绕缠一龙。多闻天王位居北方，身绿色，右手持伞，左手持吐宝鼠鼬。

Four Heavenly Kings

　　Four Heavenly Kings are also known as "Four Vajra Deities" or "Four Celestial Kings of the Quarters". According to Indian Buddhism, a mountain with four peaks lies in the area half way up Mount Sumeru. Each celestial king inhabits one peak, guarding his quarter. Four Heavenly Kings include Heavenly King of the East (Skt. Dhrtarastra), Heavenly King of the West (Skt. Virudhaka), Heavenly King of the South (Skt. Virupaksa) and Heavenly King of the North (Skt. Vaisramana). As protective deities, they guard Dharma's converts. Heavenly King of the East in white holds a lute. Heavenly King of the South in blue holds a sword. Heavenly King of the West in red intertwines a dragon around his wrist and Heavenly King of the North in green holds an umbrella with his right hand and a jewel-disgorging mongoose with his left one.

韦驮

　　韦驮（梵文：Skanda）原本是婆罗门教神祇湿婆之子，后成为佛教僧人或伽蓝（梵文：Samgharama）的守护神。他也是增长天王的八大将军之一。其塑像一般身穿古代武将服，手持金刚杵，位于天王殿弥勒佛像之后。韦驮像呈双手合十、横抱杵的姿势，表明寺院为可接纳行脚僧投宿（挂褡）的大寺院；如单手竖持杵，杵靠在肩上，则表示寺院为一般寺院，只能按寺院需要接受行脚僧投宿；如单手持杵，杵尖着地，则表示寺院较小，只可投宿三天；如双手持杵，杵尖着地，表示寺院为小庙，不能接待任何行脚僧。

Skanda

　　Skanda used to be the son of Shiva, a deity in Brahmanism. Later on, he became a protective deity to guard Buddhist monks and monasteries (Skt. Samgharama) and one of the eight generals of the Heavenly King of the South. His sculpture usually wears a suit of ancient general costume and holds a Vajra club, standing behind statue of Maitreya in the Heavenly King Hall. He clasps both his palms together, horizontally holding a Vajra club, which indicates that this is a large monastery for wandering monks to lodge. If he holds a Vajra club in a single hand and puts it on the shoulder, which means that this is an ordinary monastery for wandering monks to lodge according to its demand. If he holds a Vajra club in a single hand, and its point touches the ground, it implies that this is a small monastery for wandering monks to stay just for a few days. If he holds a Vajra club in both hands, and its point touches the ground, it makes clear that this is just a small temple unable to receive any wandering monks.

文殊菩萨

　　文殊菩萨（梵文：Manjusri）是佛教四大菩萨之一。他是释迦牟尼的左胁侍，专司"智慧"，常与司"理"的右胁侍普贤菩萨并称。其塑像通常手持宝剑，表示智慧锐利，多骑狮子，表示智慧威猛。其形象多变，其中最常见的是五髻文殊，五髻代表五种智慧。其右手一般握有智慧剑，象征以智慧剑斩烦恼结。有时亦会手持如意，象征智慧成就。他的左手持有代表纯洁无染的莲花。莲花上面放置《般若波罗蜜多经》，象征着智慧与慈悲。文殊菩萨分为白文殊、黄文殊和黑文殊三种。白文殊身面白色，形象为一面双臂，头戴天冠，披发，一手持剑，一手持莲花，莲花上置有经函。黄文殊身面黄色，一面双臂，左手持经函，右手持剑上举。相传其显灵说法的道场在山西五台山。与白文殊和黄文殊的寂静像不同，黑文殊呈愤怒相，一面二臂，三目，

□ 四臂文殊菩萨镏金铜像
Four-armed Manjusri Bodhisattva in Gilt Bronze

头戴宝冠，身着珠宝，常呈金刚跏趺坐姿，坐于智慧火焰之间。他的右手持剑，左手在胸前捻着一枝青莲花茎，青莲花（梵文：utpala）上有一函《般若八千颂》。

Manjusri Bodhisattva

Manjusri Bodhisattva is one of the four major Bodhisattvas in Buddhism. As Sakyamuni's left attendant in charge of "wisdom", he is often mentioned together with Samantabhadra (Sakyamuni's right attendant in charge of "rations"). Usually, his sculpture holds a sword and rides a lion, respectively displaying wisdom's sharpness and power. His images are varied, and Five-knot Manjusri statues are very common, and five knots represent five kinds of wisdom. He holds a wisdom sword with his right hand, which means that it is able to cut off trouble knots. Sometimes, he holds a S-shaped ornamental scepter with his right hand, which is a symbol of wisdom and achievement. He holds a lotus representative of purity. A set of *Perfection of Wisdom* is placed on it, which symbolizes wisdom and compassion. Manjursri Bodhisattva has three kinds of forms: White Manjursri, Yellow Manjursri and Black Manjursri. White Manjursri is in white, and has two arms. He wears a crown and drapes his hair, holding a sword and a lotus with a scripture book on it with his both hands. Yellow Manjursri is in yellow, and has two arms. He holds a scripture book with his left hand and lifts up a sword with his right one. Tradition has it that his meditation site lies in Mount Wutai in Shanxi Province. Unlike peaceful White and Yellow Manjursri, wrathful-looking Black Manjursri has one face, two arms and three eyes. He wears a crown and jewels, sitting in Vajraparyanka among flames of wisdom. He holds a sword with his right hand and twists the stem of a utpala in front of his chest with his left hand. On the utpala is a volume of scripture entitled *Eight Thousand Prayers of Prajna.*

五大守舍神

五大守舍神（藏文：vGo-bavi-lha-lnga）是指经常守护人体和各种器官、与寿命共存亡的一类神，分别是阳神（颇拉，藏文：Pho-lha）、阴神（莫拉，藏文：Mo-lha）、舅神（香拉，藏文：Zhang-lha）、战神（扎拉，藏文：dGra-lha）和生命神（索拉，藏文：Srog-lha）。还有另一组五位神，分别是乡土神、父族神、母族神、战神和生命神。

Five Protective Deities

Five Protective Deities (Tib. vGo-bavi-lha-lnga) refer to a group of deities who often safeguard human body and various organs and coexist with human lifespan. Five Protective Deities include masculine deity (Tib. Pho-lha), feminine deity (Tib. Mo-lha), uncle deity (Tib. Zhang-lha), deity of war (Tib. dGra-lha) and deity of life (Tib. Srog-lha). Another group of five deities respectively are native deity, paternal deity, maternal deity, deity of war and deity of life.

五佛禅冠

　　五佛禅冠是佛教密宗上师、寺院住持及得道高僧修法时所戴的象征五智如来的宝冠。在坛城和唐卡中，大日如来常常居于中央，不动如来、宝生如来、无量光如来和不空成就如来分位四方。而在五佛禅冠上，五佛横列，大日如来居中。佛像头上也常佩戴五佛禅冠。五佛禅冠一般由皮、纸、木或镂空的铜皮、银皮制成，共分五叶，连缀在一起，每一叶上都绘制着佛像、梵文字母、法轮、金刚杵、莲花、宝剑、火焰等图案。叶片中间一般绘有一个莲瓣形的佛龛，莲龛中间有代表五佛之一的梵文字符，上下镶嵌着珍珠、绿松石、珊瑚等珠宝，禅冠下部缀有长缨。还有一种由五个骷髅头骨连成的骷髅五佛冠，是藏传佛教密乘行者的头饰之一。

□ 五佛禅冠
Crown with Five
Dhyani-Buddhas

Crown with Five Dhyani-Buddhas

　　Crown with Five Dhyani-Buddhas is a symbol of Five Wisdom Buddhas. Tantric Buddhist masters, abbots and enlightened eminent monks often wear them in meditations. In Mandalas and Thang-kas, Vairocana lies in the center while Akshobya, Ratnasambhava, Amitabha and Amoghasiddhi occupy four directions. However, on such a crown, five Buddhas are arranged in a line with Vairocana in its center. Buddha statues generally wear such crowns on their heads. Such crowns are made of leather, paper, wood or hollowed-out copper or silver sheets. Each crown has five leaf blades linked together, and each leaf blade is painted with Buddha image, Dharma-wheel, lotus, sword, flames and other patterns. The center of each leaf blade is usually painted with a lotus-petal shaped niche with a Sanskrit alphabet representative of one of the five Buddhas, and pearls, turquoise, corals and other jewels are decorated on its upper and lower parts and long tassels are tied on crown's lower part. There is another five-skulled crown. As one of the headdresses worn by Tantric Buddhist practitioners, they are made of five linked skulls.

祥麟法轮

祥麟法轮亦称双鹿法轮，是藏传佛教寺院大殿楼顶上的一个标志性装饰物。祥麟法轮由一个金色法轮和一双鹿组成。法轮一般为铜质镏金，共有八个轮辐，代表佛陀的"八正道"。法轮两侧各有一头鹿，它们呈跪姿，仰视金色法轮，神态安详。双鹿代表释迦牟尼佛初转法轮（首次讲法）之地——鹿野苑。释迦牟尼觉悟成道后来到此地为其五个侍从说法，使他们成为第一批佛教信徒。

Dharma-wheel and Deer Emblem

Dharma-wheel and Deer Emblem, also named "Dharma-wheel Flanked by a Pair of Deer", serves as a decorative sign on a building roof of the great hall in a Tibetan Buddhist monastery. It consists of a golden Dharma-wheel and a pair of deer. Usually, this gilt copper wheel has eight spokes, which indicates Buddha's "Eightfold Noble Path". Both sides of Dharma-wheel are flanked by a pair of deer. In a kneeling posture, they are looking up the golden Dharma-wheel in a serene bearing. A pair of deer represents the Deer Park, where Sakyamuni gave his first sermon. After his enlightenment, Sakyamuni went there to expound Buddhist doctrines to his five attendants. As a result, they became the first Buddhist adherents.

向向鸟与共命鸟

向向鸟（藏文：Bya-shang-shang）是一种想象中的神鸟，具有鸟、人、牛的特征，专门侍奉佛和菩萨。共命鸟（梵文：Jivam-jivaka）是一个力大无比、人首鸟身的精灵，其形象手握铁链，手捧宝瓶。它一般都装饰在大屋顶上，据说可以避火。但在壁画中，共命鸟经常充当供养人的角色。

Shang-shang Bird and Jivam-jivaka Bird

Shang-shang bird is an imaginary mythological bird. It is characteristics of bird, human and ox, especially attending on Buddhas and Bodhisattvas. Jivam-jivaka bird is a powerful spirit with a human face and a bird body. It holds iron chains and precious vase with its both hands. It is usually decorated on large roofs. It is considered a protection against fire, but it often plays a role of a benefactor on murals.

□ 镏金铜共命鸟像
Jivam-jivaka Bird in Gilt Bronze

须弥山与四大部洲

　　须弥山（梵文：Sumeru）亦称"妙高山"或"善积山"，佛教宇宙结构中述及的一座著名山岳。传说，须弥山被七山七海环绕，海上有四大部洲和八小部洲。须弥山由金（北面）、银（东面）、琉璃（南面）、水晶（西面）四宝构成，高 84000 由旬（一由旬约 13 千米）。帝释天位于山顶，四天王天位于须弥山第四层级。根据《长阿含经》的说法，须弥山的四大部洲分别是北俱卢洲（梵文：Uttara-kuru）、东胜神洲（梵文：Purva-videha）、西牛贺洲（梵文：Apara-godaniya）和南赡部洲（梵文：Jambu-dvipa）。据说，人类就居住在南赡部洲。

Mount Sumeru and Four Inhabited Continents of Every Universe

Mount Sumeru, also known as "Mount Meru" or "World Mountain", is a famous mountain mentioned in Buddhist universe structure. According to legends, it is embraced by seven mountains and seven seas. At seas, there are four large and eight small subcontinents of every universe. Mount Sumeru consists of gold (north), silver (east), glaze (south) and crystal (west). It has a height of 84,000 Yojana (one Yojana is equal to about thirteen kilometers). Indra, an Indian deity, inhabits on its mountaintop while Four Heavenly Kings live its fourth level. According to *Long Discourses*, Four Inhabited Continents of Every Universe are respectively the Eastern Continent of Giant People (Skt. Purva-videha), the Southern Continent "Zam" Trees (Skt. Jambu-dvipa), the Western Continent of Animals and Jewels (Skt. Apara-godaniya) and the Northern Continent of Bad News (Skt. Uttara-kuru). It is said that human beings are inhabitants of the Southern Continent "Zam" Trees.

须弥座

须弥座亦称"金刚座"或"须弥坛"，形式与装饰均比较复杂，多用于宫殿、寺庙主殿等重要建筑中，或作为塔和幢的基座等。须弥座源自印度，是安置佛像、菩萨像的台座。"须弥"（梵文：Sumeru）指的是须弥山，在印度古代传说中，它是宇宙的中心。台座以须弥山做底，显示出佛的神圣、庄严和伟大，寓意坚固永恒。

Sumeru Throne

Sumeru thrones are also known as "Diamond Thrones" or "Sumeru Seats". They are very complicated in form and decoration. Most of them are placed in buildings, palaces, main halls and important buildings in monasteries or used as pagoda and stone pillar pedestals. Sumeru thrones originated from India, and they are used as pedestals for Buddha and Bodhisattva statues. "Sumeru" refers to Mount Sumeru. According to ancient Indian legends, it is the core of the universe. Taking Mount Sumeru as its base not only shows Buddha's holiness, solemnity and greatness, but also implies solidity and eternity.

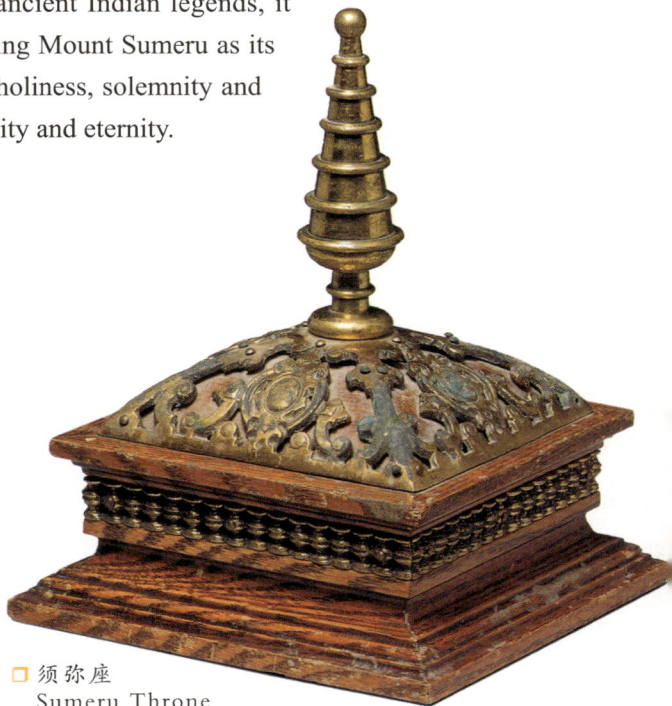

□ 须弥座
Sumeru Throne

饮血金刚

饮血金刚（藏文：dPal-kyi-rdo-rje）亦称"金刚王"（梵文：Hevajra）或"亥如迦"（梵文：Heruka），佛教无上密宗本尊之一。其塑像面相愠怒，身色洁白，八面，十六臂，四腿。八面中有两面在前，左右各三面，每面三目。他头戴骷髅冠，身挂五十骷髅项链。其主臂拥着明妃金刚无我佛母（梵文：Nairatmya）。佛母的左手勾其颈，右手上扬嘎巴拉鼓。有的塑像中，佛母右手持钺刀，与饮血金刚相拥。

Blood-drinker

Blood-drinker (Tib. dPal-kyi-rdo-rje) is also known as "Vajra King" or "Hevajra". He is one of the Yidams of Tantric Buddhism. With a wrathful facial expression and a white body, Blood-drinker has eight faces, sixteen arms and four legs. Two of his eight faces are on the front side while the other six ones are on the left and right sides, and each has three eyes. He wears a fifty-skull necklace around his body and embraces his consort Sakti Nairatmya with his principal arms. Sakti Nairatmya puts her left hand around his neck and raises a skull-drum with her right one. In some of her sculptures, she holds a curved knife with her right hand and embraces Hevajra.

拥妃佛像

　　拥妃（藏文：Yab-yum）佛像俗称"欢喜佛"，是印度密宗与西藏本土信仰结合的藏传佛教密宗的本尊神。在这样的塑像中，男身代表法，女体代表智慧，男身女体相拥，表示法慧双成。双身佛像只是一种象征性的表相，说明只有利用"空乐双运"产生的空性，才能达到"以欲制欲"的目的。拥妃佛是密宗所独有的，也只供奉在藏传佛教寺庙中。其造型源于密宗"男女双修"的教法。

Statues in a Sexual Union

　　Statues in a sexual union (Tib. Yab-yum), commonly known as Devas of Pleasure, refer to Yidams in Tantric Buddhism. Such an image came into being due to the integration of Indian Tantric Buddhism and Tibetan indigenous beliefs. In such a statue, male body and female body respectively represent Dharma and wisdom. Their embraced bodily posture shows

☐ 拥妃无量寿佛银像
Silver Statue in a Sexual Union

the union of Dharma and wisdom. Statue in a sexual union is only a symbolic appearance, which means that only by taking advantage of emptiness created by the "union of great bliss and emptiness", can people achieve the purpose of "sexual desire with repressed by sexual desire". Only Tantric Buddhism has such statues,and they are only enshrined in Tibetan Buddhist monasteries. Its modeling originated from "sexual union practice methods" mentioned in Tantric Buddhist teachings.

瑜伽、瑜伽师与瑜伽母

瑜伽（梵文：Yoga）一词源于古印度，其意为一致、结合或和谐。瑜伽行派（梵文：Yogacara）是古印度六大哲学派别之一，与中观学派并为印度大乘佛教的两大派别。瑜伽是指通过观想思悟佛教"真理"的一种修行方法。在佛教中，瑜伽师（梵文：Yogi）亦称"成道者"或"瑜伽行者"，指的是修行瑜伽宗的佛教徒。女性瑜伽行者称作瑜伽母（梵文：Yogini）。现代社会所倡导的瑜伽主要是一系列修身养性的方法。人们习得古老而易于掌握的瑜伽姿势等各种技巧以改善和提升自身生理、心理、情感和精神方面的能力，是一种能使人达到身体、心理与精神和谐统一的运动方式。

□ 瑜伽母像壁画
Yogini Mural

Yoga, Yogi and Yogini

"Yoga" in Sanskrit originated from ancient India, meaning "coherence", "combination" and "compatibility". As one of the six major ancient Indian philosophical schools, Yogacara School and the Middle Way School are viewed as major schools of Indian Mahayana Buddhism. As a practice method, Yoga practice is used for people to have a thorough insight into Buddhist "truths" through visualizations. In Buddhism, "Yogis", also known as "enlightened ones" or "Yogacara practitioners", refer to male Yoga practitioners while "Yoginis" represents female Yoga practitioners. Yoga practices advocated in modern society serve as a series of methods to cultivate people's minds. After learning some ancient, easily-mastered skills of all kinds, people are able to better and promote their physiological, psychological, emotional and mental capabilities. Therefore, it is an exercise mode for people to reach a harmonious state of body, physiology and mentality.

赞巴拉财神

赞巴拉神（藏文：Dzam-bha-la，梵文：Jambhala）是藏传佛教中的财宝之神，俗称"财神"。其塑像一般是左手抱一只象征致富的吐宝鼠鼬，右手托宝物。按颜色划分，赞巴拉神可分为黄、白、黑财神。黄财神上身袒露，遍体金黄色，左脚踩在白色大海螺上，象征他能入海探取摩尼珠宝。白财神全身洁白，呈怒相，头发似火焰直立，三目圆睁，左手持三股叉，右手持短棒，身骑张牙舞爪的巨龙。黑财神全身青黑，赤身裸体，脖颈挂着一条蛇，左手抱鼠鼬，右手托嘎巴拉碗，双脚站在一个俯卧的男子身上。

Dzam-bla-lha God of Wealth

Dzam-bla-lha God of Wealth (Tib. Dzam-bha-la; Skt. Jambhala) is Tibetan Buddhist wealth god with a trivial name of "God of Treasure". Usually, his sculpture holds a jewel-disgorging mongoose, a symbol of wealth, with his left hand and a treasure with his right one. In terms of colors, they can be classified into Yellow, White and Black Gods of Wealth. Yellow God of Wealth is in golden, and he exposes his upper body and puts his left foot on a large white conch, which symbolizes his ability to draw Mani gems from oceans. Wrathful White God of Wealth has a pure white body, flame-like straight hair and three wide-open eyes. He holds a trident and a short club with his left and right hands, riding on a giant saber rattling dragon. Black God of Wealth has a black naked body and wears a serpent around his neck. He holds a jewel-disgoring mongoose and a skull-cup with his left and right hands, standing on a man lying prostrate under his feet.

增禄佛母

增禄佛母（若君玛，藏文：Nor-rgyun-ma；梵文：Vasudhara）亦称"财续佛母"，是赐予财宝成就的佛教密乘本尊，在六道中专司人道，掌世间财富，为五路财神之佛母。根据传承的不同，财续佛母的化相不只一种，有一面二臂的，也有三面六臂的，有时她也与财神呈双身相状。常见的塑像为黄色身相，身披天衣，装饰有珠宝璎珞，神态庄严宁静，安坐莲台上。增禄佛母可以满足一切众生的心愿，其手结施予印和无畏印，表示施财和救度众生。

Goddess of Wealth

Goddess of Wealth (Tib. Nor-rgyun-ma; Skt. Vasudhara) is also known as "Wealth-increasing Goddess". She is a Tantric Buddhist Yidam with the ability to bestow wealth and achievements. She especially manages the Human Realm in the Six Kinds of Existence, controls the wealth on earth and serves as the head of Five Gods of Wealth. In light of different inheritances, she has several manifestations, including one face and two arms or three faces and six arms. Sometimes, she and God of Wealth appear together in a sexual union. Usually, she has a yellow body, drapes a garment and adorns herself with gems and pearls and jade necklaces. She sits on a lotus-moon pedestal, looking solemn and peaceful. Goddess of Wealth is able to satisfy all sentient beings' desires. She gives a gift-bestowing gesture and a fearless gesture, showing her giving money away and saving sentient beings.

尊胜佛母

尊胜佛母（南加玛，藏文：rNam-rgyal-ma）是大日如来的化身，与无量寿佛和白度母并称为藏传佛教三大长寿佛。其塑像常为三面八臂，三面上各具三眼。其身呈白色，貌如妙龄女郎。第一只右手当胸持十字金刚杵；第二只右手托着一个莲花座，座上安放着阿弥陀佛像；第三只右手持箭；第四只右手在右腿前结施愿印。第一只左手持绢索，结愤怒拳印；第二只左手上扬，结无畏印；第三只左手执弓；第四只左手托甘露宝瓶，结禅定印。她头戴宝冠，后衬背光，结金刚跏趺坐于莲台之上。

□ 尊胜佛母合金像
Goddess of Dignity in Alloy

Goddess of Dignity

Goddess of Dignity (Tib. rNam-rgyal-ma) is an emanation of Vairocana. Godden of Dignity, Amitayus and Avalokiteshvara Bodhisattva are jointly called "Trinity of Longevity" in Tibetan Buddhism. Usually, her sculpture has three faces and eight arms, and each face has three eyes. She is in white, looking like a young maiden. She holds a crossed-Vajra with her first right hand against her chest. She holds a lotus throne with a statue of Amitabha on it with her second right hand, and an arrow with her third right hand. She puts her fourth right hand in front of her right leg, giving a wish-giving gesture. She holds a rope noose with her first left hand, giving a wrathful-fist gesture. She raises her second left hand, giving a fearless gesture. She holds a bow and a vase of nectar with her third and fourth left hands, giving a meditation gesture. She wears a crown, and has a nimbus behind her body. She sits cross-legged on a lotus pedestal.

作明佛母

作明佛母被奉为藏传佛教的本尊。她貌似 16 岁妙龄少女，全身的红色代表慑服人心。其怒相表示调伏四魔。塑像为一面、三目、四臂。四臂代表息灾、增财、慑服和诛灭四种成就，或慈、悲、喜、舍四无量心。其手持的花箭、钩和绢索代表控制一切的自然力和威力。

Goddess Kurukulle

Goddess Kurukulle is praised highly as a Yidam of Tibetan Buddhism. She looks like a sixteen-year-old maiden. Her red body demonstrates convincing people while her wrathful facial expression embodies her subduing Four Demons. Her sculpture has one face, three eyes and four arms. Her four arms represent four achievements: removing ill fortunes, increasing wealth, terrifying people and subduing demons or Four Immeasurables (loving-kindness, compassion, sympathetic joy and equanimity). She holds a flower arrow, a hook and a noose with her hands, which respectively represent her natural power and formidable power to control everything.

Part 2

皈依之旅：宗教与寺院
Religions and Monasteries

八大尸林与尸陀林主

八大尸林亦称"八大寒林"，即佛书所说的八大弃尸处。分别是东方暴虐寒林、南方骨锁寒林、西方金刚焰寒林、北方密丛寒林、东南方吉祥寒林、西南方幽暗寒林、西北方啾啾寒林和东北方狂笑寒林。尸陀林主指的是出现在八大尸林、形似男女骷髅的一对鬼物。

Eight Charnel Grounds and Lords of Charnel Grounds

Eight Charnel Grounds, also known as "Eight Cemeteries"mentioned in Buddhist texts, are spots for people to cast away corpses. They are Very Ferocious Charnel Ground, Skeleton Place Charnel Ground, Blazing Vajra Charnel Ground, Dense Thicket Charnel Ground, Auspicious Charnel Ground, Intense Darkness Charnel Ground, Sounds of Kili, Kili Charnel Ground and Ha Ha Laughter Charnel Ground. Lords of Charnel Grounds refer to a pair of ghosts who appear on cemeteries and take the shape of male and female skeletons.

白居寺

　　白居寺（藏文：dPal-mchod-dgon）别名"吉祥轮寺"，位于西藏江孜。修建年代说法不一，一般认为建于 1418 年。主要建筑有措钦大殿和白居塔，大殿分有三层，供奉着近 8 米高的强巴佛（藏文：Byams-pa；梵文：Maitreya）铜像。在二层的殿堂里有一个直径 3 米左右的立体时轮坛城。白居寺内壁画和雕塑精美细腻，是研究 14 ~ 15 世纪西藏藏传佛教艺术流派及其风格的重要作品资料。

dPal-mchod Monastery

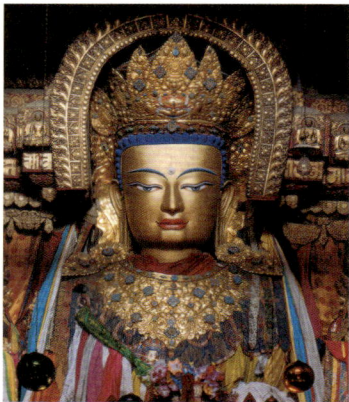

□ 白居寺主供佛像
Buddha in dpal-mchod
Monastery

Located in Gyangtse of Tibet, dPal-mchod Monastery (Tib. dPal-mchod-dgon)also enjoys another name of "Auspicious Wheel Monastery". There are different views about the date of its construction. It is generally acknowledged that it was built in 1418. The main buildings include Tshogs-chen Hall and dPal-muchod Pagoda. Three-story Tshogs-chen Hall enshrines a nearly eight-meter-high copper statue of Byams-pa(Skt. Maitreya). The hall on the second floor has a three-dimensional Time-wheel Mandala, about three meters in diameter. Elegant and exquisite murals and sculptures in this monastery serve as major works for studies of Tibetan Buddhist artistic schools and styles prevalent during the period from the fourteenth to the fifteenth century.

贝叶经

贝叶经泛指用铁笔在贝树叶上所刻写的佛教经文。它们既是当前世界古文献中极为珍贵的原始资料之一，也是人类文化的一个重要组成部分。在贝叶上刻写经文的做法源自古印度。在造纸技术尚未传到印度之前，印度人就在贝叶上进行刻写。佛教徒亦将佛经和佛画刻写或绘制在贝叶上，贝叶经因此得名。贝叶经耐磨轻便，历经千年岁月字迹依然清晰可辨。珍藏于西藏的贝叶经是藏族传统文化宝库中的璀璨明珠，也是古印度文化和藏族传统文化交往的历史见证。

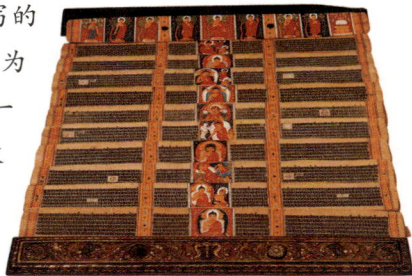

□《八千颂》贝叶经
Pattra-leaf Scriptures of *Baqiansong*

Pattra-leaf Scriptures

Pattra-leaf scriptures refer to Buddhist texts inscribed with iron pens on Pattra leaves. They are not only one of the most valuable original sources among ancient materials in today's world, but also a significant component of human cultures. The way of inscribing Buddhist scriptures originated from ancient India. Before the introduction of paper-making technique to India, Indians inscribed scripts on Pattra leaves, and Buddhist adherents also liked to inscribe Buddhist scriptures and drawings on Pattra leaves, hence the name Pattra-leaf scriptures. Pattra-leaf scriptures are wear-resisting and portable, and scripts inscribed on them are still clear and distinguishable 1,000 years later. Pattra-leaf scriptures preserved in Tibet are a bright pearl in Tibetan traditional cultural treasury as well as a historical witness to the communications between ancient Indian culture and Tibetan traditional culture.

《本生经》

　　《本生经》亦称《佛本生传记》，它是一部印度佛教寓言故事集，大约产生于公元前3世纪。根据佛教的说法，释迦牟尼成佛前只是一位菩萨，经过了无数次的转生才最终成佛。《本生经》叙述了佛陀前生曾为国王、婆罗门、商人、女人、大象、猴时所行善业功德的寓言故事，以颂扬佛陀，宣扬佛教的基本教义。现存的《本生经》共收录547个故事，绝大部分源自印度民间的寓言、故事、神话、传说。

Jatakas

　　Jatakas, also known as *Stories of Buddha's Previous Incarnations*, is a collection of Indian Buddhist fables. It probably originated in the third century B.C. According to Buddhist doctrines, Sakyamuni was only a Bodhisattva before he obtained full enlightenment. He finally became a Buddha after countless times of rebirth. *Jatakas* describes his good deeds and merits in his previous incarnations as a king, a Braham, a merchant, a woman, an elephant and a monkey, thereby praising Buddha and publicizing Buddhist doctrines. The existing *Jatakas* contains 547 stories, most of which come from Indian folk fables, stories, myths and legends.

苯教与象雄文化

苯教（藏文：Bon）亦称"苯波教"，为公元前五世纪古象雄（藏文：Zhang-gzhung）王子辛绕米沃（藏文：gShen-rab-mi-bo）创建。古象雄被视为苯教的发源地，史称"羌同"或"羊同"。它是古代横跨中亚地区及青藏高原的大国。它有着几千年悠久的历史和灿烂辉煌的远古文明，是象雄文明的真正源泉。苯教在古象雄传统文化中享有至高无上的地位，是西藏本土最古老的宗教。苯教既是古象雄文化的核心，也是藏族传统文化和藏传佛教的源泉。苯教的发展经历了笃苯（藏文：rDol-bon，意为"涌现苯"）、洽苯（藏文：vKhyar-bon，意为"游走苯"）和觉苯（藏文：bsGyur-bon，意为"翻译苯"）三个时期。苯教曾经历过佛苯并存的阶段，也经历了两次兴佛抑苯的法难。

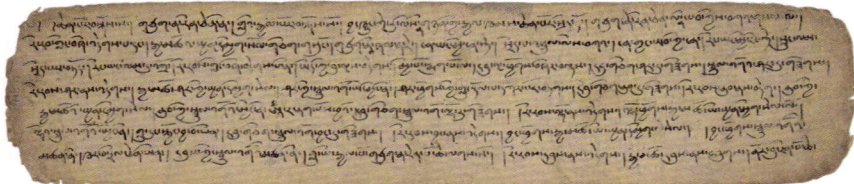

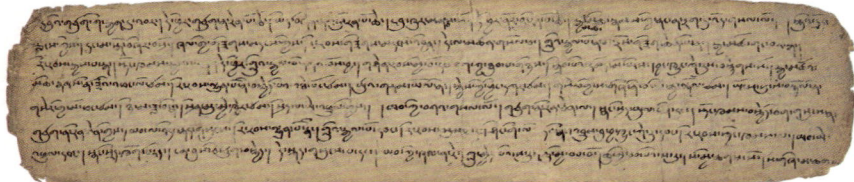

□ 苯教典籍散页
Pages of Bon Religion

Bon Religion and Zhang-gzhung Culture

Bon religion (Tib. Bon), also known as Bonpo religion, was founded in the fifth century B.C. by gShen-rab-mi-bo, a prince from ancient state of Zhang-gzhung. Zhang-gzhung is believed as the cradle of Bon religion, known as "Qiangtong" or "Yangtong". In ancient times, as a great state, it stretched its territory to the Central Asia and Qinghai-Tibet Plateau. With long history of thousands of years, it has splendid and magnificent primitive civilization and serves as the true source of Zhang-gzhung civilization. Bon religion occupies a supreme position in ancient Zhang-gzhung traditional cultures. As the oldest indigenous religion in Tibet, it is not only the core of ancient Zhang-gzhung cultures, but also the source of Tibetan traditional cultures and Tibetan Buddhism. Bon religion underwent three stages in the course of its development. They are stages of the Revealed Bon (Tib. rDol-bon), the Derived Bon (Tib. vKhyar-bon) and the Transformed Bon (Tib. bsGyur-bon). In addition, it also experienced the co-existence period of Buddhism and Bon religion as well as the periods of prospering Buddhism and suppressing Bon religion.

大乘佛教与小乘佛教

佛教创始人释迦牟尼圆寂后，佛教内部对其教义有不同的理解和阐述，因而形成了多个派别。根据教理方面的不同以及形成时期的先后，可归纳为大乘佛教（梵文：Mahayana）和小乘佛教（梵文：Hinayana）两大基本派别。大乘佛教是一世纪左右形成的一个佛教派别，自称能运载无量众生从生死大河之此岸达到菩提涅槃之彼岸。小乘佛教是早期佛教的主要流派，大乘佛教认为其教义烦琐，无法超度更多的众生，因而贬称之为小乘。在我国，大乘佛教盛行于西藏、内蒙古等地区，而小乘佛教主要流行于云南。泰国、斯里兰卡、缅甸等东南亚国家也是小乘佛教盛行之地。

Greater Vehicle of Buddhism and Lesser Vehicle of Buddhism

After the death of Buddha Sakyamuni, founder of Buddhism, different understandings and expositions on Buddhist teachings emerged in Buddhist circle. As a result, many religious sects came into being. According to various religious theories and their formation stages, Buddhism concludes two basic sects: the Greater Vehicle of Buddhism (Skt. Mahayana) and the Lesser Vehicle of Buddhism (Skt. Hinayana). Mahayana formed around the first century. It claims that it is able to carry countless sentient beings from this shore of birth and death to the other shore of peaceful detachment state (Skt. Nirvana). Hinayana was a major school in the early stage. Mahayana believed that Hinayana teachings were too tedious to enlighten more sentient beings. Therefore, Mahayana gave a disparaging term "Lesser Vehicle" to Hinayana. In China, Mahayana prevails in Tibet, Inner-Mongolia and other regions while Hinayana mainly circulates in Yunnan of China and Tailand, Sri Lanka, Myanmar and other Southeast Asian countries.

大传召法会与小传召法会

大传召法会亦称"大祈愿法会"（默朗钦莫，藏文：sMon-lam-chen-mo）。1409 年藏历正月初一，宗喀巴大师主持了大传召法会，至正月十五日才结束。大传召法会一般在藏历年后举行，拉萨三大寺及卫藏、安多和康巴等地的僧众都会聚集拉萨，参与各种宗教活动。法会期间将举行辩经、迎请护法神及摔跤、比武、赛马等各类活动。大传召法会是西藏佛教界重要的宗教活动之一。小传召法会亦称"会供法会"或"小祈愿法会"（藏文：Khrom-mchod），与大祈愿法会类似。小传召法会始于 1683 年，每年藏历二月二十八日举行。

Greater Prayer Ceremony and Lesser Prayer Ceremony

The Greater Prayer Ceremony is also called Grand Summons (Tib. sMon-lam-chen-mo). On the first day of the first month on Tibetan calendar in 1409, Tsong-kha-pa presided over the Greater Prayer Ceremony, which lasted till the fifteenth day of the same month. Usually, it is held after Tibetan New Year. And monks from three major monasteries in Lhasa and from dBus-gtsang, A-mdo and Khams regions gather together in Lhasa and participate in various religious activities. During the prayer ceremony, there are all sorts of activities, such as debating on Buddhist scriptures, greeting protective deities as well as wrestling, martial arts competition, horseracing and so on. The Greater Prayer Ceremony is viewed as the most important religious activity in Tibetan Buddhist circle. The Lesser Prayer Ceremony, known as "Multitude Offering Ceremony" (Tib. Khrom-mchod), is identical with the Greater Prayer Ceremony. Initiated in 1683, it is held on the twenty-eighth day of the second month on Tibetan calendar each year.

大昭寺与释迦牟尼十二岁等身佛像

大昭寺（祖拉康，藏文：gTsug-lag-khang）位于拉萨市中心，始建于公元七世纪吐蕃王朝松赞干布时期。它是西藏最早的大型建筑之一，是藏传佛教信众朝觐的主要佛教圣地，也是西藏地方史上重要的政治活动中心。大昭寺正殿供奉着文成公主入藏时携带的一尊释迦牟尼十二岁等身镏金佛像，寺内还保留着大量精美的塑像及各种珍贵文物。大昭寺正门前立有唐蕃会盟碑，碑的一侧有相传为文成公主所栽的一棵古柳。还有一种说法认为，此树是从释迦牟尼佛落地的头发里长出来的。

Jo-khang Temple and Statue of Twelve-year-old Sakyamuni of Life-size

Located in the central part of Lhasa City, Jo-khang Temple (Tib. gTsug-lag-khang) was set up in the seventh century during the reign of Tubo bTsan-po Srong-btsan-sgam-po. As one of the earliest large-scale buildings in Tibet, it is not only Tibetans' major Buddhist holy site for pilgrimages, but also an important political activity center in local history of Tibet. Its main hall enshrines a gilt statue of twelve-year-old Sakyamuni of life size, which was brought by Princess Wencheng in her entry into Tibet. Jo-khang Temple also preserves numerous exquisite sculptures and various valuable cultural relics. In front of its main entrance stands Tang-Tubo Peace Pledge Monument with an ancient willow on its side. According to legends, this willow was planted by Princess Wencheng herself. Another saying goes like this: This willow grew out of Sakyamuni's hair dropping on the ground.

□ 释迦牟尼十二岁等身镏金铜像
Twelve-year-old Sakyamuni Statue of Life-size in Gilt Bronze

法源

　　法源（藏文：Chos-kyi-vbyung-gnas；梵文：Dharmodaya）代表生成某些神灵的观修场所。以金刚瑜伽法源为例，它呈六角星或立体六边形，由两个相互交叠的倒等边三角形金字塔组成。法源内部呈红色，象征着大乐；外部为白色，象征着空性。交叠三角形的三个角代表"三解脱门"（空、无相、无愿）。法源的六角是六个等边小三角形，代表"六度"（戒、忍、精进、禅、慧、布施）。顶角和底角是空的，象征着一切皆空和芸芸众生的无私。四边四角上的喜旋代表"四喜"（喜、胜喜、殊喜和俱生喜）。

Reality Source

　　Reality Source (Tib. Chos-kyi-vbyung-gnas; Skt. Dharmodaya) represents meditation sites where certain deities arise. Take Vajrayoga Reality Sources as an example, it is usually depicted as six-pointed stars or hexagons and consists of two opposite equilateral triangles. Its red interior and white exterior respectively symbolize great bliss and emptiness. Three angles on the interlocking triangles represent Triple Gateways of Liberation (emptiness liberation, condition liberation and desireless liberation). Six small equilateral triangles on its six corners embody Six Perfections (precept, patience, energy, meditation, wisdom, charity). Its angels on its top and base are empty, which means that all is vanity and all sentient beings are selfless. Swirls of joy on its four corners represent "Four Joys" (joy, perfect joy, joy of cessation and innate joy).

佛经

　　佛经是佛语的汇编，也是佛教教义的根本依据。其中较为重要的佛经有《心经》和《金刚经》。《心经》是佛教徒必读必知的一部佛教经典，全经只有一卷，共有 260 个字，体现出观音菩萨的大慈大悲。《金刚经》全名为《金刚般若波罗蜜经》，源自印度大乘佛教的初期，包含"根本般若"（梵文：Prajna）的重要思想。《金刚经》存有多种译本。在西藏，蓝黑色厚纸上用金粉或银粉缮写的经书分别称作"金写佛经"和"银写佛经"。抄经是修禅定的最佳方式，而用"八珍墨"进行抄写则表现出人们对佛教经典的敬畏之心。抄好的经文可供于佛堂、赠与其他结缘人或供养在舍利塔内，不管采取哪种形式，都要谨慎对待它们，以示对佛法的尊重。

Buddhist Scriptures

　　Buddhist scriptures are collected works of Buddha's words as well as the fundamental basis of Buddhist doctrines. Among them, *The Heart Sutra* and *The Diamond Sutra* are the comparative important ones. *Heart Sutra* is a Buddhist classic work that Buddhist adherents should chant and understand. It has only one volume with 260 characters, showing Avalokiteshvara Bodhisattva's infinite compassion and sympathy. With a full name of *The Diamond Perfection of Wisdom Sutra*, *The Diamond Sutra* emerged in the early period of Indian Greater Vehicle Buddhism. It contains some essential thoughts of principal wisdom (Skt. Prajna). Nowadays, there exist a number of translated versions. In Tibet, Buddhist scriptures copied in gold or silver powders on thick black paper are known as "gold-lettered Sutra" and "silver-lettered Sutra". Copying Buddhist scriptures is regarded as the best way of meditation. "Eight-precious Ink" is used to show people's reverence for Buddhist classics. Copied scriptures should be placed in worship in halls, bestowed upon some predestined persons and inserted respectfully into funerary Stupas. Either form, people should treat them causally to show respects to Dharma.

□ 金写佛经
Gold-lettered Sutra

佛塔

佛塔代表佛的"意"并存有他的灵骨。在象征意义上，佛塔有一整套的肖像意义，每个组成部分都代表通往圆满之路的某个具体方面。佛陀释迦牟尼涅槃（梵文：Nirvana）后不久，各地徒众分别兴建佛塔，共有八座，分别是：善逝塔、菩提塔、法轮塔、神变塔、天降塔、和好塔、尊胜塔和涅槃塔。除了八大佛塔外，流行于噶当派寺院的噶当塔是元代比较典型的艺术造型。

□ 佛塔
Stupa

Stupas

Stupas are representatives of Buddha's mind and used to keep his holy relics. Symbolically, Stupas contain a whole set of iconographical meanings. Each component represents a certain aspect to the enlightened path. After his peaceful detachment (Skt. Nirvana), his disciples from all sides separately set up eight great Stupas,including Enlightenment Stupa, Bodhi Stupa, Dharma-wheel Stupa, Miraculous Stupa, Descent Stupa, Harmonious Stupa, Victorious Stupa and Nirvana Stupa. In addition, bKav-gdams Stupas prevalent in monasteries of bKav-gdams-pa Sect are a typical modeling of the Yuan Dynasty.

佛陀八相成道

　　佛陀八相成道是指佛陀一生中以成道为中心的八个重大事件。八个重大事件分指：一，降兜率（梵文：Tusita），释迦牟尼居于兜率内院，观合宜时机，下降人间；二，托胎，乘坐口含莲花的六牙白象降入母胎；三，出生，公元前623年，他从摩耶夫人的右肋出生，降生在蓝毗尼园（梵文：Lumbini）；四，出家，19岁时，因体悟到世间无常和生老病死之苦，他在公元前604年离开王宫去探究人生；五，降魔，在伽耶山（梵文：Gaya）附近菩提树下金刚石制成的金刚座上降伏魔军；六，成道，公元前588年，31岁时，他在菩提树下修成正果；七，转法轮，成道后的49年间，他一直说法度生；八，入涅槃，公元前543年，他在拘尸那迦城（梵文：Kusinagara）附近的娑罗双树间入灭。

Buddha Sakyamuni's Eight Great Deeds

　　Buddha Sakyamuni's Eight Great Deeds display eight major events in his whole life, and take the attainment of Buddhahood as its main point. Eight Great Deeds include: (1) Descending from the Palace of Prosperity (Skt. Tusita): Sakyamuni inhabiting an inner courtyard of the Palace of Prosperity, found a right time to descend onto the mortal world. (2) Entering the womb: Riding a six-toothed elephant with a lotus in its mouth, he entered his mother's womb. (3) Taking of birth: He was born from Mahamaya's right rib in Lumbini Garden in 623 B.C. (4) Ordination as a renunciation: At the age of nineteen, he knew from his experience the impermanence on earth and sufferings caused by birth, age, illness and death, so he left his royal palace in 604 B.C. to explore life. (5) Subduing evil spirits: Sitting on a diamond Vajra pedestal under a Bodhi tree near Mount Gaya, he subdued evil spirits. (6) Attainment of Buddhahood: He got enlightened under a Bodhi tree at the age of thirty-one in 588 B.C. (7) Turning of Dharma-wheel: Over the forty-nine years of his enlightenment, he insisted to preach Buddhist teachings and enlighten sentient beings. (8) Passing into Nirvana: In 543 B.C., he passed away in a detachment state between two Sal trees near Kusinagara City.

佛像

　　佛像是佛教中最主要的膜拜对象，也是佛教艺术中最基本、最主要的题材。佛像艺术形成于 1 ～ 2 世纪，是一种受古希腊文化影响、印度文化和西域文化相融合的犍陀罗（梵文：Gandharva）文化的产物。佛教大致可分为汉传、藏传和南传佛教，因地域和文化的不同，同一尊佛像的面相、服饰和手持器物都会有所差异。以姿势划分，常见佛像可分为立式、坐式和卧式三类，如：布施像常呈立姿，左手结施愿印，表示能满足众生一切愿望，右手结无畏印，表示能够施与众生勇气和无畏精神。成道像和说法像常为坐姿，即结跏趺坐。成道像结定印，表示大地做证，及为解救众生不惜牺牲一切的言行。说法像结说法印。涅槃像亦称卧佛像，为卧姿，佛像右侧面南而卧，右手支颐，自在安详。在密宗佛教中分有怒相和善相两类本尊，造型复杂多变。其中，较为著名的善相本尊是文殊菩萨、观世音菩萨、度母、无量寿佛等。大威德金刚、金刚橛神、马头金刚、金刚手菩萨是较为著名的怒相本尊神。善、怒相兼具的本尊神有密迹金刚、胜乐金刚、饮血金刚、时轮金刚和金刚亥母。此外还有众多女神像及拥妃双身像。菩萨像也归于佛像之类。

Buddha Statues

　　Buddha statues are not only major worshipped objects in Buddhism, but also the fundamental and significant themes in Buddhist art. Buddha statue art came into being between the first century and second century. As a product of Gandharva culture, it was affected by ancient Greek culture and integrated with Indian and Western Regions cultures. Buddhism can roughly be classified into Chinese Buddhism, Tibetan Buddhism and Southern Buddhism. Because of different regions and cultures, identical Buddha statue may have different facial appearance, costumes, adornments and hand attributes. In terms of postures, they can be classified into standing, sitting and sleeping postures. For example, donation statues are usually in a standing posture, giving a gesture of vow-fulfilling with his left hand, which shows that he is willing to satisfy all desires of sentient beings. He also gives a fearless gesture with his right hand, which demonstrates that he will bestow courage and fearless spirit upon all sentient beings. Usually, enlightenment statues or teaching statues all sit cross-legged. The former gives an earth-touching gesture, which implies that he summons the earth to bear witness and spares neither his words nor acts to save all sentient beings. The latter gives a teaching gesture. Nirvana statue is also known as sleeping Buddha statue. He lies rightwards, facing southwest and props up his chin with his right hand, looking at ease and calm. In Tantric Buddhism, wrathful and peaceful looking Yidams are complicated and varied in modeling. Among them, Manjusri, Avalokiteshvara, Taras, Amitayus and others are well-known peaceful-looking Yidams. And Yamantaka, Kila deities, Horse-necked Vajra deities and Vajrapani are famous wrathful-looking deities. Yidams with both wrathful and peaceful facial expressions include Guhyapadavajra, Samvara, Hevajra, Time-wheel Vajra and Vajravarahi. In addition, there are numerous goddess statues and statues in a sexual union. Moreover, Bodhisattva statues are also listed as Buddha statues.

佛像坐姿

　　佛像坐姿根据双腿的不同姿势可分为萨埵跏趺坐（梵文：Sattvaparyanka）、自在坐（梵文：Sukhasana）、金刚跏趺坐（梵文：Vajraparyanka）和半跏趺坐（梵文：Ardhaparyankasana）等。结跏趺坐时双腿盘曲，双脚脚背置于两腿之上，脚心朝上。在佛教看来，这样的坐姿最为安稳，身端心正。结萨埵跏趺坐时双腿盘曲，右腿蜷曲，左腿略伸。自在坐亦称"善跏趺坐"（梵文：Bhadrasana）。结自在坐的佛像坐在高座上，双腿不盘曲，双脚自然下垂，有的佛像则是双腿交叉。结金刚跏趺坐时双腿左内右外盘曲。结半跏趺坐时右腿盘曲，左腿略伸。

Sitting Postures of Buddha Statues

　　According to postures, Buddha statues can be classified into Sattva sitting posture (Skt. Sattvaparyanka), freestyle sitting posture (Skt. Sukhasana), Vajra sitting posture (Skt. Vajraparyanka) and one leg-crossed sitting posture (Skt. Ardhaparyankasana) and so on. In cross-legged sitting posture, Buddha statue bends his legs and places insteps of his two feet onto two legs with soles upwards. In the light of Buddhism, such a sitting posture is most steady, embodying an upright body and a good mind. In Sattvaparyanka, Buddha statue bends his right leg and slightly stretches his left one. Sukhasana is also called Bhadrasana. In Sukhasana, Buddha statue seated on a high pedestal does not bend his legs, instead, he naturally puts down his feet. Moreover, some Buddha statues cross their legs. In Vajraparyanka, Buddha statue is cross-legged with his left leg inwards and his right one outwards. In Ardhaparyankasana, Buddha statue bends his right leg and slightly stretches his left one.

甘丹寺

　　甘丹寺（藏文：dGav-ldan）坐落在西藏拉萨达孜区。它是拉萨三大寺之一，也是藏传佛教格鲁派六大寺之首寺。甘丹寺由藏传佛教格鲁派宗师宗喀巴倡建于 1409 年，历经多次扩建形成现有的规模。寺内各殿供奉着尊胜佛母、文殊菩萨像并保存着宗喀巴的经书、印章等，还存有 24 幅珍贵御赐唐卡。

dGav-ldan Monastery

　　Located in sTag-rtse County in Lhasa of Tibet, dGav-ldan Monastery is not only one of the three major monasteries in Lhasa, but also the head among the six grand monasteries of dGe-lugs-pa Sect of Tibetan Buddhism. Tsong-kha-pa, founder of dGe-lugs-pa Sect of Tibetan Buddhism, advocated the construction of dGav-ldan Monastery in 1409. The current size came into being after several expansions. The halls of this monastery enshrine statues of Goddess of Dignity, Manjusri Bodhisattva, and preserve Tsong-kha-pa's Buddhist texts, seals and twenty-four valuable Thang-kas bestowed by the emperor.

◻ 甘丹寺
　dGav-ldan Monastery

供灯与灯供

供灯俗称"酥油灯"。藏族群众大多信奉藏传佛教，故而在寺院佛堂和家中佛龛前一年四季都供有酥油灯。酥油灯一般分为金制、银制、铜制或铁制，其造型各异，种类繁多。在一些寺院里，大小不等的酥油灯排列错落有致，俗称为"灯供"或"千供"，既给大殿增添了庄重肃穆的气氛，又使整个大殿金光普照。人们常可看到藏族信众手捧酥油器皿虔诚地为酥油灯添加酥油，使灯火长明不灭。

□ 白玉供灯
White Jade
Offering Lamp

Offering Lamps and Lamp Offering

Offering lamps are commonly called oil lamps. Most of Tibetan masses believe in Tibetan Buddhism, so they always lay out oil lamps in halls of monasteries or in front of shrines in houses all the year round. Usually oil lamps are made of gold, silver, copper or iron. They have different shapes and plenty of varieties. In some monasteries, oil lamps, small or large, are well-laid out, which are commonly known as "Lamp Offering" or "Thousand Oil Lamps Offering". They not only add dignified and solemn atmosphere to halls, but also make them brilliant. People can often see Tibetan masses hold butter containers, piously add butter to oil lamps so as to make them illuminating day and night.

供养与供养人

供养亦称"供施"，供养人亦称"施主"。"供"指的是以财宝、衣物、花香对佛、法、僧三宝进行心、物两方面的供奉。因僧侣在修行时需要摈弃一切外缘，因此无法自谋生活必需品，而需要信众的布施。僧人接受别人的供养后，不要忘记替施主回向。供养人指的是通过提供资金、物品或劳力来制作圣像、开凿石窟、修造宗教场所来弘扬佛教教义的虔诚信徒。

Offering Sacrifices and Benefactors

"Offering sacrifices" and "benefactors" are respectively known as "making offerings" and "donators". "Offering sacrifices" means to provide money and valuables, costumes, flowers and joss sticks in mental and physical worship of Three Jewels. Monks need to break off all external connections in meditations, so it is hard for them to look for necessaries of life for themselves. As a result, they need donations from religious adherents. However, after receiving donations from others, they should remember to transfer merits to others. Benefactors refer to some pious religious adherents, who donate money and provide goods or labor forces to make holy sculptures, dig caves and set up religious sites so as to disseminate Buddhist teachings.

皈依与皈依处

皈依有投靠和依附之意。皈依处指的是可以皈依的场所（藏文：rTen）。因此，佛经被视为佛的皈依处，塔被视为法的皈依处，寺院被视为僧的皈依处。信仰者除皈依佛、法、僧三宝外，还须皈依上师（梵文：Guru）。佛教中还有身皈依处、语皈依处和意皈依处之说。有专家将 2015 年在西藏阿里故如甲木（藏文：Gu-ru-rgya-mo）墓出土的黄金面具视为面皈依处。

Taking Refuge and Supports

Taking refuge means "seeking refuge with sb." and "attaching oneself to". Supports (Tib. rTen) refer to spots for people to take refuge in. Therefore, Buddhist scriptures, pagodas and monasteries are respectively seen as supports of Buddha, Dharma and Sangha. In addition to taking refuge in Buddha, Dharma and Sangha, religious adherents should take refuge in masters (Skt. Guru). Buddhism has a view that there are also support of body, support of speech and support of mind. And some experts think that the gold mask unearthed in 2015 at Gu-ru-rgya-mo Cemetery in mNgav-ris of Tibet can be viewed as support of face.

慧眼

　　慧眼（梵文：Urna）亦称"天目"或"第三只眼"，源于印度教湿婆神的巨大慧眼。佛教有肉眼、天眼、慧眼、法眼和佛眼五眼之说，它们是可以观察不同对象的五种眼力。慧眼泛指能照见实相的智慧，洞察凡间的一切。在佛像（如千手千眼观音像的掌心上）、佛塔或佛教建筑上常可看到形态各异的慧眼。

Wisdom Eye

Wisdom eye (Skt. Urna), known as "divine eye" or "the third eye", originated from Hindus Shiva's huge eyes. In Buddhism, eyes can be classified into bodily vision, divine vision, wisdom vision, Dharma vision and Buddha vision, representative of five visions used to observe different objects. Wisdom eye generally refers to the wisdom to realize the real truth and see through everything on earth. Wisdom eyes in different shapes can be seen on Buddha statues (for example, on One Thousand-handed and One Thousand-eyed Avalokiteshvara's palms), pagodas or Buddhist architectures.

活佛与活佛转世

　　活佛是汉语对藏传佛教中具有转世身份僧人的称呼。藏语称"朱古"（藏文：sPrul—sku），意为"化身"，指的是由转世产生的高僧大德。活佛转世制度是藏传佛教所独有的一种宗教领袖的传承方式。随着活佛转世制度的普遍使用，在灵童认定、坐床等具体操作上逐渐形成了一套比较规范的完整制度。藏传佛教转世灵童的确认有着严格的宗教仪轨，分抓阄、护法神降神指定、高僧占卜指定或世俗统治者指定等几种方式，必须经过前世预言、自现征兆、护法神谕及前世遗物辨认等一系列认定程序。大活佛、前世活佛的近侍及寺院住持组成的寻访团负责转世灵童的寻访工作。

Rin-po-ches and Reincarnation System of Rin-po-ches

　　"Living Buddha" is a Chinese term for Tibetan Buddhist monks in reincarnated status. "sPrul-sku" in Tibetan means "incarnation", which refers to eminent monks and masters of great virtue who emerged after reincarnation. The reincarnation system of Rin-po-ches is a unique inheritance way of Tibetan Buddhist religious leading figures. Due to this system's extensive application, a complete set of comparative standard system gradually came into being in such specific operating procedures as the confirmation and enthronement of reincarnated soul boys. Tibetan Buddhist reincarnated soul boys must be confirmed according to very strict religious practices. There are several ways, including drawing lots and assigning by oracles through séance and eminent monks through divination as well as assigning by secular ruling figures. A series of selecting and identifying work relied on predictions given by their former generations, signs of their manifestations, oracles given by protective deities and their identification of former generations' remains. Usually search groups composed of Grand Rin-po-ches, previous Rin-po-che's close attendants and abbots, are responsible for the routine work.

开光与加持

开光与加持是两个不同的概念。在佛教中，只有佛像才能进行开光，其他物品只能进行加持。开光仪式类似落成典礼，新寺院建成或新塑佛像完工时均要举行开光仪式。加持是指法师对于吉祥用品的灵力灌输，使之具备有一定的灵性。经过加持的物件应随身佩戴。

Consecration and Empowerment

Consecration and empowerment are different in concept. In Buddhism, consecration is only used for Buddha statues while empowerment is used for other items. Similar to inauguration ceremonies, consecration ceremonies should be held after the completion of a new monastery or a new sculpture. Empowerment refers to some spiritual strength which religious masters transfer to lucky objects in an attempt to let them possess certain spirituality. Empowered objects should be worn at any time.

降神师与乃琼寺

　　降神师亦称"巫觋"或"神使"，指的是能传神言者。乃琼寺（藏文：gNas-chung）位于哲蚌寺下方，历史上曾是西藏著名的佛教高等学府，每年都有许多喇嘛在此获得格西学位。据传，8世纪莲花生大师将乃琼恶神多吉札丹（藏文：rDo-rje-brag-ldan）降伏，使之成为藏传佛教的护法神。因此，乃琼寺内既有法力无边的乃琼神使，也保留了一套完整的降神会的仪式。过去，每逢遇到重大事件，当时的西藏噶厦政府（藏文：bKav-shag）都会到乃琼寺请求神使明示。

Oracles and gNas-chung Monastery

　　Oracles, also known as "spirit medium" or "oracle priest", refer to those who can deliver divine messages. Located below vBras-spungs Monastery, gNas-chung Monastery used to be a well-known Buddhist institution of higher education, and many Lamas got their academic title of dGe-bshes there each year. Tradition has it that in the eighth century, Master Padmasambhava subdued vicious gNas-chung rDo-rje-brag-ldan Deity and made it a protective deity of Tibetan Buddhism. Therefore, gNas-chung Monastery not only has gNas-chung oracles of infinite supernatural power, but also keeps a complete set of séance ceremony. In the past, whenever there was a major event, the local government of Tibet (Tib. bKav-shag) would go to gNas-chung Monastery to seek oracles for their clear indications.

□ 经书架
Scripture Shelves

佛经、经书架和经书墙

佛经指的是佛语的汇编，放置佛经的架子或台座称作经书架。萨迦寺内的经书墙高 10 米、长 60 米，已有 800 多年的历史。经书墙上摆放着 8 万多卷用金、银、红珊瑚、绿松石、珍珠、象牙粉及历代法王的骨粉缮写的手抄经书。

Buddhist Scriptures, Scripture Shelves and Scripture Wall within Sa-skya Monastery

Buddhist scriptures refer to collected works of Buddha's words. Frames or pedestals used by people to lay out Buddhist scriptures are called Scripture shelves. A ten-meter-high and sixty-meter-long scripture wall within Sa-skya Monastery has a history of over eight hundred years. Over 80,000 volumes of hand-copied scriptures are laid out on the shelves on this wall.

拉卜楞寺

拉卜楞寺位于甘肃甘南州夏河县。它建于 1709 年，是藏传佛教格鲁派六大黄教寺院之一，也是甘、青、川藏传佛教的中心。寺院占地约 1300 余亩，内有六大学院（扎仓，藏文：Grwa-tshang）、十八座佛寺及金塔、辩经坛、藏经楼、印经院、经轮房等建筑。拉卜楞寺每年举行 7 次规模较大的法会：默朗钦波大法会（藏历正月初三）、跳神节（正月十四日）、酥油花供灯会（正月十五日）、浴佛节（四月初八）、敦白日扎（藏文：bDun-pavi-rigs-gra）法会（七月）、宗喀巴圆寂日（十月二十五日）及历世嘉木样活佛的圆寂日。

Bla-brang Monastery

Built in 1709 in Xiahe, South of Gansu Province, Bla-brang Monastery is not only one of the six major monasteries of dGe-lugs-pa Sect of Tibetan Buddhism, but also the center of Tibetan Buddhism in regions adjacent to Gansu, Qinghai and Sichuan Provinces. With an area of over 1,300 *mu*, it has six monastic colleges (Tib. Grwa-tshang), eighteen temples as well as golden pagodas, Sutra-debating grounds, libraries, scripture printing houses and prayer-wheel houses, etc. Each year, it holds seven large-scale prayer ceremonies, including Grand Prayer Ceremony (Tib. sMon-lam-chen-mo, on the third day of the first month on Tibetan calendar), vCham Performance Festival (on the fourteenth day of the first month), Butter Sculpture Festival (on the fifteenth day of the first month), Bathing Festival (on the eighth day of the fourth month), bDun-pavi-rigs-gra Prayer Ceremony (in the seventh month), the Death Anniversary of Tsong-kha-pa (on the twenty-fifth day of the tenth month) and the Death Anniversary of vJam-dbyangs Rin-po-ches of successive generations.

灵塔

　　灵塔一般指的是供奉和存放为藏传佛教做出巨大贡献的活佛、上师的法体或骨灰的佛塔，由佛祖释迦牟尼信徒所修的舍利塔演变而来。拉萨布达拉宫的灵塔殿就供奉着五世达赖喇嘛、十世达赖喇嘛和十二世达赖喇嘛的灵塔。五世达赖喇嘛肉身灵塔之名为"南赡部洲唯一庄严金质灵塔"，是用300多千克黄金制成的。据说灵塔内还有释迦牟尼的指骨、宗喀巴大师用过的碗及取自象脑的象宝等宝物。

Funerary Stupas

　　Funerary Stupas usually refer to pagodas which keep bodies or bone ashes of Rin-po-ches and masters who have made great contributions for Tibetan Buddhism. Funerary Stupas evolved from the Relic Stupa set up by Sakyamuni's disciples. The Funerary Stupa Hall in the Potala Palace enshrines Funerary Stupas of the Fifth, Tenth and Twelfth Dalai Lamas. The Fifth Dalai Lama's Funerary Stupa enjoys the title of "Sole Majestic Gold Funerary Stupa in the Southern Continent 'Zam' Trees". It is made of gold of over three hundred kilograms. It is said that it preserves Sakyamuni's finger bones, bowls used by Tsong-kha-pa, gems taken from an elephant's brain and other precious items.

六字真言

六字真言"唵、嘛、呢、叭、咪、吽"（梵文：Om Mani Padme Hum）源于梵文，是大慈大悲观世音菩萨咒。它象征诸菩萨的慈悲与加持，也是藏传佛教中最受尊崇的一句咒语，多用梵文或藏文描刻在建筑物、宗教器具、山崖或石板上。藏传佛教信众认为循环往返地念诵六字真言就能使人功德圆满、消灾积德。

Six Sacred Words

Six Sacred Words (Skt. Om Mani Padme Hum) originated from Sanskrit. As compassionate Avalokiteshvara Bodhisattva's incantation, it not only symbolizes compassion and empowerment, but also serves as the most revered incantation in Tibetan Buddhism. It is often engraved in Sanskrit or Tibetan on buildings, religious utensils, cliffs or slabs. Tibetans believe that chanting it repeatedly enables people to gain perfect virtues, eliminate disasters and accumulate merits.

轮回、轮回图与六道轮回

轮回（梵文：Samsara）是佛教关于善恶报应的基本学说之一。轮回图亦称"九宫八卦图"（斯贝廓洛，藏文：Srid-pavi-vkhor-lo）。在藏传佛教寺庙正殿门的外侧壁画上常可见到此图。全图呈圆轮状，分内外四层。中心层绘有代表贪、嗔、痴的红鸽、绿蛇和黑猪。外层分白黑两色，分别代表善趣和恶趣。上二区代表天界和人界，下三区正中代表地狱，右侧代表傍生，左侧代表饿鬼。六道轮回指的是佛教所说的众生依生前善恶行为在生死六种境地（天、人、非天、傍生、饿鬼和地狱）中的轮回。

Eternal Cycle of Birth and Death, Wheel of Life and Six Kinds of Existence

Eternal cycle of birth and death (Skt. Samsara) is one of the fundamental doctrines about good and evil retribution in Buddhism. Picture Depicting Wheel of Life is also known as "Figure of Nine Squares Eight Trigrams" (Tib. Srid-pavi-vkhor-lo). Such a picture often appears on murals in outer side of the major hall's entrance in a Tibetan Buddhist monastery. It is shaped like a circle ring with four layers. The central layer is painted with a red pigeon, a green snake and a black pig, respectively representative of desire, anger and ignorance. The outer layer is in white and black, standing for fortunate and inferior beings. Two upper sections signify the Celestial Realm and the Human Realm. The middle part of three lower sections represents hell while the Realm of Animal and the Realm of Hungry Ghost are on its right and left sides. Six Kinds of Existence refer to six cycles in the Realms of Celestial, Human, Denizen, Animal, Hungry Ghost and Hell mentioned in Buddhism, signifying eternal cycle of birth and death of sentient beings according to their good or evil deeds in their previous life.

曼扎

曼扎（梵文：Mantra）是藏传佛教常用供器之一，象征着须弥山，一般用于法会。曼扎盘可分为上品、中品和下品三类。上品曼扎盘用金银打造并镶嵌珠宝，中品曼扎盘用黄铜和白铜打造，下品曼扎盘用平整的木板或石板制作而成。曼扎盘内盛满五谷杂粮和各色石子。上品曼扎盘中还可放入珊瑚、玛瑙、绿松石等珠宝，以及诃子、人参等珍贵药果。曼扎呈塔形，顶部尖塔象征财富。在法会上，法师依次撒上上述各物，象征祈愿幸福吉祥。曼扎前面要摆放七只铜制供碗，以示七种供养。

Mantra Offerings

Mantra offering, one of common offering articles in Tibetan Buddhism, is a symbol of Mount Sumeru, and usually used in prayer ceremonies. Mantra offering containers can be classified into high-class, intermediate-class and low-class ones. High-class containers are made of gold or silver and inlaid with jewels. Intermediate-class ones are made of brass or cupronickel while low-class ones are made of smooth wooden boards or slabs. Mantra containers are usually full of cereals and multi-colored pebbles. Corals, agates, turquoise and other precious stones, chebules and ginsengs as well as other medical fruits can be put into high-class containers. Mantra offering takes the shape of a pagoda, and its point symbolizes fortune. In prayer ceremonies, religious masters sprinkle in succession the things mentioned above as a token of praying for happiness and auspiciousness. Seven copper bowls should be placed in front of it, representing seven kinds of offerings in sacrifice.

密宗与密宗骨饰

　　密宗是佛教的支派之一。密宗认为世界是由地、水、火、风、空和识六种力量构成，它们也构成了人类和大自然的现象世界。密宗把肉体和不可思议的、难以体验的佛的气息称作身、口、意"三密"。密宗认为"坛城"就是人与佛交流的重要渠道。密宗骨饰是举行密宗仪式时所佩戴的装饰品，大多用象牙制成，一般由头饰、项饰、耳饰、腰饰组成，头饰上常饰有金刚橛、吉祥结和骨珠。

□ 密宗骨饰
Tantric Bone Adornments

Tantric Buddhism and Tantric Bone Adornments

　　As one of the Buddhist branches, Tantric Buddhism thinks that the world is formed by six fundamental powers (earth, water, fire, wind, space and perception), which also constitute the phenomenal world of human beings and nature. Tantric Buddhism not only views physical bodies and Buddha's mysterious and inconspicuous breath as Three Kinds of Mysteries related to body, speech and mind, but also thinks that Mandalas are vary important channels for communications between men and deities. Most of Tantric bone adornments used in Tantric rites are made of ivory, consisting of topknots, neck adornments used in Tantric rites, earring adornments, waist decorations, etc. and topknots are often adorned with Kilas, endless knots and bone beads.

摩顶赐福

摩顶是佛教授戒传法时的一种仪轨。《法华经》称释迦牟尼佛以大法付嘱大菩萨时，用右手摩其顶，有加持赐福之意。

Giving Blessing Touches on Heads

Giving blessing touches on heads is a rite used in the process of ordaining monks or preaching Buddhist teachings. It is recorded in *Lotus Scripture* that Buddha Sakyamuni placed his right hand on a great Bodhisattva's head, showing his empowerment and blessings when he entrusted the latter to disseminate Dharma.

涅槃

涅槃（梵文：Nirvana）亦称"寂灭"或"圆寂"，是死亡的美称，有"不生不灭"之意。涅槃是佛教修证的最高境界。通过修道彻底地断灭烦恼，广积功德，超越生死轮回，才能达到这种"不生不灭"的涅槃状态。

Nirvana

Nirvana, also known as "still quiescence" or "in a detachment state", is a laudatory title of "death" with a meaning of "neither arising nor ceasing". Nirvana is a supreme level in Buddhist meditations and enlightenment. Only by thoroughly cutting off troubles through meditations on Dharma, greatly accumulating merits and transcending the cycle of birth and death, could people reach a "neither arising nor ceasing" Nirvana state.

青海塔尔寺

　　建于 1560 年的塔尔寺（藏文：sKu-vbum-dgon）位于青海省西宁市湟中区。相传，塔尔寺是宗喀巴大师的诞生地。1776 年修建的八大佛塔整齐地排在寺院前面。作为藏传佛教格鲁派六大寺院之一，塔尔寺以绘画、酥油花、堆绣三绝著称。藏历年期间，塔尔寺都要举行四次大型法会和两次小型法会。每年的藏历正月要举行酥油花灯会，而藏历四月和六月法会上都会举行晒佛节和跳神节，大量信徒和游客都会慕名而来。

sKu-vbum Monastery

　　Built in 1560, sKu-vbum Monastery (Tib:sKu-vbum-dgon, another name Ta'er Monastery) is located in Huangzhong County of Qinghai Province. According to legends, it is Master Tsong-kha-pa's birthplace. In front of the monastery regularly stand eight pagodas set up in 1776. As one of the six major monasteries of dGe-lugs-pa Sect of Tibetan Buddhism, it is famous for its paintings, butter sculptures and embossed embroidery Thang-kas.It will hold four large-scale and two small-scale prayer ceremonies in Tibetan New Year celebrations, and the Butter Sculpture Festival in the first month on Tibetan calendar each year. And the Festival of Displaying Buddha and vCham Performance Festival are respectively held in prayer ceremonies in the fourth and the sixth months on Tibetan calendar. Large numbers of Buddhist adherents and tourists are attracted by its fame.

萨迦寺

　　萨迦寺（藏文：Sa-skya）位于西藏日喀则萨迦县，建于 1073 年，分为南寺和北寺两座寺院，是藏传佛教萨迦派的主寺。萨迦寺内藏有元代中央政府颁给萨迦地方官员的诰命、印玺，宋元以来的各种佛像、法器、刺绣品、供品及佛教经典和与天文、地理、历算、医药、文学、历史等有关的大量藏文著作，尤为珍贵的是寺藏的 2000 余块经板及 1980 年在寺内发现的用藏、蒙、梵三种文字刻写的 20 部贝叶经。

Sa-skya Monastery

　　Built in 1073 and located in Sa-skya County in Shigatse of Tibet, Sa-skya Monastery (including Southern Monastery and Northern Monastery) is the major monastery of Sa-skya-pa Sect of Tibetan Buddhism. It preserves not only royal edicts and imperial seals bestowed upon Sa-skya local officials by the Yuan Central Government, but also various Buddha statues, ritual implements, embroideries, offering articles and Buddhist classic works as well as a large number of Tibetan works related to astronomy, geography, calculation, medicine, literature and history. The most precious are the over 2,000 pieces of scripture woodblocks kept in this monastery and twenty volumes of Pattra-leaf scriptures, which were written in Tibetan, Mongol and Sanskrit scripts and discovered in 1980.

三宝与皈依三宝

　　佛教中的三宝（公却松，藏文：dKon-mchog-gsum）指的是佛宝、法宝、僧宝。佛宝指的是成就圆满佛道的本师释迦年尼，法宝指一切教法，僧宝是依诸佛法修行、弘扬佛法、度化众生的出家人。佛教徒只有皈依三宝，即皈依佛、皈依法和皈依僧，才能真正修得解脱之道。因此，皈依三宝是成为佛教徒的根本条件。

Three Jewels and Taking Refuge in Three Jewels

"Three Jewels" or "Triple Gem" (Tib. dKon-mchog-gsum) in Buddhism represents Buddha, Dharma and Sangha, which respectively refer to the enlightened principal master Sakyamuni, all Buddhist teachings and religious adherents, who conduct meditations based on Dharma, disseminate Buddhist teachings and enlighten sentient beings. Only by taking refuge in Three Jewels (taking refuge in Buddha, in Dharma and in Sangha), could people follow the path to salvation. Therefore, taking refuge in Buddha, Dharma and Sangha is an essential condition of becoming a Buddhist adherent.

桑耶寺

位于西藏山南扎囊县雅鲁藏布江北岸的桑耶寺（藏文：bSam-yas）建于公元8世纪吐蕃王朝时期。它不但是吐蕃第一座佛法僧三宝齐全的佛教寺院，也是西藏第一座剃度僧人出家的寺院。桑耶寺仿古印度欧丹达普黎（梵文：Odantapuri）寺格局而建，与佛教宇宙观相符，并融合了汉藏的建筑风格，因此桑耶寺也被称作"三样"寺。

□ 桑耶寺碑
Stele in
bSam-yas
Monastery

bSam-yas Monastery

Located on the northern bank of the Yar-klung-gtsang-po River in Gra-nang County, Lho-kha of Tibet, bSam-yas Monastery was built in the eighth century during the Tubo Kingdom. It is not only a Buddhist monastery complete in Three Jewels (Buddha, Dharma and Sangha), but also the first monastery in Tibet to hold the tonsure ceremony. It was built by the imitation of the general pattern of ancient Indian Odantapuri Monaetery. It not only conformed to Buddhist cosmic views, but also fused Han-Tibetan architectural styles. Therefore, bSam-yas Monastery is also known as "Three-styled Monastery".

十相自在

　　十相自在（朗久旺丹，藏文：rNam-bcu-dbang-ldan）是藏传佛教时轮宗的一种极具神秘力量的图符。它由七个梵文字母和日、月、圆圈三个图形组成，包含着异常复杂的辩证关系，也标志着密乘本尊与其坛场的和合一体。图符中的五种颜色分别代表地、水、火、风、空五大要素。十相的十个部分由身、智、空、风、火、水、地、情、器、天界组成。藏传佛教信众常将十相自在绘制在房门、墙壁或房梁上。这个图符也经常出现在塔门、唐卡、岩壁或经书封面上，用以禳灾辟邪。

Mystical Seal of the Kalicakra

　　Mystical Seal of the Kalicakra (Tib. rNam-bcu-dbang-ldan) is an icon of mysterious power in the Time-wheel School of Tibetan Buddhism. It consists of seven Sanskrit alphabets and three graphs of the sun, the moon and a circle. It not only contains extreme complicated dialectical relations, but also implies the union of Tantric Yidams and their Mandalas. Its five colors respectively represent five major elements: earth, water, fire, air and space. And its ten sections are composed of body, intelligence, space, air, fire, water, earth, emotion, device and celestial realm. Tibetans usually paint them on doors, walls or beams. Such icons often appear on pylons, Thang-kas, cliff surfaces or Buddhist sculpture covers so as to avert calamity and avoid evil spirits.

手印

在佛教中，手印（梵文：Mudra）是修行者获得成就的重要一项。手印是双手与手指所结的各种手势，也是除了语言和面部表情之外的另一种表述方式。梵文 mudra 一词源自动词 mud，其意为取悦神灵。该词一般指的是印记、符号或标识。在佛教词汇中，该词主要用来指佛和神灵所结手印。在早期的大乘佛教肖像画法中，只有几个主要手印出现在佛造像上。而在后来的金刚乘佛教肖像画法中都可看到这些清晰可辨的手印。大日如来佛、不动如来佛、宝生如来佛、无量光佛和不空成就佛五佛分别结说法印、触地印、施予印、禅定印和护法印。不同的手印有不同的丰富含义。常见手印有殊胜三界印、法轮印、护法印、说法印、合十印、坛城印、期克印（梵文：Tarjani）、胜愿印、降魔印、安慰印、禅定印、触地印、无畏印、施依印、施予印、施愿印和大圆满印等。

Ritual Gestures

Hand gestures (Skt. Mudra) are very significant for Buddhist practitioners to get enlightened. They refer to various gestures made by both hands and fingers. In addition to languages and facial expressions, they also serve as another expressive way. The Sanskrit term "Mudra" derives from the verb "mud" with a meaning of "pleasing deities", and it generally refers to a seal, a mark or a sign. In Buddhist terminology, it is mainly used to present configurations or gestures given by Buddhas and deities. In early Mahayana iconography, only a few gestures were depicted upon Buddha statues, and in later Vajrayana iconography, they became distinguishing gestures of Five Buddhas. Vairocana, Akshobya, Ratnasambhava, Amitabha and Amoghasiddhi Buddhas respectively make teaching gesture, earth-touching gesture, boon-granting gesture, meditation gesture and Dharma-protecting gesture. Different gestures have different rich connotations. Common gestures include gesture of victory over the Three Realms, Wheel of Dharma gesture, Dharma-protecting gesture, teaching gesture, palms-folded gesture,

Mandala gesture, threatening gesture (Skt. Tarjani), vow-fulfilling gesture, spirit-subduing gesture, appeasement gesture, meditation gesture, earth-touching gesture, fearless gesture, refuge-giving gesture, boon-granting gesture, vow-fulfilling gesture, enlightenment gesture and so on.

受戒与灌顶

受戒指佛教徒通过一定的宗教仪式接受戒律。灌顶（梵文：Abhiseka）是修习密法时必须经历的一种宗教入门仪式。灌顶本为印度古代国王即位的一种仪式。在即位仪式上，国师以"四大海之水"灌于国王头顶，表示祝福，亦表示自此之后他可以治理国政。灌顶仪式有一整套十分严格的程序。

Ordination and Baptism

Ordination means that Buddhist adherents accept Buddhist disciplines by way of certain religious rituals. Baptism (Skt. Abhiseka) serves as an essential introductory rite for Tantric Buddhist practitioners. In the past, this rite was held when an ancient king was ready to ascend the throne. In his enthronement ceremony, a state tutor would pour "water from four oceans" onto the top of the king's head, which not only expresses the state tutor's blessing, but also accounts for the fact that the king is enabled to exercise his state administration since then. Baptist ceremony needs a whole set of very strict procedures.

赎身品与护篱

　　某些藏族仪式中要使用赎身品（藏文：gLud-gtor）以灭除邪恶精怪对芸芸众生及其财产的邪恶影响。传统上，这些"替罪羊"或"假"供品形如彩绘护篱（藏文：rGyang-bu）或是受害者的面塑像。护篱常插在所谓的"粮仓"（藏文：vBru-mdzod）上，护篱上面绘有一位身披"阳性"虎皮的男子，其"方法"右手持有一支象征男性的箭。有时护篱绘有一位身披"阴性"豹皮的女子。其"智慧"左手持有一个象征女性的纺锤。护篱的三角部分和顶部分别绘有象征阳性的金刚杵和象征女性的莲花。箭和纺锤这对截然不同的象征物源自前佛教时期。在苯教中，它们作为"真言武器"（藏文：Thun-zor）广为使用。赎身品也可按照被赎身者的模样进行捏制。在捏制时要把从受害者身上剪下的指甲、头发及从其衣物上取下的一块布揉进模拟像的面团中。

Ransom Offering and Wooden Plaques

　　A "ransom offering"(Tib. gLud-gtor) is employed in certain Tibetan rituals to divert the malignant influences of evil spirits away from human beings, their property and possessions. Traditionally, these substitute "scapegoat" and "decoy" offerings take the form of painted wooden plaques (Tib. rGyang-bu) or dough effigies of the afflicted persons. Wooden plaques would be planted upright in a "granary" (Tib. vBru-mdzod) or box of grains. Usually, the plaque depicts a male image wearing a "male" tiger-skin and holding the male symbol of an arrow with his right "method" hand. Sometimes, the plaque depicts a female image wearing a "female" leopard-skin and holding the female symbol of a spindle with her "wisdom" hand. The symbols of a male Vajra club and a female spindle respectively appear at the plaque's triangular top and its top. The polarity symbols of an arrow and a spindle of pre-Buddhist origin were extensively used as "magical weapons"(Tib. Thun-zor) in the Bon tradition. Ransom effigies (Tib. gLud) may also be molded from dough in the likeness of the person. The dough of these effigies is kneaded together with some nail clippings, hair and pieces of clothing from the afflicted victim.

四大佛教节日

佛教的四大节日指的是纪念佛祖释迦牟尼的四个主要节日，分别是每年农历二月十五日举行的神变节、四月十五日举行的成佛节、六月六日举行的说法节和九月二十一日举行的回降节。

Four Major Buddhist Festivals

Four major Buddhist festivals refer to four important festivals in commemoration of Buddha Sakyamuni, including Miraculous Festival held on fifteenth day of the second month; Becoming a Buddha Festival held on fifteenth day of the fourth month; Preaching Buddhist Doctrines Festival held on the sixth day of the sixth month; Re-descending Festival held on the twentieth-first day of the ninth month on the Lunar Calendar.

四法印

　　四法印是显示诸法真理的四个标印，可作为具有佛教特征的四种法门。四法印分别是：诸行无常、有漏皆苦、诸法无我、涅槃寂静。诸行是指身心"五蕴"（色蕴、受蕴、想蕴、行蕴、识蕴）。诸行无常指的是世间万物皆因时而变，均有出现和终结的规律。有漏皆苦指的是人对万物都有美好和苦恶之念。诸法无我指的是在一切想法中，其实都含有自己和众人的想法。涅槃寂静指因内心不会有痛苦和想法，故心宁安乐，因而达到涅槃境界。

Four Dharma-Mudras

　　Four Dharma-Mudras are four major signs in all phenomena. They are four kinds of initial approaches of Buddhist characteristics. Four verses are as follows: All products are impermanent. Contaminated things are miserable. All phenomena are empty and selfless. Nirvana is peace. All products refer to Five Aggregates related to body and mind (Five Aggregates: aggregates of form, feeling, perception, motivational factors and consciousness). The first verse indicates that everything on earth is changeable at any time, and its emergence and disappearance has its own laws. The second verse implies the fact that people may have good, miserable and evil thoughts about everything. The third verse means that all thoughts may contain yours and others'. The fourth verse demonstrates that if you have no sufferings and thoughts in your heart, you will be tranquil and peaceful, which will make you reach a Nirvana state.

坛城

　　坛城（梵文：Mandala）源于印度佛教密宗。它原是为修行所建的小土台，后为密宗所用。把这种修行场所绘制或塑造成具象的表征，以供观者观想意会，因此，它被视为密宗本尊及其眷属聚集的道场。坛城上的图案代表不同的寓意。坛城可分为观想坛城、立体坛城、彩粉坛城、图画坛城和道影方便坛城。观想坛城是密宗行者心中观想现起的自生坛城或前生坛城影像；立体坛城是用香泥等实物，按照心思构画塑造的呈立体形象的密宗坛城；彩粉坛城是用各种颜色粉末撒布而成的本尊坛城；图画坛城用各种颜料绘制而成，而道影方便坛城是根据名言名句制作而成的。

Mandala

Mandala originated from Indian Tantric Buddhism. It turned out to be small earth tables built for meditations, and later on was used by Tantric Buddhism. Such a meditation site was painted or sculpted as a figurative symbol for practitioners to visualize. It is viewed as a place for Yidams and their retinue to assemble. Patterns on Mandalas contain different meanings. Mandalas can be divided into visualized, three-dimensional, sand, painted and Means Mandalas. Visualized Mandalas are self-emerged Mandalas in minds of Tantric Buddhist practitioners after visualization or some Mandala images during their lifetime. Three-dimensional Mandalas are made of perfume clay on the basis of composition in minds of makers. Sand Mandalas are also called Yidam Mandalas, made by sprinkling various colors of sand. Painting Mandalas are painted with various pigments and Means Mandalas refer to Mandalas made according to famous sayings and phrases.

卍字符与卐字符

卍字符与卐字符在藏语中均称作"雍仲"（藏文：g·Yung-drung），是表示永恒的吉祥符号。古时译为"吉祥海云相"，是释迦牟尼三十二相之一，原为古代的一种符咒、护符或宗教标识，被认为是太阳或火的象征。在西藏，"雍仲苯"是原始苯教理论化后的主要流派。在苯教中，雍仲写成"卍"。因此，在佛教寺院，人们应顺时针方向转经，而在苯教寺院应逆时针方向转经。

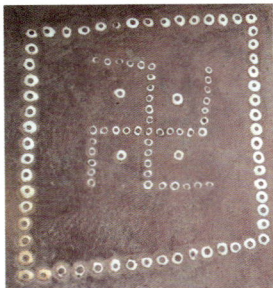

Symbols of 卍 and 卐

Symbols of 卍 and 卐 are all known as Swastikas (Tib. g·Yung-drung), an auspicious sign of eternity. In ancient times, it was translated as "auspicious signs of ocean and clouds". It is one of Sakyamuni's thirty-two marks. As an incantation, an amulet or a religious sign, it is viewed as a symbol of the sun and fire. In Tibet, g·Yung-drung Bon was a major school after primitive Bon religion was theorized. In Bon religion, symbol of g·Yung-drung is written in the shape of 卍. Therefore, people are expected to circumambulate Buddhist monasteries in a clockwise way and Bonpo monasteries in an anticlockwise way.

□ 卍字符与卐字符
Symbols of 卍 and 卐

西方极乐世界

西方极乐世界亦称"极乐世界""阿弥陀佛国"或"无量光佛刹土"，是佛经中所指的阿弥陀佛所居住的国土。佛教徒认为居住此地，即可获得光明、清净和快乐，摆脱人间的一切烦恼。

Western Paradise

The Western Paradise is also known as "Paradise", "Buddha-field of Amitabha" and "Pure Land of Buddha of Unlimited Light". According to Buddhist scriptures, it refers to the abode of Amitabha. Buddhist adherents believe that only living in such a paradise, can they gain brightness, purity and happiness and get rid of all troubles on earth.

喜旋

　　喜旋（藏文：dGav-vkhyil）形似古代中国的阴阳图，但其旋转的中心点通常由三或四个部分组成。藏文 dGav 一词用来描述各种快乐、喜悦和愉悦。藏文 vKhyil 一词的意思是"旋转"或"围转"。作为"三宝"的象征，喜旋是轮转王（梵文：Chakravartin）的如意宝。在大圆满教法（藏文：rDzogs-chen）中，喜旋的三个旋主要象征着三智：基智、道智和果智。

The Wheel of Joy

　　The Wheel of Joy (Tib. dGav-vkhyil) is depicted in a similar form to the ancient Chinese Yin-yang symbol, but its swirling central hub is usually composed of three or four sections. In Tibetan, "dGav" is used to describe all forms of joy, delight and pleasure, while "vkhyil" means "to circle" or "to spin". As a symbol of Three Jewels, it probably also appears as the Chakravartin's wish-fulfilling gem. In the rDzogs-chen tradition, three whirls in the Wheel of Joy primarily symbolize Three Kinds of Wisdom: Wisdom of the Base, the Path and the Fruit.

小昭寺

小昭寺（藏文：Ra-mo-che）建于641年，位于西藏拉萨八廓街以北大约500米处。它是松赞干布专为文成公主修建的一座寺院，也是由文成公主亲自奠基的。后来，小昭寺成为格鲁派密宗上密院所在地。小昭寺占地面积约4000平方米，寺内供奉着释迦牟尼八岁等身佛像及其他众多珍贵文物。小昭寺多次经大火毁坏，只有现存的底层神殿为早期的建筑。小昭寺的主楼共分三层，绘满无量寿佛的转经廊道环围着主楼。其屋顶的汉式金瓦在阳光下闪闪发光，蔚为壮观。

Ra-mo-che Temple

Situated at the spot five hundred meters to the north of Bar-skor Street in Lhasa of Tibet, Ra-mo-che Temple was built in 641. Srong-btsan-sgam-po especially set it up for Princess Wencheng, who personally laid a foundation stone for it. Later on, it became the location of the Upper Tantric College of dGe-lugs-pa Sect. With an area of 4,000 square meters, it enshrines a statue of eight-year-old Sakyamuni of life-size and other valuable cultural relics. Ra-mo-che Temple was destroyed by fire several times. Nowadays, only shrines on the ground floor were early architecture. Its three-story main building is surrounded by circumambulation corridors fully painted with Amitayus images, and its Han-style golden tiles are glittering under the sun, looking splendid and magnificent.

行脚僧

行脚僧亦称"游方僧"或"云水僧"。"云水"之名源自禅宗参禅学道的云水意境。行脚僧指的是或为自我修持，或为教化他人，或为寻访名师高僧而居无定所、四处云游的僧人，可独行或多人同行。

Roaming Monks

Roaming monks are called "Walking Monks" or "Yunshui Monks". The Chinese term "Yunshui" (cloud and water) originated from the poetic imagery in meditations on Zen Sect's doctrines. Roaming monks refer to a group of monks without definite residences who wander here and there for the purpose of conducting self-meditation, enlightening others or searching for great masters and eminent monks. Either a single monk or a group of monks can wander in this way.

因果报应

　　因果报应（梵文：Karma）亦称"果报"，指的是事物的起因和结果。它起源于佛教的宿命论，认为种的什么因，就会结什么果报，这也是佛教关于善恶报应的基本学说。因果报应分为现报、生报和速报三类。现报指的是现作善恶之因，现受苦乐之报，生报指的是前生作业今生报或今生作业来生报，速报就是眼前作业眼下受报。

Retribution for Sins

　　Retribution for sins (Skt. Karma) is also known as "this Karma". It refers to cause and result of things. It originated from Buddhist fatalism, which believes that a certain cause surely brings a certain result. It is also a basic Buddhist theory on retribution for good or evil deeds. Retribution for sins can be classified into retribution before our eyes, retribution for this or future deeds and quick retribution. The first retribution means that good or evil deeds will bring retribution of suffering and pleasure. The second one refers to the fact that one's deeds in his previous life will bring retribution in this life or one's deeds in this life will bring retribution in his future life. The third one reveals the fact that one's deeds in his present life will bring retribution at once.

圆光

圆光亦称"光轮""后光""灵光"或"顶上圆光"，是佛与菩萨头顶后方放出圆轮形的光明，象征佛、菩萨的光明。圆光是藏传佛教诸佛、菩萨和人物造型艺术装饰纹饰之一。

Nimbus

Nimbus is also known as "aura", "halo", "aureole" or "backrest". In the form of rays of glory around heads of Buddha statues, it is a symbol of Buddha and Bodhisattva's illumination. As one of the artistic decorative patterns, it is used on images of Buddhas, Bodhisattvas and personages.

藏传佛教及其派别

藏传佛教是中国佛教三大系之一，在10世纪后期形成于西藏。13世纪中叶藏传佛教开始传入蒙古和内地，成为藏、蒙古、土、裕固、纳西等民族信奉的宗教。在文化整合方面，经过与西藏本土宗教苯教的互相吸收和不断整合，藏传佛教的内涵更加丰富，更具地方与民族色彩。其主要派别有格鲁派（藏文：dGe-lugs-pa）、宁玛派（藏文：rNying-ma-pa）、萨迦派（藏文：Sa-skya-pa）、噶举派（藏文：bKav-rgyud-pa）等。独特的活佛转世制度是藏传佛教的一大特点。根据僧帽的黄、红颜色，格鲁派和宁玛派分别称作"黄教"和"红教"。根据僧裙的白色条纹，噶举派被称作"白教"。萨迦派寺院外墙涂有分别代表文殊菩萨、观音菩萨和金刚手菩萨的红、白、青三色，故而萨迦派也称作"花教"。

Tibetan Buddhism and Its Religious Sects

As one of the three major schools of China Buddhism, Tibetan Buddhism came into being in Tibet in the late tenth century. In the mid-thirteenth century, it was introduced to Mongolia and mainland of China, becoming a religion believed by Tibetan, Mongol, Tu, Yugur and Naxi peoples. In the aspect of cultural integration, by way of mutual assimilation and constant integration with Bon(the indigenous religion in Tibet), Tibetan Buddhism became more inclusive with more local and ethnic color. dGe-lugs-pa Sect, rNying-ma-pa Sect, Sa-skya-pa Sect, bKav-rgyud-pa Sect and others are its main sects. Tibetan Buddhism is greatly characterized by its unique Rin-po-che's reincarnation system. In terms of their yellow and red monk hats, dGe-lugs-pa Sect and rNying-ma-pa Sect are popularly called "Yellow Sect" and "Red Sect". Because of the white stripes on monks' aprons, bKav-rgyud-pa Sect is commonly known as "White Sect". Outer walls of monasteries of Sa-skya-pa Sect are painted with red, white and bluish green colors, which respectively represent Manjusri, Avalokiteshvara and Vajrapani. Therefore, Sa-skya-pa Sect is given a popular name of "Striped Sect".

扎什伦布寺

扎什伦布寺（藏文：bKra-shis-lhun-po）位于西藏日喀则，是藏传佛教格鲁派六大寺院之一，也是历代班禅大师的驻锡地。它由宗喀巴弟子根敦主巴（藏文：dGe-vdun-grub-pa）倡建于 1447 年，并在四世班禅喇嘛罗桑确吉坚赞（藏文：Blo-bzang-chos-kyi-rgyal-mtshan）时期得以扩建。扎什伦布寺由强巴佛（藏文：Byams-pa）殿、十世班禅灵塔殿、四世班禅灵塔殿、扎什南捷殿（藏文：bKras-shis-rnam-rgyal）和措钦大殿（藏文：Tshogs-khang-chen-mo）组成。强巴佛殿内供奉着一尊高达 26.2 米的强巴铜佛像，这是世界上最高、最大的铜造佛像。扎什南捷殿是五世至九世班禅喇嘛合葬灵塔殿，曾在历史上遭到严重破坏，1985 年得到了修复。五世至九世班禅喇嘛的遗骨分装在五个檀香木匣里，存放于灵塔宝瓶内。九世班禅喇嘛曲吉尼玛（藏文：Chos-kyi-nyi-ma）的铜像供奉在灵塔正中央。大殿墙壁四周的壁画描绘了藏传佛教各大教派著名高僧的功业。释颂南捷殿（藏文：Khams-gsum-rnam-rgyal）是十世班禅灵塔殿。十世班禅额尔德尼确吉坚赞（藏文：Erdeni Chos-kyi-rgyal-mtshan）于 1989 年 1 月 28 日圆寂于扎什伦布寺。该灵塔殿的修建历时 3 年，于 1993 年竣工完成。殿内灵塔高 11.52 米，塔身镏金以银箔包裹，镶满珠宝，雕饰华美，造型庄严。措钦大殿是该寺最早的建筑，是班禅喇嘛对全寺僧人讲经说法及僧人辩经的场所。

bKra-shis-lhun-po Monastery

Located in Shigatse of Tibet, bKra-shis-lhun-po Monastery is not only one of the six major monasteries of dGe-lugs-pa Sect of Tibetan Buddhism, but also the abode of Panchen Lamas of successive generations. Constructed in 1447 at the suggestion of Tsong-kha-pa's disciple dGe-vdun-grub-pa, it was extended in the reign of the Fourth Panchen Lama Blo-bzang-chos-kyi-rgyal-mtshan. bKra-shis-lhun-po Monastery consists of Byams-pa Hall, the Tenth Panchen Reliquary Stupa Hall, the Fourth Panchen Reliquary Stupa Hall, bKras-shis-rnam-rgyal

Hall and Tshogs-khang-chen-mo Hall. Byams-pa Hall enshrines a 26.2-meter-high copper statue of Byams-pa, the tallest and largest copper Buddha statue in the whole world. bKras-shis-rnam-rgyal Hall enshrines reliquary Stupas (from the Fifth to the Ninth Panchen Lamas), and their remains are preserved in five containers inside precious vases. bKras-shis-rnam-rgyal Hall was destroyed in history and renovated in 1985. A copper statue of the Ninth Panchen Lama Chos-kyi-nyi-ma is placed in the central position of this reliquary stupa. The murals around its walls portray the good deeds of well-known eminent monks of various sects of Tibetan Buddhism. Khams-gsum-rnam-rgyal Hall serves as the Tenth Panchen's reliquary Stupa hall. The Tenth Panchen Erdeni Chos-kyi-rgyal-mtshan passed away on January 28 of 1989 in this monastery. It took about three years to finish this reliquary Stupa hall, which was completed in 1993. The reliquary Stupa is 11.52 meters high, and its gilt body is wrapped with silver sheets and inlaid with various jewels. Its carved decorations are exquisite and their modelings are solemn. As the earliest building in this monastery, Tshogs-chen Hall was a place for Panchen Lamas to teach and expound Buddhist texts to monks there and for monks to conduct debates on Sutras.

□ 扎什伦布寺
bKra-shis-lhun-po Monastery

哲蚌寺

　　哲蚌寺（藏文：vBras-spungs）于 1416 年由宗喀巴之弟子所建。它坐落在西藏拉萨西郊根培乌孜（藏文：dGe-du-bdu-rtse）山下，建筑以白色为主，因此又名"白米寺"。它是拉萨三大寺之一，也是藏传佛教格鲁派六大寺中最大的一座。主要建筑包括措钦大殿、达赖喇嘛居住的甘丹颇章宫、四大扎仓（藏文：Grwa-tshang）等。哲蚌寺内供奉着宗喀巴师弟三尊、观音、文殊等佛像并保存着大量的佛教经典、壁画、法器等。哲蚌寺也被视为培养佛教人才的摇篮。

vBras-spungs Monastery

　　vBras-spungs Monastery was built in 1416 under the supervision of one of Tsong-kha-pa's disciples. It is situated at the foot of Mount dGe-du-dbu-rtse in western suburb of Lhasa, also named "White Rice Monastery" because of the white color on surfaces of its buildings. It is not only one of the three major monasteries in Lhasa, but also the largest one among the six grand monasteries of dGe-lugs-pa Sect of Tibetan Buddhism. Its main buildings include Tshogs-chen Hall, dGav-ldan-pho-brang Palace (abode of Dalai Lamas), and four major monastic colleges (Tib. Grwa-tshang), etc. It not only enshrines statues of Tsong-kha-pa and His Two Disciples, Avalokiteshvara and Manjusri, but also preserves large numbers of Buddhist classics, murals and ritual implements, etc. vBras-spungs Monastery is viewed as the cradle of training Buddhist talents.

中阴与《西藏度亡经》

从象征意义上来看，中阴（巴都，藏文：Bar-do）是死亡与转世之间的中间阶段。这段时间长达 49 天，而达到中阴要经过三个阶段。第一个"临终中阴"阶段是经历死亡的阶段。第二个"实相中阴"阶段是善相神和怒相神显现的主要阶段。第三阶段是寻求转世的"投生中阴"。《西藏度亡经》亦称《中阴得度法》，据传为 8 世纪印度高僧莲花生大师所著并传入西藏的。它依照佛教教义详细地介绍了藏传佛教神秘复杂的"中阴得度法"。目前流传的《西藏生死书》则是索甲仁波切所著，郑振煌翻译，该书旨在能使芸芸众生安详坦然地面对生死。

Intermediate State between Death and Rebirth and *Tibetan Book of Life and Death*

Symbolically, "Bar-do" in Tibetan refers to the intermediate state between death and rebirth, which is believed to last for forty-nine days. There are three phases to the Bar-do experience. The first phase "Death Bar-do" is experienced at the time of death. The second phase "Manifestation Bar-do" is the main intermediate state when peaceful and wrathful deities manifest themselves. The third phase "Seeking Rebirth Bar-do" is for the dead to seek for rebirth. *Tibetan Book of Life and Death*, also known as "*After-death Experiences of the Bar-do Plane*", was written by Padmasambhava, an Indian eminent monk in the eighth century and introduced into Tibet by himself. In terms of Buddhist teachings, it makes a detailed explanation of such a complicated and mysterious Bardo plane so as to save people in the intermediate existence mentioned in Tibetan Buddhism. *The Tibetan Book of Living and Dying* is popular in today's society. Written by Sogyal Rin-po-che and translated by Zheng Zhenhuang, it intends to help all sentient beings face their deaths peacefully and calmly.

种子字符

在密教中，种子（梵文 : bija）是具有象征意义的文字。种子是一种梵字，用以标示佛与菩萨各尊，其间亦含有哲学意味。通常每一梵字是象征某一佛或菩萨的种子。如：大日如来、不动如来、宝生如来、无量光如来和不空成就如来的种子字符分别为 Om、Hum、Tram、Hrih 和 A。

Seed-syllables

In Tantric Buddhism, seeds (Skt. bija)are scripts of symbolic meanings. Seeds are Sanskrit letters, which not only indicate different Buddhas and Bodhisattvas, but also imply philosophical significance. Usually, each Sanskrit letter is a seed embodying certain a Buddha or a Bodhisattva. For example, "Om", "Hum", "Tram", "Hrih" and "A" are respectively seed-syllables of Vairocana, Akshobya, Ratnasambhava, Amitabha and Amoghasiddhi.

转世灵童与转世灵童的寻访程序

　　藏传佛教活佛圆寂后，寺院上层通过占卜或谒湖等仪式，从活佛圆寂时出生的若干婴儿中选定的活佛继承人被称作转世灵童。谒湖亦称"观湖相"，指的是观望湖面水光天色所现幻景进行占卜的一种活动。此湖指的是拉莫拉错湖（藏文：Lha-mo-bla-mtsho），位于西藏山南地区。达赖喇嘛、班禅喇嘛两大活佛系统的转世有自己传统的程序，涉及前世生前有关转世的预言、圆寂前后的灵异征兆等。降神师的神谕是寻访灵童的主要依据。

Reincarnated Soul Boys and the Procedures in Search of Them

After the deaths of Rin-po-ches of Tibetan Buddhism, authorities of monasteries would select their successors from several babies born at the time when they passed away by way of divinations, observing visions on lake surfaces and other rites. The selected babies were called reincarnated soul boys. Observing visions on lake surfaces, also known as "observing lake visions", signifies a divination through observing various illusory visions reflected on lake surfaces. It is the lake named Lha-mo-bla-mtsho in Lho-kha of Tibet. The reincarnation systems of Dalai Lama and Panchen Lama have their own traditional procedures, involving predictions on incarnations left by their previous generations before their deaths, various odd omens before or after their deaths and so on. However, in search of reincarnated soul boys, predictions given by oracles are the most important basis.

装藏与装藏仪式

古时候，工匠在塑造佛像时会预先在佛像背后留下一个空洞。在为佛像开光时，由住持或高僧把经卷、七珍八宝、五谷、药材、经咒及象征性的内脏等放入其内，然后封之，这个过程被称作"装藏"。举行装藏仪式的地点、时间及参加的僧众均有特殊的选择和要求。

Inserting Holy Objects and Holy Object-inserting Ceremony

In ancient times, craftsmen would leave in advance hollow holes on backs of Buddha statues when they sculpted them. In consecration ceremonies, abbots or eminent monks would insert rolls of Buddhist texts, various precious gems, five cereals, medicinal herbs, incantations and symbolic internal organs into holes and then seal them. Such a procedure is called "Holy Object-inserting". For holy object-inserting ceremonies, there are specific choices and requirements of the time, the location and monk participants.

坐床仪式

坐床是指藏传佛教转世活佛升座继任的仪式。活佛地位的不同决定了坐床仪式的繁简程度。按照藏传佛教仪轨和历史定制，达赖喇嘛、班禅喇嘛的转世灵童在被认定并经中央政府批准后，均要举行坐床典礼。

Enthronement Ceremony

Enthronement ceremonies refer to Tibetan Buddhist reincarnated Rin-po-ches' throne-ascending or throne-succeeding ceremonies. Rin-po-ches' different positions decided on very complicated or very simple enthronement ceremonies. According to Tibetan Buddhist rituals and historical convention, reincarnated soul boys of Dalai Lamas and Panchen Lamas should be confirmed and approved by the Central Governments. After that, enthronement ceremonies should be held.

Part 3

发现之旅：自然与地理
Nature and Geography

阿尼玛卿山与阿尼玛卿山神

阿尼玛卿山（藏文：A-myes-rma-chen）是位于青海湖南岸的一组山系，主峰海拔6282米，共有13座山峰。"阿尼"的意思是先祖，"玛卿"有黄河源头最大山之意。阿尼玛卿山是一座神山，也是观音菩萨的道场，因此，每年会有大批朝圣者前去虔诚朝拜。阿尼玛卿山神是藏族神话中九大土著山神之一。

□ 阿尼玛卿山神
A-myes-rma-chen Mountain Deity

A-myes-rma-chen Mountain and A-myes-rma-chen Mountain Deity

A-myes-rma-chen Mountain is a mountain system located on the southern bank of Qinghai Lake. At an altitude of 6, 282 meters, it has thirteen mountains. "A-myes" has a meaning of "forefather" while "rma-chen" refers to the largest mountain at the source of the Yellow River. It is not only a holy mountain, but also Avalokiteshvara's meditation site. Therefore, large numbers of pilgrims pay respect to it every year. A-myes-rma-chen Mountain Deity is one of the nine major indigenous mountain deities in Tibetan myths.

白朗古墓群

白朗古墓群是西藏地方古代墓葬之一，位于西藏日喀则白朗县境内。考古调查证实，共有封土墓群10处，大小封土墓186座。封土大部分呈方形和圆形，有的墓前有长方形的祭祀坑。该墓群的发现和考古试挖对研究古代藏族墓葬的形成和演变及丧葬制度具有积极的学术意义。

Pa-snam Ancient Tomb Groups

Within the territory of Pa-snam County, Shigatse of Tibet, Pa-snam Ancient Tomb Groups are one of the ancient tomb groups in Tibet. Archaeological surveys have proved that they contain 10 earth-sealed tomb groups and 186 earth-sealed tombs with different sizes. Most of sealing earth appears square or round in shape, and rectangle sacrificial pits are in front of some of the tombs. Their discovery and tentative excavations are of positive academic significance for the studies on the formation and evolution of ancient Tibetan tombs as well as the funeral system.

查拉鲁甫石窟

查拉鲁甫石窟位于拉萨布达拉宫西南药王山东麓山腰。查拉鲁甫石窟是吐蕃时期（约 7 世纪 40 年代中期）依山开凿的一座佛教石窟。石窟 2.56 米高，5.5 米深，4.45 米宽。洞后部的一块巨型方柱和洞窟三面的壁画墙形成一条供礼拜者绕行的廊道。洞内有 67 尊高浮雕石像。廊道北壁下排的松赞干布、噶尔东赞、吞弥桑布扎等造像栩栩如生。

Brag-lha-klu-phug Grotto

Brag-lha-klu-phug Grotto is located in the hillside of the eastern edge of lCags-po-ri Hill, to the southwest of the Potala Palace in Lhasa. It is a Buddhist grotto excavated on the hillside during Tubo period (about 640s). It is 2.56 meters high, 5.5 meters deep and 4.45 meters wide. A huge square column in the rear of the cave and three mural walls in it form a ring-corridor for worshippers to make a detour. The cave contains 67 high relief statues, and there stand vivid statues of Song-btsan-sgam-po, mGar-stong-btsan, Thon-mi-sam-bho-ṭa and others in the bottom row on the corridor's north wall.

定日岩画

　　定日岩画位于西藏日喀则定日县（藏文：lDing-ri），是青藏高原古代岩画之一。定日岩画共分两处，相距 500 米。岩面上有岩画 30 幅，由一些坚硬的工具凿刻而成。主要有马、牛、骑马牧人等，反映了古代的放牧场景。

lDing-ri Rock Paintings

　　Located in lDing-ri County, Shigatse of Tibet, lDing-ri Rock Paintings are one of the ancient rock paintings on Qinghai-Tibetan Plateau, which have two rock painting sites 500 meters apart. Thirty pieces of rock paintings on rock surfaces were engraved with some hard tools. Horses, cattle, riding herdsmen and others were engraved on them, which shows herding scenes in ancient times.

法王修行洞

法王修行洞亦称"法王禅定宫"（曲杰竹普，藏文：Chos-rje-sgrub-phug）。吐蕃赞普松赞干布曾长期居住于此，该洞也是他的修行室。法王修行洞建于公元631年，是布达拉宫内的一座岩洞式佛堂。它坐落在布达拉山（即红山）山顶上，恰在布达拉宫中央。法王修行洞左右两侧各有一座小白塔。法王修行洞的殿堂占地约30平方米，供奉着吐蕃王朝的缔造者松赞干布像、尼泊尔尺尊公主及文成公主像。这些塑像色彩艳丽、栩栩如生、形象生动，被视为吐蕃时期的经典之作。

Dharma King's Meditation Cave

Dharma King's Meditation Cave is also known as "Dharma King's Meditation Palace" (Tib. Chos-rje-sgrub-phug). Tubo bTsan-po Srong-btsan-sgam-po lived there for a long time, and it also served as his meditation room. Built in 631, it is a cave-like hall within the Potala Palace. It lies on the top of the Potala Hill (Red Hill), just standing in the central part of the Potala Palace. Two small white pagodas stand on both its sides. With an area of about thirty square meters, it enshrines sculptures of Srong-bstan-sgam-po (founder of Tubo Kingdom), Nepalese Princess Khri-btsun and Princess Wencheng. These sculptures, bright in color, true to life, vivid in image, are viewed as a classic work sculpted in the Tubo period.

冈底斯山与冈仁波切

冈底斯山（英文：Kailas）位于喜马拉雅山脉北侧，发脉于昆仑山。在藏族文化传统中，它是最为神圣的圣地之一，具有不可替代的宗教影响。冈仁波切（藏文：Gangs-rin-po-che）在藏语中的意思是"雪山之王"，它是冈底斯山脉的主峰，被印度教、藏传佛教和苯教等视为世界的中心。据传，它也是佛祖释迦牟尼的道场。藏族传说认为，只有福报具足者才能有机会朝拜冈仁波切神山，其中更具福报者才能亲眼看见其尊容。

Mount Kailas and Gangs-rin-po-che Peak

Situated in the northern side of the Himalayas, Mount Kailas (Tib. Gangs-te-sevi-ri-rgyud) originated from Mount Kunlun. In Tibetan cultural tradition, it is viewed as one of the most sacred sites of an irreplaceable religious influence. "Gangs-rin-po-che" in Tibetan means "Snow Mountain King". As a major peak of Mount Kailas, it is considered by Hinduism, Tibetan Buddhism and Bon religion as the core of the world. Tradition has it that it was Sakyamuni's meditation site. According to Tibetan traditions, only men with enough good merits can have chances to pay pilgrimages to Gangs-rin-po-che Peak, moreover, only people with much more good merits can see its true appearance with their own eyes.

古格王朝与古格王朝遗址

古格王朝（藏文：Gu-ge）始建于 11 世纪前后，地处古老而神秘的象雄文明故地，其都城在现今西藏阿里（藏文：mNgav-ris）札达县（藏文：rTsa-mdav）境内。古格王朝在西藏历史中的地位举足轻重。它既是吐蕃王朝灭亡后实力较强的地方王朝，又是藏传佛教后弘期"上路弘法"的发祥地。古格王朝遗址位于阿里象泉河畔，遗址现存一些珍贵的壁画和雕塑。

Gu-ge Kingdom and Its Ruins

Established around the eleventh century, Gu-ge Kingdom was located at an old, mysterious spot of Zhang-gzhung civilization. Its capital was within the territory of present-day rTsa-mdav County in mNgav-ris of Tibet. Gu-ge Kingdom held a significant position in the history of Tibet. It is not only a powerful local dynasty after the demise of Tubo Kingdom, but also the birthplace of the "Upper Route of Buddhism" in the Later Prosperity of Buddhism. Situated on the bank of the Elephant-sprout River in mNgav-ris, Gu-ge Ruins still preserves some valuable murals and sculptures.

古格王朝壁画
Mural of Gu-ge Kingdom

江孜宗山抗英遗址

江孜宗山抗英遗址是西藏人民第二次抗英战争的战斗遗址。1904 年，英帝国主义者有意制造纠纷，侵占江孜。藏军与藏族百姓一道抗击外侵，以落后的武器英勇杀敌，收复了江孜城堡。他们后遭到增援英军的包围，但仍殊死搏斗，坚持奋战，直到弹尽粮绝，一些军民誓死不降，跳崖壮烈牺牲。

Site of Resistance to British Aggression at Zongshan

The Site of Resistance to British Aggression at Zongshan of Gyangtse is a combat site of the Tibetan people's second resistance to British Aggression. In 1904, the British imperialists deliberately made some disputes and then occupied Gyangtse. Tibetan soldiers and civilians used their backward weapons to resist foreign aggressors and recaptured Gyangtse Fortress. After that, Tibetan soldiers and civilians were surrounded by the British reinforcements. But they launched desperate struggles and kept on fighting till they ran out of ammunition and food supplies. Some of them refused to surrender and jumped off the cliff to sacrifice their lives.

卡若遗址

卡若（藏文：mKhar-ro）文化属新石器时代文化。卡若遗址位于西藏昌都（藏文：Chab-mdo）市卡若区，距今已有 4000 多年的历史。1978 年卡若遗址首次被发掘，出土了打制石器、细石器、磨制石器，锥、针、斧和图案精美的罐、盆、碗等。其宝贵的遗存形象地再现了青藏高原远古人类的生产和生活概貌。

mKhar-ro Ruined Site

mKhar-ro Culture belongs to the Neolithic Age Culture. With a history of over 4,000 years, mKhar-ro Ruined Site is located at mKhar-ro District, Chab-mdo of Tibet. It was excavated in 1978 for the first time. Chipped stone tools, fine stones, polished stone implements, jars, needles, axes and jars, basins and bowls engraved with exquisite patterns were unearthed there. These valuable remains vividly display a general picture of human productive and living in the distant past on Qinghai-Tibet Plateau.

绿松石

　　绿松石有着几千年的历史，是古老的宝石之一。绿松石深受藏族人的喜爱，大多数藏族女子会将绿松石与珊瑚、琥珀、珍珠等穿在一起制成项链，也会用绿松石装饰耳环、头冠等饰物。藏族男子常用几颗绿松石和珊瑚珠穿成珠串挂在脖子上，或把绿松石镶嵌在宝刀和佩饰上。绿松石的颜色和质量各异。按颜色，绿松石可分为蓝色、浅蓝色、蓝绿色、绿色、浅绿色和黄绿色。

Turquoise

　　With a history of several thousand years, turquoise is one of the ancient gemstones especially favored by Tibetans. Most of Tibetan women usually string turquoise, coral, ember, pearl beads and other jewelry together to make necklaces, or adorn their earrings, headdresses and other ornaments with turquoise. Tibetan men usually string a few turquoise and coral beads together to make bead necklaces and wear them around their necks, or they inlay turquoise on their knives and accessories. Turquoise is varied in color and quality. Its colors can be classified into blue, pale blue, blue-green, green, greenish and yellow-green.

牦牛与拉萨牦牛博物馆

牦牛是高寒地区的特有牛种，主要产于青藏高原海拔 3000 米以上的地区。由于它能适应高寒的生态环境，耐寒、耐劳，不惧陡坡险路、雪山沼泽，因而获得"高原之舟"的美誉。藏民饮用牦牛奶，食用牦牛肉，用牦牛毛和皮制作衣服和帐篷。牦牛也是高原重要的运输工具。牦牛中的白牦牛极为珍贵罕见，被视为神圣之物。拉萨牦牛博物馆于 2014 年正式开放。该博物馆占地 10000 平方米，分四个展厅，以牦牛为载体，从自然与科学、历史与人文、精神与艺术等角度，展现了牦牛与藏族人民的关系。

Yaks and Lhasa Yak Museum

As specific cattle in alpine regions, yaks mainly come from some areas at above 3,000 sea-level on Qinghai-Tibetan Plateau. Yaks deserve the highest praise of "Boat of Plateau" for their adaptive capacity to extreme cold ecological conditions. They resist cold, endure hardships and dare not fear abrupt slopes, dangerous roads, snow mountains and marshes. Tibetans drink yak milk, eat yak meat and use their hair and leather to make clothes and tents. And yaks also serve as essential transportation tools on plateaus. Among ordinary yaks, white yaks are very valuable and rarely seen, so they are seen as sacred. Lhasa Yak Museum occupies an area of 10,000 square meters, and was open to the public in 2014. Its four exhibition rooms take yaks as their carriers, displaying the relations between yaks and Tibetans from the angles of nature and science, history and humanity and spirit and art.

□ 牦牛
Yak

念青唐古拉山与念青唐古拉山神

　　念青唐古拉山（藏文：gNyan-chen-thang-lha）横贯西藏中东部，为冈底斯山向东的延续，是把西藏分为藏北、藏南、藏东南三大区域的一座山峰。根据雍仲苯教的说法，念青唐古拉山是藏地三大神山之一，也是颇具影响力的著名神山。它与纳木错湖都是修行者主要的修行圣地。念青唐拉山神是西藏最著名的山神，也是念神（藏文：gNyan）之首。念神是在山沟游荡，在石缝、森林中安家的神。

Mount gNyan-chen-thang-lha and gNyan-chen-thang-lha Mountain Deity

　　Mount gNyan-chen-thang-lha goes transversely across the mid-eastern part of Tibet and serves as a continuation of Mount Kailas in the eastern direction. It divides Tibet into northern, southern and southeastern regions. According to g·Yung-drung Bon, Mount gNyan-chen-thang-lha is not only one of the holy mountains in Tibetan-inhabited regions, but also the most famous and influential one. Buddhist practitioners view both Mount gNyan-chen-thang-lha and gNam-mtsho Lake as the most well-known meditation sites. As the most famous mountain deity in Tibet, gNyan-chen-thang-lha Mountain Deity is the head of a group of gNyan deities, who usually loaf about in valleys and settle down in cracks of stone or forests.

□ 念青唐古拉山
Mount gNyan-chen-thang-lha

钦浦静修地

钦浦（藏文：mChims-phu）静修地在西藏山南桑耶寺东北 7.5 千米处。相传，这里有 108 个修行洞、108 座天葬台和 108 处泉水。据传，莲花生大师、赤松德赞等吐蕃时期的著名历史人物均在此地修行过。藏传佛教信众中流传着这样一种说法，人若一生能在钦浦静修三次就会获得无量功德。钦浦所处的山沟呈 U 字形，三面环山。在寂静的山林中可以听到潺潺的流水声和鸟儿欢快的鸣叫声，可以看到无数大师留下的足迹和自然显现的圣迹。山上的静修洞星罗棋布，整个静修地透出超脱的宁静，让人感受到静修者与生俱来的淡定和坚韧及他们希望往生净土的意愿和修持的决心。钦浦既是藏传佛教最著名的修行地，也是朝圣者、旅游者向而往之的胜地之一。

mChims-phu Meditation Site

mChims-phu Meditation Site is 7.5 kilometers away from bSam-yas Monastery in Lho-kha of Tibet. Tradition has it that it has 108 meditation caves, 108 celestial burial platforms and 108 fountains. According to legends, Padmasambhava, Khri-srong-lde-btsan and other distinguished historical figures of Tubo period once meditated there. A saying among Tibetans goes like this: you are able to achieve boundless beneficence if you meditate in mChims-phu Meditation Site three times in your whole life. The valley where mChims-phu Meditation Site is located is in the shape of "U" and surrounded by three mountains. Such a silent site is filled with sounds of running water and cheerful chirps of birds as well as numerous masters' footprints and naturally emerged holy marks. Meditation caves, like stars in the sky, are scattered all over the mountain. mChims-phu shows detached serenity, meditators' innate tranquility and tenacity as well as people's desires to be reborn in the Pure Land and resolutions to conduct meditations. It is not only the most famous Tibetan Buddhist meditation site, but also one of scenic spots that pilgrims and tourists long to visit.

青海和日石经墙

　　石经墙指的是刻满"六字真言"和佛教经文、咒语的经石堆。和日石经墙位于青海黄南藏族自治州泽库县，是迄今为止发现的中国最大的雕刻石群。石经墙的文字与佛像是寺院艺僧和民间艺人历时28年完成的，（1923年～1951年）。和日石经墙长约200米、宽3米，由刻着经文、图案的石片堆砌而成，石片上的字数多达20多亿，石雕作品多达5000余件，上面刻有各类佛像、精美的图案及描述风土人情的各种场景等。

Heri Stone Scripture Wall in Qinghai

Stone Scripture Wall refers to piles of stones carved with Six Sacred Words, Buddhist texts and incantations. Located in Zeku County of Huangnan Tibetan Autonomous Prefecture in Qinghai Province, Heri Stone Scripture Wall is the largest stone carving groups found in China so far. It took monk artisans and local craftsmen twenty-eight years (from 1923 to 1951) to finish carving scripts and Buddha images on the slates. The Stone Scripture Wall, about two hundred meters long and three meters wide, consists of piles of slates engraved with various Buddha images, exquisite patterns and all sorts of scenes about local customs and practices.

青海湖

青海湖亦称"库库诺尔"（蒙文：Kokonor），地处青藏高原东北部，湖面海拔 3196 米，全长 105 千米，宽 63 千米，是中国最大的内陆湖泊和咸水湖。有关青海湖的传说很多，一种说法是文成公主因思念家乡，便用其父赐给她的日月宝镜观看，但为了不辱使命，她毅然将宝镜扔掉，宝镜落地时闪出一道金光，变成了青海湖。青海湖景色迷人，著名的鸟岛位列中国八大鸟类保护区之首。

Qinghai Lake

Qinghai Lake, known as Kokonor, lies in the northeastern part of Qinghai-Tibet Plateau. Its lake surface is at an attitude of 3,196 meters. As the largest inland lake and saltwater lake in China, Qinghai Lake is 105 kilometers long and sixty-three kilometers wide. There are many legends about it. One legend goes like this: Princess Wencheng missed her hometown very much, so she took out her precious sun-moon mirror given by her father to look at it. However, in order to carry out her mission successfully, she resolutely threw it out. As soon as it fell onto the ground, the mirror sent out a golden light and became Qinghai Lake. The lake has a beautiful view, and the well-known Bird Island takes the lead among the eight major bird sanctuaries in China.

□ 青海湖
Qinghai Lake

青瓦达孜山摩崖造像

　　青瓦达孜山摩崖造像是西藏古代摩崖石刻造像之一，位于西藏山南琼结县青瓦达孜山南端。崖面呈三角形状，面积不大，共有两处摩崖石刻，但年代不详，形制不一。石刻主要分人物石刻和文字石刻两种。56 尊人物石刻主要表现的是藏传佛教诸佛、菩萨和一些著名人物。文字石刻主要是六字真言。

vPhying-ba-stag-rtse Hill Cliff Carvings

　　As one of the ancient cliff carvings in Tibet, vPhying-ba-stag-rtse Hill Cliff Carvings stand erect on the southern edge of vPhying-ba-stag-rtse Hill in vPhyongs-rgyas County, Lho-kha of Tibet. On its small area of cliff surfaces, there are only two groups of cliff carvings of unknown age and different shapes. Its carvings can be divided into two types: figure carvings and script carvings. Its fifty-six figure carvings mainly display Tibetan Buddhist deities, Bodhisattvas, Dharmapalas and some famous figures while script carvings are mostly inscribed with Six Sacred Words.

青藏铁路

　　青藏铁路是全球最长的、海拔最高的高原铁路，被誉为"天路"。它全长 1956 千米，2006 年 7 月 1 日正式通车运营。铁路沿线共设有 45 个富于民族特色的车站。青藏铁路东起青海格尔木，西至西藏拉萨，大部分线路处于高海拔地区和"无人区"，途中还要翻越海拔 5072 米的唐古拉山。在青藏铁路的修建过程中，建筑者攻克了多年冻土、高原缺氧、生态脆弱三大难点并解决了许多难题。

Qinghai-Tibet Railway

　　As the longest plateau railway at the highest altitude in the whole world, Qinghai-Tibet Railway is honored as "Sky Road". It is 1,956 kilometers long. On July 1 of 2006, it officially started operating. Forty-five stations with ethnic features stand along the railway. Golmud in Qinghai Province is its starting point in the east while Lhasa of Tibet is its ending point in the west. Most of its lines lie in high-altitude localities and "depopulated zones". On its way, it crosses Tanggula Mountain at an altitude of 5,072 meters. In the process of its construction, builders overcame such three major difficulties as frozen earth, oxygen deficit and fragile ecology and solved other difficult problems.

曲贡遗址

　　曲贡遗址位于拉萨北郊，是西藏新石器时代文化遗址。该遗址东西约150 米，南北约 30 米，总面积约 5000 平方米。1984 年和 1990 年的两次发掘出土了大量的骨器、打制石器和为数众多的陶片。曲贡遗址证明，早在4000 年前，拉萨一带就是藏族先民繁衍生息的重要地区之一，这对研究藏族的起源具有十分重大的意义。

Chu-gong Site

　　Located in the northern suburbs of Lhasa, Chu-gong Site serves as a cultural site of the Neolithic Age in Tibet. It is about 150 meters from east to west and 30 meters from south to north, occupying an area of about 5,000 square meters. Large numbers of bone objects, polished stone tools and countless pottery pieces were unearthed during two excavations in 1984 and in 1990. Chu-gong Site has proved that as early as 4,000 years ago, Lhasa and its surroundings were one of the major regions lived and multiplied by Tibetan ancestors.

日月山

　　日月山（藏文：Nyi-zla-ri-bo）坐落在青海省湟源县西南 40 千米处，属祁连山脉。日月山山口海拔为 3520 米。在历史上，日月山是唐朝与吐蕃的分界，也是内地赴藏的咽喉之道。公元 643 年，吐蕃赞普松赞干布迎娶了唐文成公主。据传，进入吐蕃之前，日月山山顶就是文成公主伫望故乡的最后一站。

The Sun-moon Mountain

　　The Sun-moon Mountain (Tib. Nyi-zla-ri-bo) is situated at a spot forty kilometers away from the southwest of Huangyuan County in Qinghai Province. It is part of Qilian mountain range, and its mountain mouth is at an altitude of 3, 520 meters. In history, it used to be a dividing line between the Tang Dynasty and Tubo Kingdom and an essential path from hinterland to Tibet. In 643, Tubo bTsan-po Srong-btsan-sgam-po married Princess Wencheng. As it is said, the Sun-moon Mountaintop was the last spot where Princess Wencheng stopped and stood looking at her hometown on the way before her entry into Tibet.

四河源

四河源指的是从冈底斯山主峰附近流出的四条大河的水源，位于西藏阿里地区。象泉河、孔雀河、马泉河和狮泉河分别位于东、南、西、北方向，因泉口状似巨象、孔雀、骏马和雄狮而得名。

Four Rivers

Located in mNgav-ris region of Tibet, Four Rivers refer to four major water sources near the highest peak of Mount Kailas. Elephant-spouted River, Peacock-spouted River, Horse-spouted River and Lion-spouted River respectively lie in the east, south, west and north. They are named after their spouts shaped like a giant elephant, a peacock, a fine horse and a lion.

唐蕃古道

　　唐蕃古道是 1300 年前的一条入藏之路。在中国古代历史上，它也享有盛名，是唐代以来中原内地前往青海、西藏等地乃至尼泊尔、印度等国的必经之路。文成公主远嫁吐蕃赞普松赞干布时，其送亲队伍走的就是这条大道。其起点是唐朝的国都长安（今陕西西安），终点是吐蕃都城逻些（今西藏拉萨），横跨今天的陕西、甘肃、青海、四川和西藏 5 个省区，全长约 3000 千米，其中一半以上的路段在青海境内。

Tang-Tubo Ancient Road

　　Tang-Tubo Ancient Road was a route for people to enter Tibet 1,300 years ago. In the history of ancient China, it enjoyed a high reputation. Since the Tang Dynasty, it was the only route for people to go to Qinghai, Tibet and other regions, even to Nepal, India and other countries from interior areas of the Central Plains. The bridal procession took this route when Princess Wencheng went to Tubo in a marriage with Tubo bTsan-po Srong-btsan-sgam-po. Chang'an, the capital of the Tang Dynasty (present-day Xi'an of Shaanxi Province) and today's Lhasa were respectively its starting and ending points. It stretched over today's Shaanxi, Gansu, Qinghai, Sichuan Provinces and Tibet Autonomous Region. Its overall length was about 3,000 kilometers. and one half was within the territory of Qinghai Province.

唐古拉山

唐古拉山有多个称谓，其藏文名字意为"高原上的山"。它坐落在西藏自治区东北部，与青海毗邻。它向东南延伸，与横断山脉的云岭和怒山相连。唐古拉山终年风雪弥漫，海拔多在 5000 ~ 6000 米，有民谣唱道："唐古拉，伸手把天抓。"

gTang-la Mountain

gTang-la Mountain has many different names, and its Tibetan name means "mountain on the highland". It lies in the northeastern part of Tibet Autonomous Region and adjoins Qinghai border. It extends to the southeast and links Yunling and Nushan of Hengduan Mountains. It is covered with snow all the year round, and most sections are at an altitude of 5,000~6,000 meters. A folk song goes like this: "gTang-la reaches for the sky."

□ 纳木错湖
gNam−mtsho Lake

西藏的三大圣湖

    圣湖专指可以进行观湖圆光的一些重要湖泊。观测湖面呈现的光色幻景是进行占卜的一种方法。西藏的三大圣湖分别是纳木错湖（藏文：gNam−mtsho）、羊卓雍错湖（藏文：Yar−vbrog−g·yu−mtsho）和玛旁雍错湖（藏文：Ma−pham−g·yu−mtsho）。纳木错湖亦称"天湖"或"腾格里湖"，位于藏北当雄（藏文：vDam−gzhung）西北。羊卓雍错亦称"珊瑚湖"，位于雅鲁藏布江南岸山南市浪卡子县（藏文：sNa−dkar−rtse）。玛旁雍错湖亦称"玛法木错湖"，位于西藏普兰县（藏文：spu−leng）。在藏族人心中，它们具有至高无上的神圣地位。根据藏族"羊年转圣湖"的说法，每逢藏历羊年都会有大量的朝圣者和来自世界各地的游客到此转湖。

Three Major Holy Lakes in Tibet

    Holy lakes specially refer to some significant lakes used to observe visions for divinations. Observing colored lights and illusions reflected on a lake surface is a divination method. gNam-mtsho Lake, Yar-vbrog-g·yu-mtsho Lake and Ma-pham-g·yu-mtsho Lake are three major holy lakes in Tibet. Located in northwestern of vDam-gzhung, north of Tibet, gNam-mtsho Lake is also known as "Celestial Lake" or "Tengery Lake". Yar-vbrog-g·yu-mtsho Lake, also called

"Coral Lake", lies in sNa-dkar-rtse County of Lho-kha, on the southern bank of the Yar-klung-gtsang-po River. With another name of "Manasarova Lake", Ma-pham-g·yu-mtsho Lake lies in sPu-leng County. These three holy lakes occupy supreme lofty positions in the minds of Tibetans. According to a Tibetan saying of "people should go for circumambulations around holy lakes in the year of sheep", large numbers of pilgrims and tourists from all over the world are willing to go there for circumambulations in the year of sheep on Tibetan Calendar.

□ 羊卓雍错湖
Yar-vbrog-g·yu-mtsho Lake

西藏的摩崖石刻

石刻造像遍及西藏各地。药王山（藏文：
lCags-po-ri）摩崖造像、昂仁（藏文：Ngam-
ring）摩崖石刻及昌都摩崖石刻颇具代表性。药王
山摩崖造像位于拉萨布达拉宫西南侧。据记载，
它最早开凿于吐蕃时期。药王山山体长约两千米，
大小石刻组像数量达数万，石像形神兼备，栩栩
如生，气势磅礴。昂仁摩崖石刻位于西藏昂仁县，
摩崖石刻造像有多处，还有众多大卵石、板石浮
雕造像。昌都摩崖石刻位于西藏昌都境内，分有
两处，一处有一尊释迦牟尼佛，另一处有一尊
十一面千手千眼观音菩萨造像。

□ 摩崖石刻诏文
Cliff Carvings

Cliff Carvings in Tibet

Cliff carvings extend everywhere in Tibet. Medicine King Hill (Tib.
lCags-po-ri) cliff carvings, Ngam-ring cliff carvings and Chab-mdo cliff carvings
are the most representative ones. Medicine King Hill cliff carvings are located in
southwestern side of the Potala Palace in Lhasa. It is recorded that it was excavated in
the Tubo period. About two-kilometer-long massif is covered with tens of thousands
of groups of different-sized stone carving statues. In unity of form and spirit, they are
as vivid as life, looking powerful and grand. There are several cliff carving statues
and relief sculptures engraved on large pebbles or slabs in Ngam-ring cliff carvings in
Ngam-ring County. Located within the territory of Chab-mdo of Tibet, Chab-mdo cliff
carvings stay at two spots where separately stand a statue of Sakyamuni and a statue
of Eleven-faced, One-thousand-armed and One-thousand-eyed Avalokiteshvara.

香跋拉与香格里拉

□ 香跋拉
Sham-bha-la

香跋拉（藏文：Sham-bha-la）是佛教一净土之名，亦称"香格里拉"（英文：Shangri-la）。

据传，此世界地为圆形，雪山环绕，状似八瓣莲花，花瓣间流水潺潺。香格里拉原意是心中的日月，其原名为中甸（藏文：rGyal-thang）。现在的香格里拉市是云南迪庆藏族自治州下辖市。据传，它与巴塘（藏文：vBav-thang）和理塘（藏文：Li-thang）是藏王三子的封地。1933年，英国作家詹姆斯·希尔顿在其长篇小说《消失的地平线》中第一次描绘了这个地处东方崇山峻岭中的永恒的和平宁静之地。1937年该书被拍成同名电影，自此，香格里拉成为一个特有的地名，也是人们心目中十分向往的世外桃源。

Sham-bha-la and Shangri-la

Sham-bha-la, name of the Pure Land in Buddhism, is also known as Shangri-la. Tradition has it that this spherical world surrounded by snowy mountains is shaped like an eight-petalled lotus with water gurgling between petals. With a meaning of "the sun and the moon in one's mind", Shangri-la was originally given the name of Zhongdian (Tib. rGyal-thang). Now, it is a city under the jurisdiction of bDe-chen Tibetan Autonomous Prefecture of Yunnan Province. As it is said, rGyal-thang, vBav-thang and Li-thang used to be manors of a Tibetan king's three sons. In 1933, James Hilton, a British writer described this eternal peaceful and quiet place in mountains in the East for the first time in his novel entitled *Lost Horizon*. In 1937, this novel was turned into a movie. From then on, Shangri-la not only became a distinctive place name, but also a paradise that people yearn for in their heart.

小恩达遗址

小恩达遗址（藏文：dNgul-mdav）位于西藏自治区昌都市，是西藏地区新石器时代的重要遗址之一。1986 年进行发掘，出土了大量的打制石器、细石器、磨制石器和骨器。据推测，小恩达遗址的年代与卡若遗址相近，距今应当有 4000 ~ 5000 年。

dNgul-mdav Ruined Site

As one of the major ruined sites of the Neolithic Age in Tibet, dNgul-mdav Ruined Site is situated in Chab-mdo region of Tibet. It was excavated in 1986, and large numbers of chipped stone tools, fine stones, polished stone implements and bone implements were unearthed there. Presumptively, it is close in age to mKhar-ro Ruined Site. It probably has a history of 4,000 to 5,000 years.

□ 药王山摩崖造像
Cliff carvings of Medicine King Hill

药王山

　　药王山（藏文：lCags-po-ri）意为"铁围山"，因其山上有建于1676年的一座药王庙而得名。药王山位于拉萨布达拉宫西南，地势十分险要，海拔高度为3725米，只有一条小道通往山顶。药王庙曾经是专门传习藏医藏药知识的场所，培养过众多的藏医人才。后来，药王庙成为西藏地方政府门孜康（藏文：sMan-rtsis-khang）所在地。令人遗憾的是，它在近代遭到损毁。药王山上巨大的崖壁上刻有千尊佛像，蔚为壮观。

Medicine King Hill

　　Medicine King Hill (Tib. lCags-po-ri) means "Iron Enclosure Hill". It was named after the Medicine King Temple built in 1676 on its top. Situated southwestern to the Potala Palace, it has a strategic geographical location at an altitude of 3,725 meters. Only a single narrow path goes up to its top. The Medicine King Temple used to be a spot to impart science of Tibetan medicine and medicinal herbs and to train Tibetan medicine talents. Later on, it became the site of Tibetan Medicine and Calculation College (Tib. sMan-rtsis-khang). Unfortunately, it was destroyed in modern times. The huge cliff surfaces of the Medicine King Hill are engraved with 1,000 Buddha images, looking very spectacular.

雅鲁藏布大峡谷

中国西藏的雅鲁藏布大峡谷是地球上最深的峡谷，全长 504.6 千米，最深处达 6,009 米。它不仅以其深度、宽度名列世界峡谷之首，更以其丰富的科学内涵和宝贵资源引起世界科学界的瞩目。山峰与拐弯峡谷相连的自然奇观在世界峡谷河流发育史上实属罕见。科学考察证实，大峡谷地带是生物多样性最为丰富的山地，被赞誉为"植物类型天然博物馆"。雅鲁藏布大峡谷有着无穷的魅力，独特的自然环境和丰富的自然资源不仅是我国的珍贵财富，也是全人类的自然遗产。

Yar-klung-gtsang-po Canyon

Yar-klung-gtsang-po Canyon in Tibet of China is the deepest canyon on earth. Its length is 504.6 kilometers and its largest depth is 6,009 meters. As the head of worlds' canyons, it is not only famous for its depth and width, but is also the focus of global scientific circle for its rich scientific values and valuable resources. Natural wonder displayed by connections between peaks and turning canyons is rarely seen in the development history of world's canyons and rivers. Scientific surveys have verified that canyon zones are hilly areas rich in biological variety, so they are praised as "natural museum of various plant types". Of infinite charm to common people, Yar-klung-gtsang-po Canyon's unique natural environment and rich natural resources are not only our valuable wealth, but also mankind's natural heritage.

藏獒

藏獒（藏文：vBrog-khyi）原产于青藏高原，属大型犬，分为长毛型（狮型）和短毛型（虎型）两类。藏獒具有以下典型特征：警觉性高，地域意识极强，对主人极为忠诚，对陌生人充满敌意。在危急关头，它们会奋不顾身地保护主人和财物。与其他犬类相比，藏獒的体形更为高大，骨骼粗壮，肌肉丰满结实。藏獒的表情威严、气质高尊、动作敏捷矫健、耐力持久、有着极强的记忆力，是藏族牧民忠实的朋友。

□ 藏獒
Tibetan mastiff

Tibetan Mastiffs

As a kind of large dog, Tibetan mastiff (Tib. vBrog-khyi) was indigenous to Qinghai-Tibet Plateau. They can be classified into long coat (lion type) and short coat (tiger type). They are very alert to intruders and strangers, and are loyal to their owners. In crises, they protect their owners and property regardless of dangers. Tibetan mastiffs are taller and larger than other dogs, and their bones are thick and strong, and their muscles are abdominal. With dignified facial expressions and temperament, Tibetan mastiffs are agile and swift, and they have strong endurance and long-term memory. They are faithful friends to Tibetan herdsmen.

藏地的传统桥梁

　　藏地的地形特点大多为山高林密，交通不便，因此，山谷和河流之间常可看到铺架的各式桥梁，如藤索桥、铁索桥、悬臂桥等。藤索桥或铁索桥都是原始吊桥，藤桥上的藤索是用抗力比较好的藤、竹、皮绳等绞拉而成，而铁索桥则用锻铁铁链建造，铁索链之间铺搭上木板，便于人畜行走。汤东杰布（藏文：Thang-stong-rgyal-po）被视为西藏铁索桥之父。悬臂桥也是藏族地区渡河设施之一，桥身分为长而坚固的数段，其相接处都会有一个桥墩。除了各种桥梁外，还有一种更为原始的渡河方法，那就是溜索。它们经常出现在峡谷两侧的村落之间，人或货物被悬挂在索上即可溜放过江。拉萨河上的琉璃桥相传为唐代古迹。

Traditional Bridges in Tibetan-inhabited Regions

　　Landforms in Tibetan-inhabited regions are characterized by their high mountains, dense forests and inconvenient transportation. Therefore, various bridges were put up between valleys and rivers, such as rattan bridges, iron-chained bridges and cantilever bridges. Both rattan bridges and iron-chained bridges are primitive. Rattan bridges are often made of durable materials such as twisted rattan, bamboo, and leather ropes while iron-chained ones are made of forged iron chains with wooden boards paved on. In that case, they are convenient for people and domestic animals to pass through. Thang-stong-rgyal-po is believed as forefather of iron-chained bridges. Cantilever bridges are also one of the river-crossing facilities in Tibetan-inhabited regions. The bridge structure is divided into several long and solid sections, and each interface has a pier. In addition to bridges of all sorts, there is another primitive river-crossing method by way of zip-lining. Zip-lines often appear in villages on both sides of valleys, and people and goods are suspended on zip-lines to cross rivers. Tradition has it that the Turquoise-roofed Bridge over the Lhasa River is an ancient site of the Tang Dynasty.

藏羚羊与索南达杰自然保护站

藏羚羊是青藏高原的一种稀有动物，也是国家的重点保护动物，它们生活在青藏高原海拔 4500 ～ 5000 米的高寒草原上。藏羚绒轻软纤细，弹性好，保暖性极强，是制作美丽华贵的沙图什（英文：Shahtoosh）披肩的重要原材料。而一条长 2 米、宽 1 米，仅重 100 克的沙图什披肩就需要杀害三只藏羚羊。根据历史记载，藏羚羊曾达到百万只之多。但在 20 世纪最后的 20 年间，大量的偷猎活动使藏羚羊的数量急剧下降。为保护藏羚羊，杰桑·索南达杰（藏文：rGyas-bzang bSod-rnam-dar-rgyas）在与偷猎者的斗争中壮烈牺牲。1996 年 5 月在可可西里自然保护区建立起了"索南达杰保护站"及一座纪念碑。

Tibetan Antelopes and bSod-rnam dar-rgyas Nature Preserve Station

Tibetan antelopes are a kind of rare animals on Qinghai-Tibet Plateau as well as a key state-protected animal. Usually, they live on high and cold grassland at an altitude of 4,500~5,000 meters. Its hair is light, soft, tenuous, elastic and thermal, so it is an important rare material to make pretty and luxurious Shahtoosh shawl. However, three Tibetan antelopes will be killed just for a piece of two-meter-long, one-meter-wide and only ten grams of Shahtoosh shawl. According to historical records, the number of Tibetan antelope once reached as many as over one million. In the last twenty years of the twentieth century, a large number of poaching resulted in their decline in number. In order to protect Tibetan antelopes, rGyas-bzang bSod-rnam-dar-rgyas sacrificed his life bravely and gloriously in the fights against poachers. In May of 1996, "bSod-rnam-dar-rgyas Nature Preserve Station" and a monument were set up in Kekexili Nature Preserve.

六大黄教寺院

西藏拉萨的哲蚌寺、甘丹寺、色拉寺和日喀则的扎什伦布寺，甘肃的拉卜楞寺及青海的塔尔寺是六大黄教寺院。

Six Major Monasteries of the Yellow Sect

vBras-spungs, dGav-ldan and Se-ra Monasteries (Lhasa of Tibet) and bKra-shis-lhun-po Monastery (Shigatse of Tibet), La-brang Monastery (Gansu) and sKu-vbum Monastery (Qinghai) are six major monasteries of the Yellow Sect.

札达土林与日土岩画

　　札达（藏文：rTsa-mdav）土林位于西藏阿里地区札达县境内。它是古格王国宫殿和寺院的遗址，土林蜿蜒曲折达数十里长，距今约有 1100 百年的历史。日土岩画是西藏日土县境内的一处重要的文化遗址。岩画是用坚硬的石头或其他坚硬的工具在岩面或岩石上刻凿而成，线条笔画流畅、飘逸，深浅不一，还有一些彩

□ 日土岩画
Ru-tog Rock Paintings

绘的画面。岩画内容广泛，有狩猎、骑乘、放牧、农耕及宗教祭礼，还有日、月、山、牛、马、羊、驴、羚羊、房屋、人物等精美图案。

rTsa-mdav Earth Forest and Ru-tog Rock Paintings

　　Located within the territory of rTsa-dmav County in mNgav-ris region of Tibet, rTsa-mdav Earth Forest is ruins of palaces and monasteries of Guge Kingdom. With a history of about 1,100 years, it twists and turns, extending several *li*. As an important cultural site within the territory of Ru-tog County, Ru-tog rock paintings were chiseled or carved on rock surfaces or rocks with rigid stones or other hard tools. The lines and strokes on them are fluent, elegant and irregular, and there are also some color-painted pictures. Rock paintings are extensive in content, including hunting, riding, herding, farming scenes, religious rites as well as the sun, the moon, mountains, cattle, horses, sheep, donkeys, antelopes, houses, people and other exquisite patterns.

珠穆朗玛峰

珠穆朗玛峰（藏文：Jo-mo-glang-ma）亦称"世界第三极"。它位于喜马拉雅山中段西藏定日县中尼边境处。珠穆朗玛峰是喜马拉雅山的主峰，海拔 8844.43 米，被视为地球第一高峰。藏语"珠穆"和"朗玛"分别含有"女神"和"第三"之意。"珠穆朗玛"意为"第三女神"，因在其周边的四座山峰中，珠穆朗玛峰高居第三。

Jo-mo-glang-ma Peak

Jo-mo-glang-ma Peak (Tib. Jo-mo-glang-ma), also known as "The Third Pole of the World" is located in the middle section of the Himalayas in lDing-ri County on the China-Nepal border. As the main peak, Jo-mo-glang-ma Peak is at an altitude of 8,844.43 meters, and believed as the first highest peak on earth. The Tibetan words "Jo-mo" and "glang-ma" respectively represent "goddess" and "the third". "Jo-mo-glang-ma" means "The Third Goddess", because it ranks the third in height among four mountains around it.

Part 4

徜徉之旅：民俗与习惯
Customs and Habits

八宝

八宝，亦称"八吉祥表象"，是藏族传统吉祥图案之一。它由宝伞、金鱼、宝瓶、妙莲、右旋海螺、吉祥结、胜利幢和金轮组成。宝伞象征遮蔽魔障，也象征佛陀教义的权威，可保护众生在轮回中不受烦恼、痛苦和阻障。金鱼象征自由与超越，代表富裕和祥和，同时象征着复苏、永生、再生等。宝瓶象征财运和吉顺，代表财富汇聚和长寿。莲花象征清净，代表心灵纯洁。莲花出淤泥而不染，能助人免于污秽之染，因此，在佛教中，妙莲清净、圣洁、吉祥，象征解脱一切烦恼。右旋海螺极为罕见，象征法音遍扬十方。吉祥结象征能够往返循环的无尽佛法。胜利幢象征降伏烦恼获得解脱，它是与财富和权力有关之众神的手持器物。金轮象征永不停息地度化众生。

Eight Auspicious Signs

As one of the traditional Tibetan auspicious patterns, Eight Auspicious Signs is also called Eight Auspicious Symbols. It consists of parasol, gold fishes, treasure vase, lotus, white right-spiraling conch shell, endless knot, victorious banner and golden wheel. The parasol is not only a symbol of protection from obstacles and harmful forces, but also a sign of authority of Dharma. It protects sentient beings from troubles, sufferings and obstacles in their rebirths. Goldfish not only symbolizes freedom and transcendence, but also represents happiness and spontaneity. It is also a symbol of revival, eternity and rebirth. Treasure vase shows fortune and luckiness, representing wealth's accumulation and longevity. As a symbol of purity, lotus represents pure mind. Lotus, emerging unstained from the filth, is able to help people free from impurities. Therefore, in Buddhism, lotus is viewed as a sign of calmness, purity and auspiciousness, symbolizing extrication from all troubles. White right-spiraling conch shell is rarely seen, it symbolizes dissemination of Dharma to all directions. Endless knot shows endless circulation of Dharma. Victorious banners are held by many deities related to wealth and power as their hand-attributes, and they symbolize free from troubles and liberation. Golden wheel symbolizes continuously enlightening sentient beings.

白算、黑算与历算图

　　白算（藏文：dKar-rtsis），亦称"星宿算"（藏文：sKar-rtsis），是以太阳月亮运行周期为依据，在实际应用中已成为时轮历的同义语。藏历中的"白算"就是天文历算，其主要成分是科学的。"黑算"（藏文：Nag-rtsis）是占卜术，其主要成分是迷信的。第司·桑结嘉措1687年主编的《白琉璃》是有关西藏天文历算的一部综合性的重要文献，也是西藏地方政府使用的一部历书。

White Calculation, Black Calculation and Picture Depicting Calculation

　　White Calculation (Tib. dKar-rtsis), also known as "Constellation Calculation"(Tib. sKar-rtsis), is based on the cycle of the movement of the sun and the moon. In actual application, it has become a synonym of "Time-wheel Calculation". In Tibetan calendar, White Calculation refers to astronomy and calculation, whose main contents are scientific. Black Calculation (Tib. Nag-rtsis) is a kind of divination with superstitions as its major contents. *White Glaze*, compiled in 1687 by sDe-srid Sang-rgyas-rgya-mtsho, the editor-in-chief, is not only a very influential, comprehensive work on Tibetan calculation and astronomy, but also an almanac used by the local government of Tibet.

多玛与抛撒多玛仪式

多玛（藏文：gTor-ma）是一种供神施鬼的食品丸子，用糌粑粉、酥油和水糅合而成。日常制作的多玛称作常例多玛。多玛还可分为供养多玛、会供多玛和神灵多玛三种，供养多玛用于怀柔、增长和除障仪式，会供多玛用于精神护佑仪式，神灵多玛用于供神。在传统上，多玛上也常饰有日月饰物等象征物。抛撒多玛仪式是依靠咒力镇伏魔鬼的一种宗教活动。

gTor-ma and gTor-ma Casting Rituals

gTor-ma is a kind of ritual cake offering for deities and ghosts. It is made by mixing barley flour, butter and water together. Common gTor-mas are known as daily-made gTor-mas. Usually, gTor-mas can be classified into offering, prayer ceremony and deity-offering gTor-mas. Offering gTor-mas are used in peaceful, enriching or obstacle-removing rites. Prayer ceremony gTor-mas are used in spiritual blessing rites while deity-offering gTor-mas are offered to various deities. Traditionally, they are often decorated with sun-moon decorations and other symbols. gTor-ma casting rituals is a kind of religious activity of driving out and subduing demons and evil spirits by way of spell forces.

风马旗

风马旗（隆达，藏文：rLung-rta）亦称"经幡"，其中 rLung 为风，rta 为马。风马旗是藏族民间宗教信仰的信物之一，常有黄、白、蓝、绿、红五种颜色，分别代表大地、白云、蓝天、江河水和空间护法神。风马旗上的符咒、祈祷文和吉祥符号是用木制雕版印制在方形布上的。背驮

风马旗
Wind-horse Flags

佛、法、僧三宝的宝马居中，四角是龙、金翅鸟、老虎和狮子。五种动物象征着五行的循环往复，表示生命的经久不衰。风马旗常常插于屋顶和嘛呢堆顶上。人们常常将印有风马旗图案的纸片从山顶上往下抛撒，以祈福禳灾。

Wind-horse Flags

Wind-horse Flag (Tib. rLung-rta)is also called "prayer banner". "rLung" and "rta" in Tibetan respectively represent "wind" and "horse". Wind-horse flags are one of Tibetan folk religious tokens. Its colors of yellow, white, blue, green and red respectively represent the earth, white clouds, blue sky, rivers and celestial protective deities. Incantations, prayers and auspicious signs on wind-horse flags are printed on pieces of square cloth in a wood engraving technique. The fine horse carrying the Three Jewels (symbols of Buddha, Dharma and Sangha) on its back lies in the central part of a wind-horse flag, and a dragon, a Garuda, a tiger and a lion are on its four corners. These five animals symbolize the repeated circle of the Five Elements as well as the eternity of life. Wind-horse flags are often erected on roofs or tops of Mani stone piles. Usually, people scatter scraps of paper painted with wind-horse patterns from mountaintops in the hope of bringing blessings and averting calamity.

哈达

□ 哈达
Ceremonial Scarf

　　哈达（藏文：Kha-btags）是藏族人作为见面礼使用的一种长条丝织物或麻织物，也是藏族人民社交活动中的必备之物。根据质量可分为四等，有多种颜色，以白色为主。哈达的内涵十分丰富，既可用于婚嫁或节日，也可用于丧葬仪式中以示哀悼。敬献哈达有很多规矩，不同场合方式有所不同。敬献时要双手向上捧着哈达。地位高者一般把哈达挂在对方的脖颈上，而地位相同者则把哈达捧送到对方的手中。

Ceremonial Scarves

　　Long ceremonial silk or liner scarves (Tib. Kha-btags) are not only gifts used by Tibetans on their first meetings, but also necessities in their social interactions. They can be classified into four classes in terms of qualities, and have many colors, mainly white. Ceremonial scarves contain rich connotations. People use them in weddings or festivals as well as funerals to express condolence. There are many rules in presenting ceremonial scarves and various ways on different occasions. When presenting them, people should hold them up in both hands. Usually, people of higher status wear them around other persons' necks. And people of the same status present them into other persons' hands.

护摩仪式

护摩仪式（梵文：Homa）亦称"火供"或"烧祭"等，是密宗的一种修法。将有浆的树枝等物料放入炉中燃烧以供养本尊。护摩仪式根据功能分为怀柔护摩、增长护摩、息灭护摩和诛灭护摩四种。佛教密宗举行火祭仪式时所用柳木被称作"护摩木"。

Burning Rituals

Homa Ritual (Skt. Homa), also known as "fire rite" or "ceremony of burnt offerings", is a Tantric Buddhist rite. Branches containing pulps and other materials are burnt in hearths to make offerings to Yidams. In terms of functions, ones can be classified into peaceful, enriching, subduing and fierce ones. Willow wood used in Tantric Buddhist Homa rituals is called "Homa wood".

护身符与辟邪物

藏族的护身符亦称"护轮",分铜或白铜质地两种。该护轮的层层纹样结构代表着复杂的多重象征意义。在小小的护轮上,西藏原始宗教苯教文化、密宗佛教文化与中原文化的阴阳五行等文化符号水乳交融、相辅相成,构成一个和谐的组合。护轮外圈上的八瓣莲花与八卦一一对应。第三圈雕有十二生肖属相,北方为猪鼠,南方为马蛇。最外圈的树、火山、刀剑和水波分别象征木、火、金、水,中间的九宫代表土。藏文化的五行方位与传统意义上的五行方位完全一致。藏族人佩戴的辟邪物形状各异,最常见的是类似铜镜圆片的辟邪物。

Amulets and Talismans

Amulet, also known as "protective wheel", is made of copper or whitish metal. Its structure with multilayer patterns represents numerous complicated symbolic meanings. On such a small amulet, various cultural symbols overlap each other, including primitive Bonpo cultures, Tantric Buddhist cultures and Yin-yang and Five Elements Cultures from the Central Plains. They coexist side by side, and constitute a harmonious assembly. On its outer circle, eight-petalled lotus corresponds to Eight Diagrams. The third circle is incised with animals representing twelve zodiacs. Among them, pig and mouse point to the north while horse and snake point to the south. Trees, flaming mountains, knives and swords on its outmost layer symbolize wood, fire, metal and water while the Nine Palaces in its center represents earth. Five Elements in Tibetan culture are completely identical in location with traditional Five Elements. Talismans worn by Tibetans are varied in shape, and copper mirror-like circular ones are commonly seen.

吉祥天女游幻节

　　吉祥天女游幻节亦称"白拉日珠节"（藏文：dPal-lhavi-ri-rab），是一个宗教节日。每年藏历十月十五日，僧众从大昭寺抬出吉祥天母像在拉萨市区游行。游至拉萨南城时，吉祥天母像必须面对拉萨河南岸的赤尊赞（藏文：khri-btsun-btsan）庙。传说认为，赤尊赞是她的丈夫，而这一天是他们夫妻相会的日子。

Goddess Festival

　　Goddess Festival, also known as "dPal-lhavi-ri-rab Festival", is a religious festival. Every year, on the fifteenth day of the tenth month on Tibetan calendar, monks take out the statue of Goddess dPal-ldan-lha-mo and carry it in the parade around Lhasa urban districts. Whenever they arrive at the southern part of the city, they make the statue face Khri-btsun-btsan Temple on the southern bank of Lhasa River. Legend has it that Khri-btsun-btsan is her husband, and only on that day, the couples can meet each other.

夹经板

夹经板亦称"经板",是一种装帧用具。藏文典籍多为散页,常用布或缎包裹着,用上下两块夹经板夹住,再由宽布带捆牢。夹经板一般有雕刻式和彩绘式两种。精美的木雕夹经板被视为典籍装帧的首选。

Scripture Binders

Scripture binders, also called "scripture covers", are a kind of binding and layout utensils. Most of Tibetan classics are unbound pages and wrapped with cloth or brocade. Two pieces of scripture binders are used to press them from both sides, and then, broad straps are used to tie them as a whole. Usually, scripture binders can be classified into two kinds: carving and colored drawing. Exquisitely carved wood scripture binders are viewed as the first choice to bind and arrange classic works.

□ 木雕夹经板
Scripture Binder Woodcarving

金瓶与金瓶掣签制度

　　金瓶掣签制度是确定藏传佛教最高等大活佛转世灵童所实行的一项特殊制度。1792年，清政府规定达赖喇嘛、班禅喇嘛等大活佛的转世灵童须在大昭寺释迦牟尼像前并在中央政府代表的监督下，通过金瓶掣签加以确认。历史上，第十、十一、十二世达赖喇嘛和第八、九、十一世班禅额尔德尼以及第

□ 金瓶
Gold Urn

五、六、七、八世哲布尊丹巴呼图克图均是经金瓶掣签仪式产生的。金瓶（奔巴，藏文：Bum-pa）共有两只，一只存于北京雍和宫，专为确认蒙古大活佛转世灵童之用。另一只金瓶存于西藏拉萨大昭寺，专门用于确认西藏、青海等地大活佛的转世灵童。

Gold Urns and Lot-drawing Ceremonies

As a unique system, the method of drawing lots from a gold urn was used to confirm reincarnated soul boys of the highest-ranking Rin-po-ches of Tibetan Buddhism. In 1792, the Qing Government stipulated that reincarnated soul boys of Dalai Lamas, Panchen Lamas and other grand Rin-po-ches shall be confirmed by drawing lots from a gold urn in front of the statue of Sakyamuni in Jo-khang Temple under the supervision of the Central Government's representatives. In history, the Tenth, Eleventh and Twelfth Dalai Lamas, the Eighth, Ninth and Eleventh Panchen Erdenis, the Fifth, Sixth, Seventh and Eighth Grib-brtson-vgrus-bstan-pa Hutuktus were confirmed through the method of drawing lots from a gold urn. There are two gold urns (Tib. Bum-pa). The one kept in Yonghe Lamasery in Beijing was used to confirm reincarnated soul boys of Mongolian grand Rin-po-ches. The other kept in Jo-khang Temple in Lhasa was applied to confirm reincarnated soul boys of grand Rin-po-ches from Tibet, Qinghai and other places.

磕长头、磕短头与磕响头

　　磕头是藏族传统的礼节之一，可分为磕长头、磕短头与磕响头三种。磕长头是最为虔诚、最独特的一种磕头方式。磕头时，双手合掌过头，自顶至额、胸，拱揖三次，再匍匐在地，双臂伸直，双手平放于地，划地为号。一些虔诚的佛教徒会三步一拜，一磕几年到拉萨朝佛。磕长头一般用于拜谒佛像、佛塔和活佛及尊者和长者。磕短头是手足及额部等五处屈俯着地的敬礼姿势。发出响声的磕头方式俗称磕响头。

All-body, Short-length and Bumping Prostrations

　　As one of the Tibetan traditional etiquettes, prostrations can be classified into three ways: full-body, short-length and bumping, and full-body prostration is the most pious and unique one among them. In making an full-body prostration, a person first clasps both his hands and lifts them overhead, and then makes kowtow three times with his hands on the top of his head, forehead and chest. After that, he prostrates himself on the ground, stretches forward both his arms, places both his hands on the ground and then draws a circle. Some pious Buddhist adherents prostrate themselves on the ground after each three steps, and spend several years doing so in their way to Lhasa for pilgrimages. Usually, full-body prostrations are used for people to make pilgrimages to statues of Buddha, Stupas and Rin-po-ches as well as the honored and the elderly. Short-length prostration is a solute posture with one's hands, feet and forehead touching the ground, and prostrations making a lot of noise are commonly known as bumping prostrations.

□ 磕长头
All-body Prostrations

六长寿图

六长寿图是藏传佛教艺术壁画题材之一。图中绘有长寿老人、长寿树、长寿岩、长寿水、长寿鹤和长寿鹿。长寿老人居住在经过无量寿佛加持过的长寿岩。他白眉白发，一手持拐杖，一手捧寿桃。长寿岩经众生踩踏，能祛除一切烦恼。长寿树根深叶茂，长寿水经过长寿老人的加持，能免除生老病死，长寿鹤常行财施和无畏施，长寿鹿尽享此处肥美的水草。六长寿图常被用作建筑物内装饰的壁画。

Picture Depicting Six Symbols of Long Life

Picture Depicting Six Symbols of Long Life is one of the mural themes in Tibetan Buddhist art. This picture is painted with an old man of long life, a tree of long life, a rock of long life, water of long life, cranes of long life and deer of long life. The old man of long life lives in a rock of long life empowered by Amitayus. He has white hair and beard, holding a walking stick and a longevity peach with both his hands. Having tramped by sentient beings, the rock of long life can eliminate all troubles. The tree of long life has thick leaves and a deep root. Water of long life empowered by the old man of long life can relieve birth, old age, illness and death. Cranes of long life often give wealth and fearless power to others while deer of long life enjoy plump plants here. Pictures Depicting Six Symbols of Long Life are often used as murals in interiors of buildings.

沐浴节

沐浴节是藏族的一个传统节日。一般在每年藏历八月六日至十二日的初秋之际举行，历时一周左右。据藏族天文历书记载，初秋之水具有凉、香、轻、柔、清、无垢、饮之不损腹和饮之不伤喉八种特性，被称作"八德甘泉"。在西藏，这种具有鲜明民族特色的沐浴活动已有 700 ~ 800 年的历史。

Bathing Festival

Bathing Festival is a traditional Tibetan festival. Usually, it is held in the early autumn from the sixth day to the twelfth day of the eighth month on Tibetan calendar, which stretches over about one week. According to Tibetan astronomy and almanacs, water in the early autumn is also known as Eight Kinds of Virtuous Water, which contains the following qualities: cool, sweet, soft, light, pure, clean, not vulnerable to abdomen and throat after drinking. In Tibet, such a bathing activity of extinct ethnic characteristics has a history of seven hundred to eight hundred years.

燃灯节

燃灯节是为纪念藏传佛教格鲁派创始人宗喀巴圆寂日而设立的一个宗教节日。每年藏历十月二十五日举行，在两天的节期里，寺院僧人都要上供、上香、燃灯、诵经、叩拜、祈祷并做法事。拉萨甘丹寺举行的燃灯节最为隆重，故而在藏语中，该节日亦称作"甘丹阿曲"（藏文：dGav-ldan-lnga-mchod）。

Lamp Festival

The Lamp Festival is a religious festival established for the death anniversary of Tsong-kha-pa, the founder of dGe-lugs-pa Sect of Tibetan Buddhism. It is held on the twenty-fifth day of the tenth month on Tibetan calendar every year. On these two days, monks from various monasteries would lay out offerings, burn joss sticks, light up lamps, chant Buddhist texts, worship and hold various religious rituals. The Lamp Festival held in dGav-ldan Monastery is the most grand and solemn one, so it is given a Tibetan name "dGav-ldan-lnga-mchod".

日月宝焰图

在古老藏族文明中，具有象征意义的符号为数众多，日月宝焰图就是十分常见的一个图形。宝焰亦称"喷焰末尼"，象征消灾和吉祥。日月宝焰图由太阳、月亮、宝焰组成。太阳象征法身（梵文：Dharmayaka），月亮象征色身（梵文：Rupakaya），宝焰象征悲慈双运或乐空双运。

Sun-moon and Flaming Gem Pattern

Symbols and signs are in great quantity in old Tibetan civilization. Among them, Sun-moon and Flaming Gem Pattern is a common graph. Flaming gem, also known as "flaming jewel", symbolizes removing ill fortunes and bringing good luck. Sun-moon and Flaming Gem Pattern is composed of the sun, the moon and flaming gems, respectively representative of Dharma body (Skt. Dharmakaya), physical body (Skt. Rupakaya) and the union of compassion and kindness or the union of bliss and emptiness.

萨嘎达瓦节

　　萨嘎达瓦节（藏文：Sa-ga-zla-ba）是纪念佛祖释迦牟尼入胎、诞生、圆寂和成佛的一个节日。萨嘎达瓦节在藏历每年四月十五举行，节日期间要举行各种隆重的纪念活动，如斋僧礼佛、朝圣敬香和封斋放生等。这个节日已经逐步演变成了一个民俗节日。

Sa-ga-zla-ba Festival

　　Sa-ga-zla-ba Festival is a festival in commemoration of Buddha Sakyamuni's entry into her mother's womb, birth, Nirvana and becoming a Buddha. It is held on the fifteenth day of the fourth month on Tibetan calendar each year. During the festival, there are various grand commemorative activities, such as giving alms to monks, pray to Buddha, going on pilgrimages to holy sites, burning joss sticks, fasting and ransoming of living creatures from death, etc. It has gradually become a folk festival.

瑟珠

　　瑟珠是藏文"gZi"的音译，亦称"天珠"。据认为与原始苯教文化习俗渊源很深。有些藏族人认为瑟珠是超自然之物。瑟珠纹路各异，除了两眼、三眼、六眼和九眼瑟珠外，有些瑟珠还有圆形和方形图案。九眼瑟珠最受人尊崇，常被誉为"具有奇效的如意珠"。远古先民将瑟珠奉为护身符佩戴在身，以防病驱邪。

gZi Beads

　　gZi beads (Tib. gZi) are also known as "celestial beads". It is said that they were greatly related to primitive Bonpo cultural customs. Some Tibetans believe that they possess supernatural power and have various veins and eyes. In addition to two, three, six and nine eye gZi beads, some of them have round and square patterns. And nine eye gZi beads are greatly valued and viewed as amazingly powerful wish-fulfilling gems. Primitive ancestors wore them around their necks as amulets so as to prevent themselves from diseases and eliminate evil spirits.

晒佛节

　　晒佛节亦称"晒大佛"或"瞻佛节"，是藏族人民的传统宗教节日。晒佛节大都在藏历二月初、四月中旬或六月中旬举行。晒佛节期间，各地寺院将寺内珍藏的做工精致、色泽鲜艳的巨幅布画或锦缎织绣佛像取出，展示在寺院附近的晒佛台或山坡、巨岩石壁上。成千上万的善男信女和观者不远万里前来观瞻、朝拜。佛像展开时，万众齐声诵经的场景、缭绕的桑烟及飘扬的五彩经幡构成了一幅激动人心的宏伟壮观的画面。

Buddha Image Displaying Festival

　　Buddha Image Displaying Festival, also known as "Sunning Buddha Image Festival" or "Hanging Large Buddha Image Festival", is a traditional religious festival celebrated by Tibetans. Usually, it is held in the early second month, the mid-fourth month or the mid-sixth month on Tibetan calendar. During these periods, monasteries in different areas usually take out their huge cloth paintings or embroidery Buddha images, which are well preserved, bright in color and exquisite in craftsmanship. Monks display them on display platforms near monasteries, on mountain slopes or on huge rock surfaces. Thousands of devout Buddhist adherents and viewers travel thousands of miles to view and worship them. When Buddha images are unfolded, the scene of millions of people's chanting, curling bSang smokes and fluttering colorful prayer flags constitute an exciting, grand and spectacular picture.

酥油花与灯节佛供

　　酥油花是一种形式独特的油塑艺术。制作的初衷是替代原始苯教中祭祀用的牺牲，以避免杀生。酥油花是塔尔寺的"艺术三绝"之一。它的制作工序十分复杂，亦十分艰辛，因为为了防止酥油融化变形，艺僧们需要在严寒的冬季把双手浸入冰水之中。酥油花以酥油为原料并加入各种矿物颜色，其油塑作品题材广泛，雕塑工艺精湛，具有经久不褪色的特点。酥油花油塑的佛像色彩艳丽、形象端庄，各色人物栩栩如生，山水风光绮丽多姿，飞禽走兽和花草树木种类繁多，亭台楼阁气势恢宏。每年藏历正月十五，在藏地各大寺院均会举行酥油花灯会。

Butter Sculptures and Butter Sculpture Display

　　Butter sculptures are a unique butter sculpture art. Making butter sculptures originally intended to replace sacrificial animals used in primitive Bonpo rites so as to avoid killing livestock. Butter sculptures are one of the "Three Artistic Absolutes" in sKu-vbum Monastery. Its handcraft procedure is very complicated. In order to prevent butter from dissolution and deformation, monk artists have to put their hands into icy water in cold winter. Sculptures are mainly made of butter mixed with various mineral colors. Sculptures are extensive in theme and exquisite in craftsmanship, and their colors will never fade. Butter sculptures include gorgeous colorful Buddha statues with solemn facial expressions, animated figures, beautiful scenery, all sorts of birds and beasts as well as magnificent pavilions, terraces and towers. Grand monasteries in Tibetan-inhabited regions hold Butter Sculpture Display on the fifteenth day of the first month on Tibetan calendar each year.

唐卡

唐卡（藏文：Thang-ka）是流行于藏地的一种宗教卷轴画，分"国唐"（藏文：Gos-thang）和"止唐"（藏文：Bris-thang）两类。国唐指的是以丝绢绸缎等为材料制作的唐卡，共分绣制、丝面、丝贴、手织和版印五种，并

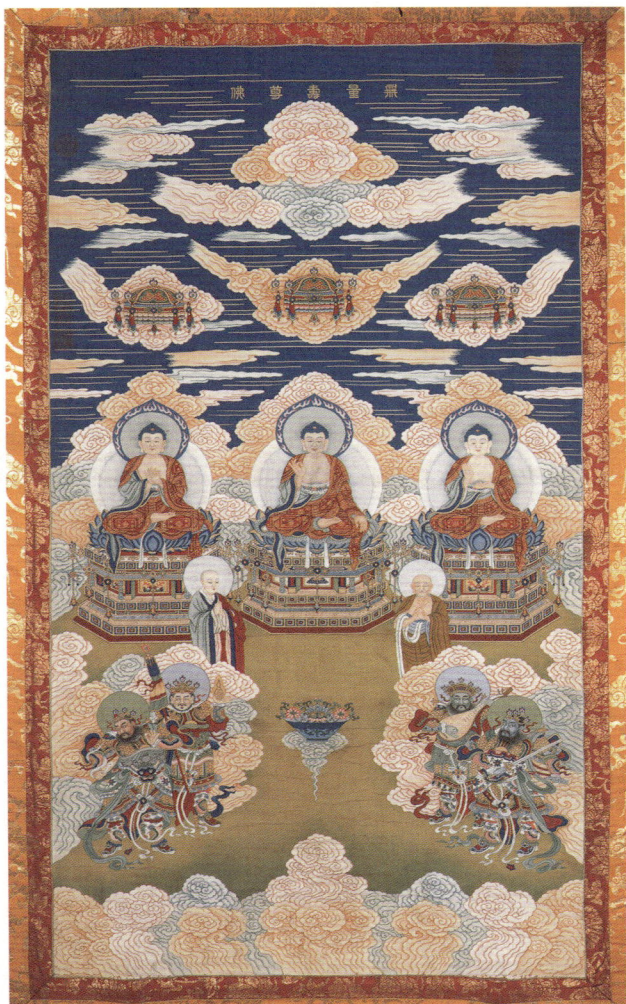

□ 无量寿佛像缂丝唐卡
Budhha Amitayus, Cut Silk Thang-ka

采用了手工刺绣、缝合、编织和套版印刷等多种工艺进行制作。止唐指的是用颜料绘制在画布上的唐卡。根据《四部医典》绘制的唐卡称作"门唐"（藏文：sMan-thang），这种挂图式医药唐卡是藏医学中具有鲜明民族色彩的医学教具。除了纸绘、布帛和丝绢唐卡外，还有更为珍贵的缂丝唐卡。"扎嘎里"（藏文：Tsak-li）是一种尺幅更小的画作，被称作袖珍唐卡画片，属于在布面、纸面上绘制神佛像的绘画艺术，因此也可归类于唐卡绘画艺术。

Thang-kas

Thang-kas are a kind of religious scroll paintings prevalent in Tibetan-inhabited regions. They can be classified into "Gos-thang" and "Bris-thang". Gos-thang refers to Thang-kas made of silk, satin and other fabric materials, including embroidered, silk screen printed, silk pasted, hand woven and bolck-printed Thang-kas, and hand embroidery, sewing, knitting, block-printing and other craft skills are used. Bris-thang refers to Thang-kas painted on canvas with pigments. "sMan-thang" refers to Thang-kas painted in terms of *Four Medical Tantras*. Such hanging medical Thang-kas are Tibetan medical aids of distinct Tibetan features. In addition to paper, cloth and silk Thang-kas, cut silk Thang-kas are more valuable. As a form of miniature painting, pocket-sized Tsak-li Thang-ka belongs to a painting art of drawing images of Buddha and deities on cloth and paper. Therefore, it also falls under the category of Thang-ka painting art.

投石带

投石带（乌尔都，藏文：Vur-rdo）亦称"抛石绳"，是藏族牧民经常使用的一种放牧用具，既可防身亦可制敌。制作毛编投石带时，先要把牦牛毛搓捻成粗毛线，然后再编织成毛辫。毛辫上端有一个直径约为 10 厘米的套环，中间编有一个巴掌大小的椭圆形。在驱赶牛羊时，先将石块或土块置于椭圆形上，然后将套环套在中指上，双手抓住投石带两端，使劲抡之，然后骤然松开一端。于是，石块或土块便可朝牛羊方向飞去使其改变方向。

Slingshots

Slingshots (Tib. Vur-rdo), also known as "stone launchers", are a kind of herding tool frequently used by Tibetan herdsmen. It is also used in self-defense and subduing the enemy. In its making process, first, yak hair is twisted into coarse yarn, and then the yarn is plaited. A ring of about ten centimeters diameter is placed on the top of the plait and a palm-size oval-shaped area is in its central part. When driving cattle, a herdsman first places stones or clods on oval-shaped areas, and then fixes the ring on his middle finger. He grasps both slingshots' ends and forcibly swings it, and then suddenly loosens one of the ends. In that case, stones or clods fly towards cattle so as to make them change their directions.

望果节

望果节（藏文：Vong-skor）是藏族人民庆祝农业丰收的节日，于每年秋收前择吉日举行。"望"（藏文：Vong）意为田地，"果"（藏文：skor）为转圈，因此其字面含义是"转田垄"。望果节已有1500多年的历史。届时，身着盛装的男女老幼手持青稞穗，扛着彩旗，毕恭毕敬地抬着系有白色哈达的丰收塔，绕行于田间地头，庆祝丰年吉祥。

Bumper Harvest Festival

As a festival to celebrate agricultural harvest, Bumper Harvest Festival (Tib. Vong-skor)is held on an auspicious day before autumn harvest each year. "Vong" and "skor" in Tibetan respectively mean "fields" and "circling". Therefore, literally, "Vong-skor" indicates "circling around field ridges". This festival has a history of over 1,500 years. In celebrations, people, men and women, old and young, are all dressed up. They hold barley ears, lift up flags, carry in awe pagoda-shaped harvest towers and go around the fields in celebration of the auspicious harvest year.

煨桑仪式

　　煨桑仪式（藏文：bSang）是指一种焚香祭祀的仪式。藏文"桑"本意为清洗、消除、驱除之意。藏族人焚烧松柏枝用焚烟祀天地诸神。每逢藏历年的大年初一，人们会起得很早，第一件要做的事情就是煨桑祭神。人们常以成为煨桑第一人为荣，而后到的人就在已经燃起的煨桑堆上添加松枝、柏枝、糌粑粉等。这种宗教祈愿仪式也是宗教场所不可或缺的形式之一。瓶形泥灶称作"桑康"（藏文：bSang-khung），亦称"香炉"或"神香炉灶"。按照藏族习俗，几乎每家每户都备有桑康，桑康位于精心挑选的最洁净之地，如院子中央或屋顶上等。

bSang Ritual

　　bSang ritual refers to an incense-burning rite. "bSang" in Tibetan means "cleaning, dispelling and driving out". Tibetans burn pine and cypress branches to make smoke in worship of earthly and heavenly deities. On the first day of the Tibetan New Year, people get up very early, and the first thing to do is to burn incenses in worship of deities. People are very proud of being the first person to burn branches. And latecomers put pine and cypress branches, rTsam-pa flour and others onto piles of branches. Such a religious praying ritual is one of the indispensable forms on religious venues. Vase-shaped clay hearth (Tib. bSang-khung) is also known as "incense burner" or "juniper hearth". In light of Tibetan customs, each household has to prepare a vase-shaped clay hearth and places it on a most pure and elaborately selected spot, for example, in the central part of a courtyard or on roofs.

西藏的货币

　　1959 年之前，西藏共有硬币和纸币两种货币。硬币从产生直至消亡都与西藏的重大历史事件紧密相联。每一种硬币都反映出那一时期的政治、经济、军事及近代历史上的许多重大事件，其记录历史的功能大大超过其他货币，其意义也绝不仅限于经济领域。格桑章嘎（藏文：sKal-bzang-tam-ka）币被称作"幸运银币"，面值为白银一钱五分，是原西藏地方政府发行的货币。1913 年～1959 年，西藏地区流通的纸币被称作"藏币"，单位为两和章嘎，面额为五、十、二十五、一百两和五、十、十五、二十五、五十章嘎。

Tibetan Currency

　　Two kinds of currency (coins and paper money) existed in Tibet before 1959. Coin was closely connected with major historical events in Tibet from its emergence to its disappearance. Each coin reflected politics, economy and military affairs as well as lots of major events in modern history. Therefore, as far as its function of recording history is concerned, it greatly exceeds all other currencies, and is by no means confined to its economic function. "sKal-bzang-tam-ka" Coin is also called "Lucky Silver Coin" in denomination value of one *qian* and five *fen*. It was a currency issued by the former local government of Tibet. From 1913 to 1959, paper money circulated in Tibet was called "Tibetan Currency", and its monetary unit includes "*Liang*" and "*Tam-ka*". The former is in denomination value of 5, 10, 25, 100 *Liang* while the latter is in 5, 10, 15, 25, 50 Tam-ka.

响铜

响铜（黎，藏文：Li）是以铜、铅、锡按照一定比例混合炼成的金属。它发出悦耳的声音，可用来制造乐器、法器和其他器物。响铜也是藏传佛教艺术造像的重要材料。响铜可分为紫响铜或红响铜（黎玛尔，藏文：Li-dmar）、白响铜（黎嘎尔，藏文：Li-dkar）和黄铜（黎斯，藏文：Li-ser）。

Bell Metal

Bell metal (Tib. Li) is a kind of cast copper smelted with copper, lead and tin according to a certain proportion. Bell metal can issue a sweet sound, so it can be used to make musical instruments, items and ritual implements. It is a very important material used in Tibetan Buddhist statue-making art. Bell metal can be classified into reddish bell metal or orange reddish bell (Tib. Li-dmar), whitish bell metal (Tib. Li-dkar) and yellowish bell metal (Tib. Li-ser).

凶神会

凶神会亦称"九刹毕集"。传说认为，藏历十一月初六、初七日间的一昼夜是土地神大黑日曜与另外八个凶神共同值日。九位凶神对应九曜指的是九大天体，包括日曜、月曜、火曜、水曜、木曜、金曜、土曜、罗曜和计都。人们迷信地认为，此日诸事不宜，只应闭门家居，以避开凶神。

Gathering of Nine Vices

Gathering of Nine Vices is also known as "Assembly of Nine Wrathful Deities". Tradition has it that the earth god (Great Black Sun Deity) and other eight wrathful deities are on duty round the clock between the sixth and seventh days in the eleventh month on Tibetan calendar. Nine luminaries refer to nine celestial bodies, including Sun, Moon, Mars, Mercury, Jupiter, Venus, Saturn, Rahu and Ketu. People believe superstitiously that that day is always an off-day, and people are expected to stay at home so as to keep away from wrathful deities.

雪顿节

　　雪顿节（藏文：Zho-ston）亦称"藏戏节"或"酸奶节"，是藏族的一个重要节日。雪顿节从每年藏历七月一日开始,节期达 5 ~ 7 天。在藏语中,"雪"是酸奶之意,"顿"是宴的意思。节日期间,藏族群众喝酸奶,观看藏戏演出并参加规模盛大的晒佛仪式。雪顿节的起源有如下说法：格鲁派戒律规定,寺院僧人每年夏季要有三个月的"坐夏"期,以避免在万物复苏时节踩杀生命,直到藏历六月僧人方可出寺下山。百姓为了犒劳僧人,为他们准备酿好的酸奶,并开始郊游和野宴。

Yogurt Festival

Yogurt Festival (Tib. Zho-ston) is an important Tibetan festival. It starts on the first day of the seventh month on Tibetan calendar and lasts for five to seven days. In Tibetan, "Zho" means "yogurt" while "ston" refers to "banqueting". During this period, Tibetan masses drink yogurt, watch Tibetan opera performances and participate in large-scale ceremonies of displaying Buddha. As for its source, a saying goes like this: according to the precepts of dGe-lugs-pa Sect, monks have to spend a three-month summer recess so as to avoid crushing creatures in the period of the recovery of all things. Monks are neither allowed to leave monasteries nor go down hills until the sixth month. Common people prepare brewed yogurt to reward monks and to start their own outings and barbecues.

浴佛节

浴佛节亦称"浴佛诞"，始于东汉，盛行于唐宋，传延至今。据传，释迦牟尼降生时，一手指天，一手指地，口说："天上天下，唯吾独尊"。于是大地震动，九条巨龙吐水为其沐浴。自此，各地佛教徒均以浴佛的方式纪念佛祖的诞辰。每逢此日，僧尼都会供奉香花灯烛，并将铜佛置于水中，进行清理洗浴。届时，普通信众会争舍财钱、放生、求子，祈求佛祖的保佑。

Buddha Bathing Festival

Buddha Bathing Festival, also known as "Buddha's Birth Festival", originated in the Eastern Han Dynasty and prevailed in the Tang and Song Dynasties. It is still popular up to today. Tradition has it that Sakyamuni pointed at the sky and the earth with both his hands after his birth, saying:"Me, myself and I rule the world." As a result, the ground shook and nine giant dragons spat out water to bathe him. From then on, Buddhist adherents from all directions would wash Buddha statues in commemoration of his birthday. On that day, monks and nuns would offer joss sticks, flowers, lamps and candles and place copper Buddha statues into water to wash and clean them. On these occasions, common people would try to be the first to give donations, free captured animals, seek for babies and pray for Buddha's blessings.

元宵供

　　元宵供亦称"十五供"，是藏族人民传统的宗教节日。佛经描述释迦牟尼诞生在藏历正月十五，在这天，各方神灵手捧各种供品向他的塑像顶礼膜拜。每年藏历正月十五，藏族僧俗群众会在拉萨大昭寺释迦牟尼像前摆花添灯，设置供品，以纪念佛祖释迦牟尼的诞辰。当天夜晚，各寺院都会摆设桌架，供奉酥油灯、精美的酥油花及其他各类供品。大批人聚集在八廓街，载歌载舞，彻夜不眠。

Butter-lamp Festival

　　Butter-lamp Festival, also called "Fifteenth Day's Offering", is a Tibetan traditional religious festival. It is described in Buddhist scriptures that Sakyamuni was born on the fifteenth day of the first month on Tibetan calendar. On that day, deities from all directions held various offerings to prostrate themselves in worship in front of his statues. Every year, Tibetan monks and laymen go to Jokhang Temple in Lhasa on that day. They put flowers, add lamp-oil and place offerings in front of his statues in commemoration of his birthday. At night on that day, monks in monasteries lay out tables or stands and put oil lamps, exquisite butter-sculptures and all sorts of offerings on them. At night, a great number of people assemble in Bar-skor Street, singing and dancing joyously and sitting up all night.

藏地歌舞

　　藏族是一个能歌善舞的民族。按舞蹈类型分类，藏族舞蹈大致可分为卓谐（藏文：Bro-gzhas）、果谐（藏文：sGor-gzhas）或锅庄（藏文：sGor-bro）、堆谐（藏文：sTod-gzhas）、谐（藏文：gZhas）四种。卓谐起源于古代祭祀，历史悠久，分为两种，一种是鼓者不舞，只唱吉祥颂歌；另一种是鼓者边唱边舞。果谐是由多人围成圆圈队形围篝火而舞的弦歌舞蹈。堆谐最早流传于雅鲁藏布江两岸，后逐渐盛行于拉萨，是最早的用六弦琴乐器伴奏的舞蹈，后又逐渐演变成在小型乐队伴奏下的男子踢踏舞。谐也称为弦子，由男舞者边领舞边以弦乐二胡或牛角琴伴奏而得名，四川的巴塘弦子声名远扬。热巴舞（藏文：Ral-pa）亦称铃鼓舞，是一种民间歌舞。牦牛舞则是重大节日演出的一种具有浓郁民族风格和鲜明艺术特色的舞蹈。此外，还有供藏族宫廷和上层贵族欣赏的囊玛（藏文：Nang-ma）及全部由男孩演奏的宫廷音乐噶尔（藏文：Gar）。

Songs and Dances in Tibetan-inhabited Regions

　　Tibetans are good at singing and dancing. In terms of dance styles, Tibetan dances can be roughly classified into four types: Bro-gzhas, sGor-gzhas or sGor-bro, sTod-gzhas and gZhas. With a long history, Bro-gzhas originated from ancient sacrificial rites. It is performed in two ways: drummers only sing auspicious songs without dancing; drummers sing while dancing. Many people circle around bonfires, performing sGor-gzhas to the accompaniment of stringed musical instruments. sTod-gzhas originally circulated in the valley of the Yar-klung-gtsang-po River, and then gradually prevailed in Lhasa. As the earliest dance performed to a six-stringed plucked musical instrument accompaniment, Tod-gzhas gradually became a kind of male tap dance accompanied by small-sized bands. gZhas, also known as "Xianzi", is named after its performing form: a man dances while playing a two-stringed bow instrument or an ox-horn bow musical instrument. Ba-thang Xianzi in Sichuan enjoys a widespread reputation. Ral-pa dance, also known as tambourine dance, is a kind of folk singing and dancing. With rich and strong ethnic style and distinct artistic features, Yak dance is performed in important festivals. In addition, Nang-ma was performed for Tibetan court and upper level nobles while court music (Tib. Gar) was performed only by boys.

藏历

藏历以 12 年为一小循环，60 年为一大循环，称作"饶迥"（藏文：Rab-byung）。藏族的传统历法基本上与农历相同。藏历采用干支纪年，以"阴阳"与五行相配代替十干，以十二生肖代替十二支，形成了"阳火虎年""阴木牛年"等。藏文历书可为两类，一类为计算用书，另一类为民用年历。

Tibetan Calendar

Tibetan calendar respectively takes twelve years and sixty years as a small and a large circulation, which is called one sixty-year circle (Tib. Rab-byung). Tibetan traditional calendar is basically identical with lunar calendar. It adopts the Heavenly Stems, and Earthly Branches as its way of numbering the years, in which Yin-yang matches up with Five Elements to substitute the Ten Heavenly Stems, and twelve animals replace Twelve Earthly Branches, for example, Yang fire-tiger year or Yin wood-ox year, etc. Tibetan almanacs can be classified into two categories, one for calculation and the other for civil use.

藏历年

　　藏历年是藏族人民最隆重的传统节日。从藏历十二月开始，人们就开始准备吃、穿、玩的东西。每家每户都要准备一个五谷斗（切玛，藏文：Phye-mar）和彩色酥油花塑的羊头，预祝新的一年风调雨顺。除夕前两天，家家要进行大扫除，换上崭新的卡垫或年画。二十九日晚饭之前，要在灶房正中墙上用干面粉画上八宝图案和卍字符。晚饭时，一家人围坐在一起，吃年夜饭、喝腊九粥（古突，藏文：dGu-thug）。腊九粥的面团里包有石子、辣椒、羊毛、木炭和硬币，分别代表"心肠硬""刀子嘴""心肠软""黑心肠"和"发大财"。吃到的人要即刻吐出，这往往会引起哄堂大笑，增添了节日的气氛。大年初一，人们要顺次祝长辈"扎西德勒"。从初二开始，亲戚好友要相互拜年，新年活动会持续三至五天。

Tibetan New Year

　　Tibetan New Year is the grandest traditional festival celebrated by Tibetans. It usually starts in the twelfth month on Tibetan calendar. People begin to prepare food, clothes and other things for it. Each household prepares a container with a mixture of rTsam-pa and other grains as well as a colored sheep's head sculpted with butter and rTsam-pa flour to congratulate beforehand a good weather for crops in the coming year. Two days before the eve, many households usually do a thorough cleaning and change brand new cushions or New Year paintings. Before the supper on the twenty-ninth day, people draw Eight Auspicious Symbols and symbols of 卍 with dry wheat flour on kitchens' central walls. During supper time, all family members sit together and eat dGu-thug dough porridge. Cobbles, peppers, wool, corals and coins are put into dough, which respectively represent "hard mind", "sharp tongue", "soft mind", "evil mind" and "big fortune". And those who eat them immediately spit them out, which will set the whole room with laughter and add festival atmosphere. On the first day of the New Year, people say "Good luck to you" to the elderly in succession. From the second day on, relatives and friends pay New Year calls. The celebrations continue for three to five days.

藏文书法

藏文书法是藏族文化艺术的一个重要组成部分。藏文文体可分为"有头字"和"无头字"两大类。"有头字"和"无头字"都是根据字体的不同形式而得名。"有头字"相当于楷书，一般用于印刷、行文和雕刻等。"无头字"相当于行书，主要用于手写。据《布顿佛教史》记载，吞弥桑布扎（藏文：Thon-mi-sam-bho-ṭa）仿兰扎体创制了藏文印刷体，仿乌尔都字创建了书写体。在藏文中，用来表示每段文字开头的形如象鼻的符号被称作云头符。

Tibetan Calligraphy

Tibetan calligraphy is an essential component of Tibetan culture and art. It can be classified into Tibetan regular script and Tibetan cursive script. Both of them are named after their handwriting forms. Tibetan regular script is equal to formal script, mainly used in printing, writing and carving while Tibetan cursive script is equal to running script, mainly used in handwriting. It is recorded in *Bu-ston's History of Buddhism* that Thon-mi-sam-bho-ṭa imitated Lhanda script and Urdu script to create Tibetan printing and handwriting forms. In Tibetan scripts, elephant trunk-like letters, called "cloud signs", are used to indicate the beginning of each paragraph.

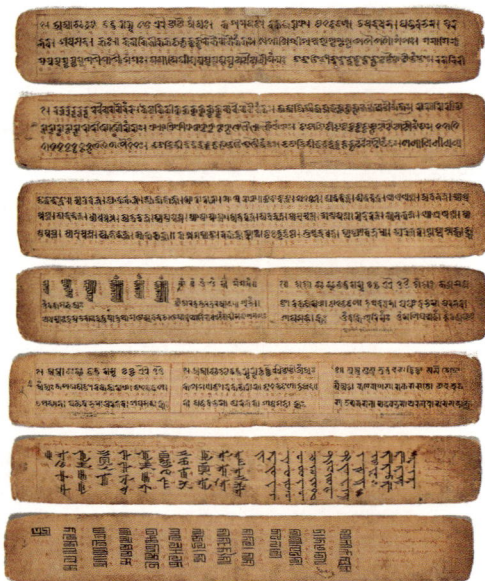

□ 清代藏文书法字帖
Tibetan Calligraphy Copybook in Qing Dynasty

藏戏与藏戏面具

　　藏戏（藏文：A-ce-lha-mo）产生于 8 世纪。噶举派著名僧人汤东杰布被尊奉为藏戏的祖师。17 世纪，它被五世达赖喇嘛从宗教跳神仪式中分离出来，专门表演经过艺术加工的民间故事和佛经故事。其中影响广远、颇具代表性的八大剧目是：《文成公主》《朗萨姑娘》《卓瓦桑姆》《赤美更登》《顿月顿珠》《诺桑王子》《苏吉尼玛》和《白玛文巴》。按照最先出场的男演员所戴面具的颜色，藏戏可分为白面具和蓝面具藏戏两种。与宗教面具相比，藏戏面具造型具有浓郁的世俗倾向和民间色彩。不同色彩象征着不同的角色特征。如深红色象征国王，淡红色代表大臣，黄色象征活佛，蓝色代表反面人物，而半黑半白象征两面派。较为常见的是带有神秘微笑笑容的蓝黑色大面具，其前额饰有金色日月，两颊有黄色短须，鼻子上挂着贝壳和珠串。相传，这是汤东杰布的形象。

Tibetan Operas and Tibetan Opera Masks

　　Tibetan opera (Tib. A-ce-lha-mo) came into being in the eighth century. Thang-stong-rgyal-po, a well-known monk of bKav-brgyud-pa Sect, was revered as its forefather. In the seventeenth century, it was separated from religious dances by the Fifth Dalai Lama. In that case, it especially gave performance of folktales and Buddhist stories after artistic modification. The far-reaching and most representative eight major Tibetan operas are *Princess Wencheng*, *Bu-mo-snang-gsal*, *vGro-ba-bzang-mo*, *Dri-med-kun-ldan*, *Don-yod-don-grub*, *Prince Nor-bzang*, *gZugs-gyi-nyi-ma* and *Pad-ma-vod-vbar*. In terms of colors on masks worn by performers on the first stage, Tibetan operas can be divided into "White-masked" and "Blue-masked". Compared with religious masks, Tibetan opera masks are secular-leaning with strong folk tastes. Different colors represent different roles' characteristics. For example, dark red, pale red, yellow and blue respectively represent kings, ministers, Rin-po-ches and negative figures. And half-black and half-white color implies double-dealers. Blue-black mask with a mysterious smile is very common. It has a gold sun-moon decoration on its forehead, yellow short beard on its checks as well as shells and strings of beads on its nose. It is told that this is Thang-stong-rgyal-po.

□ 藏戏面具
Tibetan Opera Mask

藏香

　　藏香使用青藏高原特有的纯天然、无污染的30余种藏草药制成。不仅可用于佛事活动，还具有杀菌、驱浊、预防感冒和其他传染性疾病及促进睡眠之功效。尼木（藏文：sNye-mo）藏香指的是西藏尼木县生产的藏香，它以制作历史悠久、工序繁杂和工艺严格而著称，因此该地生产的藏香被誉为"西藏第一圣香"。

Tibetan Joss Sticks

　　Tibetan Joss Sticks are made of over thirty kinds of pure natural and non-polluted Tibetan herbs from Qinghai-Tibet Plateau. They are not only used in religious rites, but also have the efficacy of sterilizing, driving pollution, protecting against the cold, preventing other infectious diseases and promoting sleep. sNye-mo Tibetan Joss Sticks refer to those made in sNye-mo County of Tibet. sNye-mo Tibetan Joss Sticks is famous for its long history of manufacturing, multifarious processes and very strict craftsmanship. Therefore, Tibetan Joss Sticks made in sNye-mo are honored as "Tibet's Top Holy Joss Sticks".

藏语

　　藏语是藏族使用的主要语言，属于汉藏语系藏缅语族，我国主要使用人群分布在西藏自治区、青海，以及四川甘孜藏族自治州、四川阿坝藏族羌族自治州、甘肃甘南藏族自治州和云南迪庆藏族自治州。藏语方言很多，主要有卫藏方言（拉萨话）、康巴方言（德格话、昌都话）和安多方言。随着藏学研究的国际化，出现了藏文－拉丁文转写系统。该系统是指将藏文字母转换成拉丁文，从而使藏文罗马化的一套文字转写系统。目前通用的是威利转写方案。

Tibetan Language

　　As a major language used by Tibetans, Tibetan language belongs to Tibetan-Burma branch of the Sino-Tibetan language family. It is distributed in China's Tibet Autonomous Region, Qinghai, Sichuan Gantse Tibetan Autonomous Prefecture, Aba Tibetan and Qiang Autonomous Prefecture, Gansu Gannan Tibetan Autonomous Prefecture and Yunnan bDe-chen Tibetan Autonomous Prefecture. There are many dialects in Tibetan language, mainly including dBus-gtsang dialect (Lhasa dialect), Khams dialect (bDe-dge and Chab-mdo dialects) and A-mdo dialect. The internationalization of Tibetan studies resulted in the formation of the Tibetan-Latin transcription system. Such a system is a script-transcription system used to make Tibetan Romanized so as to transfer Tibetan letters to Latin scripts. Today, Wylie transcription system is in common use.

藏语吉祥话

与其他语言一样，藏语中也有一些人们耳熟能详的吉祥话，在祷神时的常用语"拉加啰"（藏文：Lha-rgyal-lo），其意为愿善神得胜或神的旨意胜利了。在通过金瓶掣签确定活佛的场合里，众僧也会高呼"拉加啰"，表示庆贺。"扎西德勒"（藏文：bKra-shis-bde-legs）是人们经常使用的互致问候的吉祥话，意为吉祥如意，也用于多种场合。

Tibetan Auspicious Words

Like in other languages, there are a number of very familiar auspicious words in Tibetan language. "Lha-rgyal-lo" is often used in worship of deities. It means "Glory to the Gods!" or "Victory to the Gods' Wills!" On occasions when Rin-po-ches are confirmed through the method of drawing lots from a gold urn, numerous monks also shout loudly "Lha-rgyal-lo" to express their congratulations. As an auspicious word, "bKra-shis-bde-legs" has a meaning of "Good luck to you". It is frequently used for people to say hello to each other and also used on many occasions.

藏纸

　　藏纸产生于7世纪中叶，是西藏特有的文化产品。文成公主入藏带来了造纸术，其后，在当地没有中原造纸所使用的竹、稻、渔网等原料的情况下，藏汉两族工匠经过多年摸索，生产出工艺独特的藏纸。他们采用十分独特的瑞香狼毒草的根部纤维作为藏纸原料。这种纤维很长，质地坚韧，具有不易虫蛀、遇水不化烂、耐折、耐拉、耐磨的特点。布达拉宫、大昭寺、萨迦寺等处珍藏的大部分经典都是印在藏纸上的。

Tibetan Paper

　　As a unique cultural product, Tibetan paper was made in the mid-seventh century. Princess Wencheng brought with her paper-making techniques when she entered Tibet. Afterwards, though Tibet had no such raw materials as bamboo, rice straws and fishing nets (materials for paper-making in the Central Plains), Tibetan and Han craftsmen explored paper-making techniques for several years and created something unique. They adopted very unique Re-lcag (root fabric of a special grass) as its raw materials. Such a fabric is very long, tough and tensile. It is neither easy to be damaged by moths nor easy to be mashed in water, and is fold-resistant, pull-resistant and wear-resistant. Most of Buddhist scriptures preserved in Potala Palace, Jo-khang Temple, Sa-skya Monastery and other places were all printed on Tibetan paper.

□ 藏纸
Tibetan Paper

藏族的日常饮食

　　茶（包括甜茶和酥油茶）、青稞酒（藏文：Chang）、糌粑（藏文：rTsam-pa）和风干肉是藏民重要的日常饮食。酥油茶是藏族日常生活中不可缺少的饮料，它是用酥油、砖茶和盐制成。酥油茶热量很高，饮用后可抵御严寒。甜茶也是一种常见的饮料，大小城镇星罗棋布的甜茶馆是藏民对甜茶钟爱有加的佐证。青稞酒是用青稞酿制的酒，是藏族人非常喜爱的传统饮料。糌粑是用青稞粒磨出的面做的，它具有不易变质、营养丰富、携带方便的特点。风干牛肉是藏民在放牧或远行时喜欢携带的肉食。

Tibetan Daily Diet

　　Tea (including sweet tea and butter tea), barley beer (Tib. Chang), barley flour(Tib. rTsam-pa)and dried meat are Tibetan's essential diet. As an indispensable drink in their daily life, butter tea is made of butter, brick tea and salt. Due to its great heat, drinking butter tea enables people to resist cold. Sweet tea is a common drink, and Tibetans have a special liking to it, which can be proved by the scattered sweet teahouses all over cities and towns. Barley beer is a traditional drink extremely favored by Tibetans. rTsam-pa is a kind of flour ground from barley grains, and it is non-perishable, affluent in nutrition and more portable. Dried beef are what Tibetans like to carry in their herding or long journeys.

藏族的丧葬习俗

　　藏族的丧葬方法依个人的经济能力和社会地位不同而异，一般分为天葬、塔藏、火葬、土葬、水葬等。天葬是藏族较为普遍的一种葬俗,亦称"鸟葬",而专门从事天葬的人被称作天葬师。藏传佛教信众认为，天葬寄托着一种上"天堂"的愿望。在举行天葬仪式的过程中,要点燃桑烟招引称作"神鸟"的秃鹫争相啄食拌以糌粑的骨肉团，如若食尽，示意吉祥，说明死者没有罪孽，灵魂已安然升天。如若未尽，要将剩余部分捡起焚化，同时念经超度。天葬仪式一般在清晨举行,未经许可切勿前去观看。火葬是高尚的丧葬仪式,德高望重的活佛、喇嘛圆寂焚尸后，将其骨头灰烬捡起带到高山之巅顺风播撒或者撒入大江大河之中，随流水漂走，或用其骨灰和泥制成"擦擦"供奉在宗教场所。塔藏亦称"木乃伊葬"，是级别最高的一种丧葬方法，分为两种。一种是大活佛圆寂后，尸体用盐水、藏红花及其他特殊药物抹擦处理，进行整容修饰置于塔内。另一种是大活佛圆寂后，将其骨灰与经书、佛像、法器、金银财宝一起置于金质或银质灵塔内。土葬大部分用于麻风、炭疽、天花等传染病人及强盗、杀人犯和被刀砍死者。水葬用于乞丐及鳏寡孤独者。

Tibetan Burial Customs

　　Tibetan burial ways are different in terms of personal economic ability and social status. Usually, they include celestial burial, pagoda burial, cremation, burial in the ground, water burial and so on. As a common burial, celestial burial is also known as "bird burial", and those who conduct celestial burial are called corpse cutters. Tibetan Buddhist adherents believe that celestial burial is loaded with a hope of "going to heaven". In the process of celestial burial, people burn joss sticks and use the smoke to call vultures. These so called "divine birds" will vie to eat bones and flesh balls mixed with barely flour. If balls are eaten up, it not only symbolizes auspiciousness, but also implies that the dead has no sin, and his soul has safely gone to heaven. If not, people have to pick up remaining parts and burn them, and in the meanwhile, they have to chant Buddhist scriptures so as to redeem the dead. Usually, celestial burials are held in the early morning, and nobody is allowed to watch without permission. Cremation is viewed as a noble burial. Bodies of Rin-po-ches or Lamas are cremated after their deaths, and then, their bones and ashes are carried to mountaintops and thrown about with winds or thrown into rivers. Or, their ashes mixed with clay are made into Tsha-tshas enshrined in religious sites. Pagoda burial, also known as "Mommy Burial", is the highest level. There are two ways: if a grand Rin-po-ches passes away, his body is smeared with salt water, saffron and other special medicine and then decorated. After that, it is inserted into a pagoda. Another way is after his death, a grand Rin-po-che's bone ash, together with Buddhist scriptures, Buddha statues, ritual implements, gold, silver and other jewels are inserted into a gold or silver stupa. Burial in the ground is used for leprosy, anthrax and smallpox patients or other contagious patients as well as murderers, robbers and those who have been killed by a knife. Water burial is often used for beggars, widowers, widows or other loners.

藏族服饰

藏族服饰具有鲜明的地域特色和民族风格，与青藏高原的自然环境、气候条件及生产生活方式关系极为密切，也反映出藏民族独具特色的审美意识和审美情趣。藏族服饰色泽艳丽，式样繁多，装饰性极强，地域差异悬殊。常见的服饰有皮帽、金丝花帽、翘尖彩靴，还有各种丰富多彩的饰物，如腰饰、耳饰、胸饰、辫桥、珠冠（巴珠，藏文：sPa-phrug）等，包括金、银、铜、珠宝等饰物。"嘎乌"是藏族人主要的胸饰之一。藏族妇女腰间围的彩色围裙（邦典，藏文：Pang-gdan）色彩斑斓，极具特色，分有长、短、梯形等式样。缝在藏靴后跟花边上的红色三角花是藏靴独特的装饰物。

☐ 高筒靴
Knee-Length Boots

Tibetan Costume and Adornments

With distinct regional features and ethnic styles, Tibetan costume and adornments are not only closely related to natural environment, climate conditions as well as productive and living ways on the Qinghai-Tibet Plateau, but also reflect the unique

☐ 皮毛冬帽
Fur Hat

aesthetics of the Tibetan people. Tibetan costume and adornments have bright colors and many styles; they are decorative and varied in different regions, including fur hats, hats with gold thread patterns, rainbow-braided boots with toe ends pointing upwards and plenty of rich and colorful adornments, such as waist decorations, eardrops, breastplates, hairpins, jeweled tiaras (Tib. sPa-phrug) and gold, silver, copper decorations and jewels. Amulet boxes (Tib. Gavu) are one of the major breastplates. Color aprons (Tib. Pang-gdan) worn by Tibetan women around their waists are multicolored and very unique, and can be classified into long, short and ladder-shaped ones. Red triangular patches on heels of Tibetan boots are very unique decorations.

藏族谜语

谜语主要指暗射事物或文字等的隐语，供人猜测，有时也指一些蕴含奥秘的事物。藏族谜语最初起源于藏族口头文学，是表现藏族人民幽默、智慧和机智的一种口头艺术，也是藏族人民集体智慧创造的文化产物。藏族谜语多以与日常生活息息相关的事物作为谜材，因此，藏族谜语具有朴实无华的特质，极具民族特色。如谜面：百人一根肠是什么？谜底：佛珠。又如谜面：一个珊瑚盒，内装九枚金币。谜底：红辣椒。

Tibetan Riddles

Riddles mainly refer to enigmas to hint at something or words for people to guess, and sometimes, to some mysterious things. Originating from Tibetan oral literature, Tibetan riddles are not only a verbal art reflecting Tibetan people's humor, wisdom and wit, but also a cultural product created by way of collective intelligence of Tibetans. Tibetan riddles often select some things related to daily life as part of mystery materials. Therefore, Tibetan riddles are always unadorned and simple, and have distinctive local features. Here are two examples. Riddle: One hundred people own one intestine. Answer: A string of rosary. Riddle: A coral container has nine gold coins inside. Answer: A red pepper.

藏族面具

　　藏族面具（巴，藏文：vBag）可分为羌姆、悬挂、藏戏、歌舞、折嘎演唱（藏文：vBras-dkar，过去是一种"乞讨"性的表演）、傩仪等6种面具，可用动物毛皮、布、纸板、绸缎等制成。2015年，与象雄文化有关的重要文物信息公布于众，其中就有关于黄金面具的资料。黄金面具四厘米见方，用压成薄片的金片制成，正面由红、黑、白三色绘出面部，黑色双目大睁，鼻翼、牙齿、胡须轮廓清晰，周边均匀分布八个小圆孔。黄金面具缝缀在较软质地的材料上。某些学者认为黄金面具除了美化逝者，还有一定的宗教功能。它与西藏原始宗教苯教祭祀习俗密切相关，是研究古代象雄的生动资料。

Tibetan Masks

　　Tibetan masks, called "vBag" in Tibetan, can be divided into vCham mask, hanging mask, Tibetan opera mask, talking-singing mask, vBras-dkar begging performance mask as well as dancing mask. Usually, they are made of fur, cloth, cardboards and silk fabric, etc. In 2015, some important cultural relics information related to Zhang-gzhung culture was made public, including the information about a gold mask. The four centimeters square mask was made of a piece of pressed thin gold slice. Its front face is outlined in red, black and white. It has black open-wide eyes and very clear outlines of nose wings, teeth and beard. Eight small holes are distributed evenly around the mask. It is sewn on a piece of soft fabric. Some scholars believe that it can be seen as support of the face. Therefore, in addition to beautifying the dead, it has certain religious functions. It has not only close relations to primitive Bonpo sacrifice rites, but also serves as a vivid material for studies of ancient Zhang-gzhung.

藏族民歌与谚语

　　西藏民歌的产生、发展与它在藏族人民生产和生活中的特殊地位密不可分。藏族人民喜爱唱歌，在劳动、饮酒和过节时都离不开歌声，甚至在行走途中都是歌不离口。他们用歌声表达自己的情感、希冀和追求。如"羊卓雍湖畔的姑娘啊！请剪下白云般的羊毛，给我这孤独的旅行人，做一件最美丽的衣衫"。藏族谚语言简意赅、形象生动，是藏族人民经验和智慧的结晶。如"没有盐巴茶难喝，没有智慧事难成"和"磨盘重了糌粑细，父母严了儿女贤"等。

Tibetan Folk Songs and Proverbs

　　Tibetan folk songs are closely related to their unique position in Tibetans' production and life. Very fond of singing songs, Tibetans sing songs during laboring, drinking or celebrating festivals, even walking on the way. Their songs express their emotions, hopes and pursuits. For example, "The girl on the bank of Yar-vbrog-g·yu-mtsho Lake, please cut off sheep's wool as white as clouds, make a beautiful clothes for me, a lonely wanderer!" Tibetan proverbs, concise and comprehensive, vivid and lively, are a crystal of Tibetans' experience and wisdom. For example, "Tea tastes bad without salt, things are none without wisdom." "Heavy millstones enables grind barley flour well, strict parents can cultivate virtuous children."

藏族人取名

藏族人早期是有姓的，但现今大多数藏族人是无姓的。藏族人的名一般由四个字组成，如扎西多吉、次仁旺姆等。佛教的盛行也影响到孩子的取名上。作为一种藏俗，婴儿降生后要在其舌面上加盖舌面印，所用阴文刻制的图章要用藏红花末充填。而后父母将婴儿抱到活佛那里，在举行简单的取名仪式后，活佛要念经，对孩子说些吉利话，然后才会取名。因此，许多人的名字都带有浓烈的宗教色彩，如多吉（金刚）、群培（兴教）、拉姆（仙女）等。还有用自然界的物体、出生日或星期为孩子起名的，如达瓦（月亮）、次松（初三）巴桑（星期五）。还有些人会在名字前加上自己庄园的名字以示尊贵的身份，如帕拉·扎西旺久，表明该人是帕拉庄园的后人。

Tibetan's Naming

In the early periods, Tibetans had family names, but nowadays, most of them have no surnames. Their names usually consist of four words, such as bKra-shis-rdo-rje, Tshe-ring-dbang-mo, etc. The prevalence of Buddhism also affected people when they name their children. As a Tibetan custom, a letter was sealed on a baby's tongue after his birth, and the seal cut in intaglio is filled with saffron powders. And parents would carry their babies to a Rin-po-che. After a brief naming ceremony, Rin-po-che would chant Buddhist scriptures and say some auspicious words before giving a name to a child. As a result, many names enjoy strong religious overtones, such as rDo-rje (Vajra), Chos-vphel (prospering religions), Lha-mo (fairy), etc. Also, some are named after objects in nature as well as their birthdays or birthweeks, for example, Zla-ba (moon), Tshe-gsum (lunar third day) or Pa-sangs (Friday) and so on. Some people would like to add their own manors' titles to their names in an attempt to imply their honorable status, for example, the name of vPhags-lha bKra-shis-dbang-phyug means that this person is a descendant of the vPhag-lha Manor.

藏族日常生活用品

　　酥油桶、僧帽壶、木碗和藏毯都是藏族日常的生活用品。酥油桶用来打制酥油，一般由木板箍制或圆木挖空而成，内有长柄木制活塞，塞上有孔。僧帽壶因其造型宛如僧帽而得名。木碗是藏族群众随身携带的物品，随时用来喝茶、搅拌糌粑（藏文：rTsam-pa）。木碗一般由桦木或杂木节雕制而成，其质地结实、花纹细腻，十分美观。称作"卡垫"（藏文：Kha-gdan）的藏毯亦是藏族人最常使用的坐垫或卧垫，也是寺院、宫廷和民居最重要的陈设。西藏江孜是卡垫重要的产地，其生产的藏毯以色泽艳丽、图案精美、编制技艺高超而著称。

Tibetan Articles for Daily Use

　　Butter churns, monk-hat shaped bottles, wooden bowls and Tibetan carpets are all Tibetan articles for daily use. Butter churns used to churn butter are usually made of laths with hoops or hollow round logs. The piston inside has a long handle and a hole. Monk-hat shaped bottle is named after its shape. Tibetans carry around wooden bowls with them and use them in drinking tea or churning barley flour (Tib. rTsam-pa) at any time. Usually they are cut out of birch or hardwood warts, sturdy, refined and elegant. Tibetan carpets, also called "Kha-gdan", are not only cushions or bed cushions, but also major furnishings in monasteries, courts or civilian residences. Gyangtse is an important manufacturing location, and carpets produced there are famous for their splendid colors, exquisite patterns and excellent knitting skills.

藏族乐器

种类繁多的藏族民族乐器分为打击乐器、吹管乐器、弹拨乐器和弓弦乐器四类。打击乐器有大鼓、热巴鼓（藏文：Ral-pa）、锣、镲、串铃柄鼓、铙钹等。吹管乐器有笛、低音大号（筒钦，藏文：Dung-chen）、海螺、口弦、唢呐（甲林，藏文：rGya-gling）等。弹拨乐器有扬琴、弦子或胡琴（比旺，藏文：Pi-wang）和六弦琴。弓弦乐器有牛角胡琴（扎年，藏文：sGra-snyan）和弦胡等。

Tibetan Musical Instruments

A wide variety of Tibetan musical instruments can be divided into percussion instruments, wind instruments, plucked instruments and bowed string instruments. Percussion instruments include big drums, Ral-pa drums, gongs, small cymbals, stringed bells, handled drums and big cymbals, etc. Wind instruments include flutes, double bass tubas (Tib. Dung-chen), conch, jew's harps and Sonas (Tib. rGya-gling). Plucked instruments include dulcimers, three- or two-stringed plucked instruments (Tib.Pi-wang) and Tibetan guitars. Bowed string instruments include ox-horned two-stringed bowed instruments (Tib.sGra-snyan) and four-stringed bowed instruments, etc.

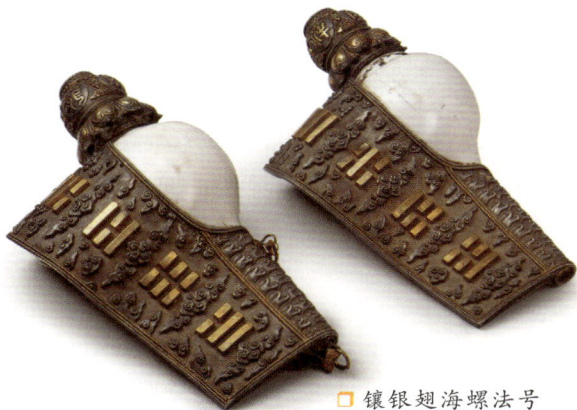

□ 镶银翅海螺法号
Conch Horns Inlaid
with Silver

藏族宗教乐器

藏族宗教乐器独具特色，种类繁多。在宗教仪式中，它们是不可或缺、无法替代的。常见的宗教乐器有低音法号（筒钦，藏文：Dung-chen）、唢呐（甲林，藏文：rGya-gling）、苏那、海螺号（筒嘎，藏文：Dung-dkar）、神鼓和鼗鼓（达玛茹，藏文：Da-ma-ru）、胫骨号筒（康令，藏文：rKang-gling）和金刚杵铃（藏文：rDo-rje-dril-bu）。低音法号长约3米，音色低沉而庄重威严，由红铜、铜、黄铜和银制成。唢呐与法号是藏佛传教乐器中两个主要的旋律性乐器。苏那形似唢呐，是阿里地区民间歌舞的伴奏乐器。在佛教寺院迎请仪仗、法会和仪式活动中常用海螺号。镶翅海螺号的螺身镶有铜片或银片制成翅状装饰物。西藏原始宗教苯教的神鼓带有手柄，常与钹和其他寺院乐器一起使用，既是各种宗教仪轨和羌姆表演的伴奏乐器，也是藏戏的主要伴奏乐器。铙钹的形状基本相近，但音量有别。胫骨号筒是用人腿胫骨制成的，是西藏密宗佛教的乐器之一，主要用于密宗仪式、羌姆表演和"断行"（藏文：gChod）修法中。金刚杵铃的上半部是金刚杵，下半部是铃，分别代表智慧和方便，主要用于佛教密宗修习和诵经等活动。

Tibetan Religious Musical Instruments

There're a wide variety of Tibetan religious musical instruments, which are not only unique, but also indispensable and irreplaceable in religious rites.

Common religious musical instruments include bass ritual trumpets (Tib. Dung-chen), Suona (Tib. rGya-gling), Suna, conch-shell trumpets (Tib. Dung-dkar), divine drums, rattle drums (Tib. Da-ma-ru), shin-bone trumpets (Tib. rKang-gling), Vajra clubs and bells (Tib. rDo-rje-dril-bu). About three-meter-long bass ritual trumpet is made of pure copper, copper, brass and silver with a long and solemn sound. Suonas and ritual trumpets are two major melodious instruments among Tibetan Buddhist musical instruments. Sunas, similar in form to Suonas, are used as accompaniment instruments in folk singing and dancing performance in mNgav-ris Region. Conch-shell trumpets are mainly used in greeting ceremonies, prayer ceremonies and other rituals in Buddhist monasteries. Bodies of winged conch-shell horns have wing-shaped decorations made of brass or silver slices. Primitive Bonpo handle divine drums are used together with cymbals and other monastic musical instruments as accompaniment musical instruments in various religious rituals and vCham performance. Big and small cymbals are identical in shape, but are different in volume. As one of the Tantric Buddhist musical instruments, shin-bone trumpets are made of human shin bones and mainly used in Tantric Buddhist rites, vCham performance and "gChod" practices. Vajra club (upper) and bell (lower) respectively represent wisdom and method, usually used in Tantric Buddhist practices as well as in chanting Buddhist texts and other activities.

转山与转湖

转山与转湖是藏地盛行的习俗，也是庄严而神圣的宗教仪式。在转神山和圣湖时，人们常会抛撒风马旗，悬挂五彩经幡，在嘛呢堆上置放刻有经文咒语的嘛呢石等。据说朝圣者转圣山或转圣湖一圈，可洗尽一生罪孽。藏传佛教信众有个说法："马年转神山，羊年转圣湖，猴年转森林，平时转一圈，可以洗净一生的罪孽，这是佛祖留给人间的旨意。"在康巴和安多地区的嘛呢长调就是转山或转湖时吟唱的六字真言歌。

嘛呢堆，亦称"神堆"，是用石块或石板垒成的祭坛。石块或石板的规格与形状不一。表面鋻刻有六字真言、慧眼、造像、咒语及各种吉祥图纹的石块或石板统称"嘛呢石"。

Circumambulations around Mountains and Lakes

Circumambulations around mountains and lakes are customs prevalent in Tibetan-inhabited regions as well as solemn and holy religious rites. When doing so, people usually disperse wind-horse flags, suspend five-colored prayer banners and lay out stones engraved with Buddhist texts and incantations on piles of Mani stones. It is said that circumambulating around a mountain or a lake once enables a person to eliminate all sins in his whole life. A Tibetan saying goes like this: "People should go for circumambulations around holy mountains in the year of horse; around holy lakes in the year of sheep and around forests in the year of monkey. At ordinary times, making a circumambulation eliminate all sins in one's whole life. This is Buddha Sakyamuni's decree to this world." In Khams and A-mdo areas, Mani wordless melodies are songs of Six Sacred Words sung by people on their circumambulations around mountains and lakes.

Mani stone piles, also called "divine piles", refer to altars piled up with stones and slabs in different size and shape. The stones and slabs carved with the Six Sacred Words, the Third Eye, statues, incantations and various auspicious patterns are collectively known as "Mani stones".

Part 5

追寻之旅：人文与人物
Society and Humans

阿底峡

　　阿底峡（梵文：Atisa，982～1054）是一位古印度僧人和佛学家，也是藏传佛教噶当派的祖师。他曾著有《密宗道次第解说》及《菩提道灯论》等佛学著作，解答了人们对密宗教法的疑惑并讲说了从学法到成佛的修习内容和阶段。他所撰写的其他著作对藏传佛教教理的发展起了重要的作用。

Atisa

　　Atisa (982~1054) was an ancient Indian monk, a Buddhist scholar and the forefather of bKav-gdams-pa Sect of Tibetan Buddhism. He wrote *Explication on the Path to Enlightenment of Tantric Buddhism*, *Lamp That Shows The Path to Enlightenment* and other Buddhists works, which not only explained people's doubts about Tantric Buddhism, but also told about the contents and the stages from learning Buddhist teachings to getting enlightened. His works played a significant role in the development of Tibetan Buddhist fundamental principles.

□ 阿底峡合金像
Atisa in Alloy

□ 八廓街
Bar-skor Street

八廓街

　　"八廓"（藏文：Bar-skor）意为"转中经"，位于拉萨市旧城区，它是拉萨著名的转经路和商业中心。1300多年前，赞普松赞干布迁都拉萨，并在称作"乳湖"的一片沼泽上修建了大昭寺。自此，拉萨城以大昭寺为中心逐渐向四周扩延。藏传佛教认为，围着大昭寺顺时针转经，表示对供奉在内的释迦牟尼佛像的敬拜并能给人们带来福报。因此，环绕大昭寺的转经路就逐渐形成了一条繁华热闹的街道。

Bar-skor Street

　　"Bar-skor" in Tibetan means "circumambulation around an inner ring-road". Located in the old town of Lhasa City, Bar-skor Street is a celebrated circumambulation road and a business center. Over 1,300 years ago, bTsan-po Srong-btsan-sgam-po had his capital moved to Lhasa and supervised the construction of Jo-khang Temple on a piece of marsh named "Milk Lake". From then on, taking Jo-khang Temple as its center, Lhasa City gradually extended around. It is believed in Tibetan Buddhism that circumambulating clockwise around Jo-khang Temple shows people's worship to statue of Sakyamuni enshrined in it and also brings good merits to them. Therefore, the circumambulation road around Jo-khang Temple gradually became a prosperous and boisterous street.

八思巴与八思巴文

八思巴（1235～1280）是藏传佛教萨迦派第五代祖师。1260 年，元朝开国皇帝忽必烈即位，赐予八思巴"国师"和"大宝法王"称号。1264 年，忽必烈迁都北京。元廷设立总制院统领天下释教和吐蕃境内行政事务，授令八思巴兼掌总制院院务。1269 年，八思巴奉忽必烈之命创制了八思巴文，亦称"蒙古新字"。次年，八思巴为忽必烈灌顶，忽必烈赐予八思巴"帝师"称号并赐玉印。

vPhags-pa and vPhags-pa Script

vPhags-pa (1235~1280) is the fifth forefather of the Sa-skya-pa Sect of Tibetan Buddhism. In 1260, Kublai, the founding emperor of the Yuan Dynasty, ascended the throne and conferred the titles of "State Tutor" and "Great Treasure Prince of Dharma" upon vPhags-pa. In 1264, Kublai moved his capital to Beijing. The Yuan Court set up the General Council to take charge of Buddhist and administrative affairs within the territory of Tibet and ordered vPhags-pa to be concurrently in charge of the affairs of the General Council. In 1269, by order of Kublai, vPhags-pa formulated vPhags-pa script, also known as Mongolian quadratic script. In the following year,

□ 八思巴玉雕像
Jade Statue of vPhags-pa

vPhags-pa conducted baptism for Kublai, who conferred upon vPhags-pa the title of "Imperial Tutor" and bestowed upon him a jade seal.

布达拉宫

　　布达拉宫始建于 7 世纪吐蕃赞普松赞干布时期，距今已有 1300 年的历史。为迎娶唐朝的文成公主，松赞干布迁都拉萨后，在红山之上修建了布达拉宫。据史料记载，红山内外围城三重，一条银铜桥连接着松赞干布和文成公主的宫殿。当吐蕃王朝灭亡时，布达拉宫的大部分毁于战火。1645 年，五世达赖喇嘛为巩固政教合一的甘丹颇章地方政权，由第司·索朗绕登（藏文：bSod-nams-rab-brtan）主持重建了布达拉宫的白宫及宫墙城门角楼等。1690 年，第司·桑结嘉措开始为五世达赖喇嘛修建灵塔，并扩建了红宫。1936 年，十三世达赖喇嘛的灵塔殿建成。自此之后，布达拉宫的规模保持至今。

The Potala Palace

　　With a history of 1,300 years, the Potala Palace was originally built in the seventh century during the reign of Tubo bTsan-po Srong-btsan-sgam-po. In order to marry Princess Wencheng from the Tang Court, Srong-btsan-sgam-po made the Potala Palace built on the top of the Red Hill after he moved the capital to Lhasa. According to some historical records, there used to be three enclosures and a silver-bearing copper bridge which connected Srong-btsan-sgam-po and Princess Wencheng's palaces. A large part of the Potala Palace was destroyed by fire at a time when Tubo Kingdom perished. In 1645, the Fifth Dalai Lama intended to consolidate dGav-ldan-pho-brang Regime (a local regime fused with political and religious affairs), so he ordered sDe-srid bSod-nams-rab-brtan to supervise the reconstruction of its White Palace as well as palace walls, city gates and towers. In 1690, sDe-srid Sangs-rgyas-rgya-mtsho supervised the construction of a reliquary Stupa for the Fifth Dalai Lama and the expansion of the Potala Palace's Red Palace. In 1936, the Thirteenth Dalai Lama's Reliquary Stupa Hall was completed. Since then, the Potala Palace's current size has remained up to now.

布达拉宫印经院

布达拉宫印经院是历史上最大的藏文印经院之一，与德格印经院和那塘印经院齐名。明末清初，由五世达赖喇嘛阿旺·罗桑嘉措（藏文：Ngag-dbang Blo-bzang-rgya-mtsho）创建。1920 年，十三世达赖喇嘛土登嘉措（藏文：Thub-bstan-rgya-mtsho）加以扩建。布达拉宫印经院藏有完整的藏文《大藏经》。

Potala Scripture Printing House

Potala Scripture Printing House is not only one of the largest scripture printing houses in history, but also equally famous with sDe-dge Scripture Printing House and sNar-thang Scripture Printing House. The Fifth Dalai Lama Ngag-dbang Blo-bzang-rgya-mtsho advocated its construction in the late Ming Dynasty and the early Qing Dynasty. In 1920, the Thirteenth Dalai Lama Thub-bstan-rgya-mtsho supervised its expansion. Now, it preserves Tibetan *Tripitaka* of a full version.

□ 长生牌位
Longevity Tablet

布达拉宫中的长生牌位

　　长生牌位为在世人而立，指的是写有恩人姓名、为恩人祈求福寿的木牌。布达拉宫殊胜三界殿（萨松郎杰，藏文：Sa-gsum-rnam-rgyal）中供奉着一个用藏、汉、满、蒙四种文字书写的"当今皇帝万岁万万岁"的牌位，牌位上方供奉着清乾隆皇帝的肖像。

Longevity Tablet in the Potala Palace

Longevity tablets, usually placed for the living, refer to wooden memorial tablets with benefactors' names, which are used to pray for their longevity and wealth. In the Triumph over Three Realms Hall (Tib. Sa-gsum-rnam-rgyal) in the Potala Palace, there stands a longevity tablet with inscriptions of "Long live present-day Emperor, a long, long life to him" in Tibetan, Han, Manchurian and Mongol. A portrait of Qing Emperor Qianlong hangs above it.

财神牵象图

　　财神牵象图亦称"牵象行脚僧"，是藏地寺院大殿等处的墙壁上常绘的吉祥图案之一。画面上，一名行脚僧牵着背驮如意宝的大象，面向里屋行走，含有"招财进宝"之意。但此图必须面对正门，以强调进宝，避免资财外流。

Picture Depicting God of Wealth Leading an Elephant

Picture Depicting God of Wealth Leading an Elephant, also called "Picture Depicting a Wandering Monk Leading an Elephant", is one of the auspicious patterns. It is often painted on walls of halls or other places in monasteries in Tibetan-inhabited regions. In the picture, a wandering monk leads an elephant with a wish-fulfilling gem on its back. He walks towards an inner room, which implies "bringing in wealth and treasures". However, this picture must face the main entrance to stress the inflow of wealth and to avoid the outflow of it.

□ 财神牵象图
Picture Depicting God of Wealth Leading an Elephant

长寿五姐妹峰

　　长寿五姐妹原为西藏民间所信奉的女神。公元8世纪印度莲花生大师入藏后，将其收服，自此成为佛教的护法神。她们的身色、手持器物和坐骑有所不同。神话故事认为，长寿五姐妹降伏了五头毒龙，变成了喜马拉雅山脉的五座山峰。她们分别是祥寿仙女峰、翠颜仙女峰、贞慧仙女峰、冠咏仙女峰和施仁仙女峰，为首的翠颜仙女峰就是世界最高峰珠穆朗玛峰。

Peaks of Five Sisters of Longevity

　　The Five Sisters of Longevity used to be goddesses worshipped in folk beliefs. In the eighth century, Indian master Padmasambhava subdued them after he entered Tibet. After that, they became Buddhist protective deities. They are different in their bodily colors, hand attributes and mounts. According to legends, they subjugated five poisonous dragons, which became five peaks of the Himalayas. They are Peak of Auspicious Longevity Goddess, Peak of Blue Joyful Goddess, Peak of Constant Benevolent Goddess, Peak of Harmonious-voice Goddess and Peak of Reliable Passionate Goddess. As their head, Peak of Blue Joyful Goddess is Jo-mo-glang-ma Peak, the highest one in the world.

传统的西藏绘画流派

传统的西藏绘画流派分为勉唐（藏文：sMan-thang）画派、噶玛噶赤（藏文：Karma-sgar-bris）画派和钦则（藏文：mKhyen-rtse）画派三派。勉唐画派亦称"门赤画派"，主要流行于卫藏地区，它是近代影响最大的绘画流派。该派以蓝绿色为主调，兼用红色，还大量使用金色，这使得画面金光灿灿，富丽堂皇。噶玛噶赤画派亦称"噶赤画派"，形成于 16 世纪下半叶。该画派设色偏重青绿色，背景上的风景多采用写实主义的表现方式。钦则画派形成于 15 世纪中期以后。该派擅长绘制坛城和怒相神，善于使用对比色，其绘画作品的画面装饰性更强。

Traditional Tibetan Painting Schools

sMan-thang, Karma-sgar-bris and mKhyen-rtse Painting Schools are three traditional Tibetan painting schools. sMan-thang Painting School, also known as "sMan-khri Painting School", is not only popular particularly in dBus-gtsang regions, but also of greatest influence in modern times. It takes color of bluish green as its main tone and also uses colors of red and gold, which makes general appearance of pictures glittering, splendid and imposing. In the second half of the sixteenth century, Karma sGar-bris Painting School (also sGar-bris Painting School) came into being. It lays emphasis on color of dark green and favors to express landscapes on backgrounds in a realistic approach. mKhyen-brtse Painting School was formed after the second half of the fifteenth century. It is skilled at painting Mandalas and wrathful deities and proficient in using contrast colors, which makes general appearance of pictures more decorative.

达扎路恭纪功碑

达扎路恭（藏文：sTag-sgra-klu-khong）纪功碑位于西藏拉萨西城。由于布达拉宫脚下的无字碑为"内碑"，因此该碑就被称作"外碑"。它是公元 8 世纪吐蕃赞普赤松德赞（在位期 755～797 年）为吐蕃大臣达扎路恭纪功所立之碑，是现存最早的吐蕃时期的石碑。碑文描述了平定内乱和兴兵攻唐这两个重大事件，是研究赤松德赞时期吐蕃历史及西藏地方政权与唐朝中央政权关系史的重要文物。

Stele with the Records of sTag-sgra-klu-khong's Meritorious Service

Stele with the Records of sTag-sgra-klu-khong's Meritorious Service stands in the western part of Lhasa City. This stele is commonly known as "Outer Tablet", for Wordless Memorial Tablet at the foot of the Potala Palace is named "Interior Tablet". It was erected for Tubo minister sTag-sgra-klu-khong in the eighth century in the reign of Tubo bTsan-po Khri-srong-bde-btsan (reigned from 755 to 797). It is the earliest existing stele of the Tubo period. Its inscriptions describe two major events: pacifying civil strife and sending an army against Tang forces. It is a significant cultural relic for the studies on Tubo history in the reign of Khri-srong-bde-btsan as well as the relations between local regimes of Tibet and the central political power of the Tang Dynasty.

大五明、小五明和色达喇荣五明佛学院

　　大五明指的是五大类学问，是寺院僧人的修学课程，包括工巧明（工艺、绘画、雕刻、建筑、天文、历法）、医方明（医疗学和药物学）、声明（语言、文学、音韵学）、因明（逻辑）和内明（佛学）。小五明指的是五小类学问，包括修辞学、辞藻学、韵律学、戏剧学和星象学。色达喇荣五明佛学院（藏文：gSer-thang-bla-rung-lnga-rig-nang-bstan-slob-gling）创建于 1980 年，坐落在四川甘孜色达县境内。佛学院分长期和短期两种进修方式，亦可授予堪布（藏文：mKhan-po）学位。

Five Major Treaties of Buddhist Doctrine, Five Minor Treatises of Buddhist Doctrine and Ser-thar-bla-rung Buddhist Institute of Five Kinds of Knowledge

Five major treaties of Buddhist doctrine refer to five major fields of knowledge and serve as courses for monks to study, including technology (craft, painting, sculpting, architecture, astronomy and calendar), medicine (medicine science and pharmacology), phonology (languages, literature and phonology), logic and Buddhism. Five minor treatises of Buddhist doctrine refer to five kinds of lesser knowledge, including rhetoric, words and expressions, syntax, drama and astrology. Located within the territory of Ser-thar County in Gantse of Sichuan, Ser-thar-bla-rung Buddhist Institute of Five kinds of Knowledge was built in 1980. It offers both long-term and short-term research studies, and also awards mKhan-po academic degrees.

德格印经院

位于四川德格（藏文：sDe-dge）县的德格印经院（藏文：sDe-dgevi-par-khang）亦称"更庆寺印经院"。它建于1729年，是藏地著名的印经院。德格印经院由藏经库、储纸库、晒经楼和洗版台等建筑组成。其保存的经板多达217000多块，且印制的经书版本精良、印刷技术考究、文本内容丰富。因此，德格印经院不仅是藏传佛教印经中心和藏文典籍的刻印中心之一，也是在历史上与拉萨布达拉宫印经院和那塘印经院齐名的三大藏文印经院之一。

sDe-dge Scripture Printing House

Located in sDe-dge of Sichuan, sDe-dge Scripture Printing House is also known as "dGon-chen Monastery Scripture Printing House". As a famous scripture printing house in Tibetan-inhabited regions, it was built in 1729. It consists of scripture warehouses, paper warehouses, scripture-sunning buildings, woodblock-cleaning courtyards and other buildings. sDe-dge Scripture Printing House now preserves more than 217,000 pieces of woodcut printing blocks, and the scripture versions printed there are fine in quality, exquisite in printing technique and rich in content. Therefore, sDe-dge Scripture Printing House is not only one of the Tibetan Buddhist scripture printing centers and Tibetan classic engraving centers, but also equally famous in history with Potala Scripture Printing House and sNar-thang Scripture Printing House.

第司·桑结嘉措

第司·桑结嘉措（藏文：sDe-srid Sangs-rgyas-rgya-mtsho，1653 ～ 1705）是一位政治家和学者。1679 年，他出任第五任第司（行政长官），掌管西藏地方政务。举世闻名的布达拉宫扩建工程就是在他的任期内于 1693 年完工的。他还是一位学术造诣颇深的著名学者。他对《四部医典》进行了整理、校对、修订和注解，还编著了《五世达赖喇嘛传》《六世达赖喇嘛仓央嘉措传》《黄教史》等 20 多部有关藏族历史、宗教、文化、医学、天文、历算、法律的著作。他在拉萨的药王山上倡建了藏医学院，培养了一大批著名的藏医学者。

sDe-srid Sangs-rgyas-rgya-mtsho

sDe-srid Sangs-rgyas-rgya-mtsho (1653~1705) is a politician and scholar. In 1679, he acted as the Fifth sDe-srid (governor) and took charge of the whole local affairs in Tibet. The expansion program of the world-famous Potala Palace was completed in 1693 during his administration. He is also a well-known scholar with great academic achievements. He not only arranged, proofread, revised and annotated *Four Medical Tantras*, but also compiled *Biography of the Fifth Dalai Lama*, *Biography of the Sixth Dalai Lama Tshangs-dbyangs-rgya-mtsho*, *History of dGe-lugs-pa Sect* and more than twenty books involving history of Tibet, religions, culture, medicine, astronomy, calculation and laws. He advocated the construction of Tibetan Medical College on top of the Medicine King Hill and trained large numbers of famous Tibetan doctors.

伏藏与掘藏师

伏藏（藏文：gTer-ma）指的是苯教和佛教遭受迫害时期，一些被藏匿起来、后又被后世重新挖掘出来的宗教典籍。根据内容，伏藏可分为经文伏藏（藏文：Chos-gter）和圣物伏藏（藏文：rDzas-gter）。圣物伏藏指的是法器、圣贤大德的遗物、唐卡等。著名的伏藏有《玛尼宝训》《五部遗教》等。掘藏师（藏文：gTer-ston）指的是发现和挖掘出伏藏的人。西藏历史上著名的大掘藏师仁增·晋美林巴（藏文：Rin-vdzin vJigs-med-gling-pa）生于 1730 年，28 岁时，他发掘了莲花生大师的教法，被视为掘藏师。

Rediscovered Texts and Treasure-finders

Rediscovered texts (Tib. gTer-ma) refer to classic works which were buried under the ground at a time when Buddhism and Bon religion were persecuted, and then were rediscovered and unearthed by later generations. In terms of their contents, they can be classified into rediscovered texts (Tib. Chos-gter) and rediscovered treasures (Tib. rDzas-gter). *Five Mani Lectures*, *Five Volumes of Biography* and others are well-known rediscovered texts. Rediscovered treasures include ritual implements, saints and great men's remains, Thang-kas and so on. Treasure-finders (Tib. gTer-ston) refer to those who found and unearthed rediscovered texts. Rin-vdzin vJigs-med-gling-pa born in 1730 was a well-known treasure-finder in the history of Tibet. At the age of twenty-eight, he unearthed Padmasambhava's teachings, so he was viewed as a treasure-finder.

噶厦政府

　　噶厦（藏文：bKav-shag）是原西藏地方政府办公机构的总称。因其办公地点在大昭寺一个叫作噶厦的地方而得名。七世达赖喇嘛执政后，在奏请乾隆皇帝批准后，噶厦于1751年正式设立。它由噶伦（藏文：bKav-blon）四人（一僧三俗）主持，共有秘书处和审计处两个主要办事机构。秘书处（译仓，藏文：Yig-tshang）由四名僧官组成，直接由达赖喇嘛或摄政掌管，负责管理所有的寺庙及僧官的调迁和任命并负责代达赖喇嘛或摄政起草文件。审计处（仔康，藏文：rTsis-khang）由四名俗官组成，管理着财政和俗官及贵族的事务。

The Former Local Government of Tibet

　　The local government of Tibet (Tib. bKav-shag) was a general title for offices of the former local government of Tibet. It was named after its office location called bKav-shag in Jo-khang Temple. After the Seventh Dalai Lama was in power, bKav-shag was established in 1751 with the approval of Qing Emperor Qianlong. It was under the jurisdiction of four ministers (Tib. bKav-blon), including one monk and three laymen. It consisted of two offices: secretariat (Tib. Yig-tshang) and audit division (Tib. rTsis-khang). The former was composed of four monk officials under the direct leadership of Dalai Lamas or regents. It was responsible for the administration over all monasteries, the transfer of monk officials and the drafting of documents on behalf of Dalai Lamas or regents. Audit division was made up of four lay officials in charge of finance and affairs related to lay officials and noblemen.

格萨尔与《格萨尔王传》

　　《格萨尔王传》是一部著名的藏族长篇英雄史诗。史诗的主人公格萨尔是一位岭国国王。为了拯救岭国百姓、降伏妖魔，他投胎人间。一般认为，这部史诗是广大藏族群众根据藏族古老的神话、传说、故事、歌谣、谚语等民间文学集体创作的，形成于 11 世纪。依据唱本和灵感，《格萨尔王传》的说唱艺人可分为掘藏艺人和神授艺人。《格萨尔王传》的主要章节包括：《安定三界》《地狱救母》《地狱救妻》《门岭大战》《北地降妖》《诞生之部》《霍岭大战》《姜岭大战》《赛马称王》和《天界卜筮》等。

King Ge-sar and *King Ge-sar*

　　King Ge-sar is a well-known Tibetan heroic epic. Ge-sar, the protagonist in the epic, was a king of gLing Kingdom. In order to save his people and subdue various devil spirits and demons, he was reincarnated on earth. Generally considered, the epic was created in the eleventh century by broad Tibetan masses on the basis of ancient Tibetan myths, legends, stories, ballads, proverbs and other folk literature. According to songbooks and inspirations, bards can be classified into common bards and deity-empowered bards. Its main chapters include *Stabilizing Three Realms, Rescuing His Mother from Hell, Saving His Wife from Hell, A Fierce Battle between Mon and gLing, The Birth of a Hero, A Battle between rDzongs of Hor and gLing, A Battle between rDzongs of Byang and gLing, Winning the Title of King through a Horse Race, Divination in the Fairy Realm*, etc.

和气四瑞图

　　和气四瑞图亦称"四兽和睦图"，是藏民族独特的文化载体。它既是藏族传统吉祥图案之一，也是藏传佛教绘画艺术常用的主题之一。和气四瑞图有几个不同的版本，均取材于《本生经》。佛陀讲述了《本生经》中的寓言故事：大象、猴子、山兔和鹧鸪为所栖大树的年龄争执不休，后鹧鸪把树上果实啄了下来，猴子把果实收捡起来，山兔将它们分发给大家，自此，四个朋友和睦相处，过着欢乐、祥和的日子。和气四瑞图上绘有一头大象，大象背上蹲着一只猴子，猴子肩上扛着一只山兔，山兔头顶上站着一只鹧鸪。在寺庙或家庭中常可看到各类和气四瑞图，甚至还有雕像。

Picture Depicting Harmonious Four Brothers

As a unique Tibetan cultural carrier, Picture Depicting Harmonious Four Brothers, also known as "Allegory of Cooperation", is not only one of the traditional auspicious patterns, but also one of the main themes in Tibetan traditional painting art. It has several versions, all based on *Jatakas*. Buddha once told the fable written in *Jatakas*: an elephant, a monkey, a hare and a partridge endlessly argued over the ages of the tree they roosted. And then, the partridge pecked off all fruits from the tree, the monkey picked them up and the hare distributed the fruits among them. From then on, they lived together in peace, living a joyous and auspicious life. Usually, such a picture is painted with an elephant with a monkey on its back. The monkey carries a hare with a partridge standing on the top of its head. All sorts of Pictures Depicting Harmonious Four Brothers, even sculptures, can be seen in monasteries or houses.

□ 和气四瑞图
Picture Depicting Harmonious Four Brothers

吉祥回环诗

在西藏寺院的壁画上经常可以看到吉祥回环诗。它的表格式图案由许多方块组成。每个方块上写有一个藏文音节，既可横向读，也可斜向读，亦可转圈读，无论采取何种方式来读，它均会表达出吉祥的寓意。这类诗文的写作难度较大，格子愈多写作就愈难。壁画上的吉祥回环诗一般呈方形，有时也可以呈圆形。

Auspicious Revolving Prayers

Auspicious Revolving Prayers are often seen on murals in Tibetan monasteries. Its tabular pattern is composed of many squares. Each square is written with a Tibetan syllable. Viewers can read syllables vertically, diagonally or circularly. Whatever the angle is, they all express auspicious meanings. Writing such a kind of poetry is rather difficult, and the more squares, the more difficult for its writing. Auspicious revolving prayers on murals usually assume a square shape, but sometimes, they also take a circular shape.

拉萨的清真大寺

　　拉萨共有五座清真寺，其中拉萨清真大寺最具代表性，其现存建筑为1959年重建。据藏文史籍记载，清乾隆初年来自甘肃、青海、云南、四川等地的商人中有一部分穆斯林逐渐在拉萨定居。征得西藏地方政府的准允后，他们集体捐资在拉萨创建了这座清真寺。1793年，这座清真寺进行了维修和扩建。该寺占地面积1600多平方米，大门上悬挂着一块横书匾额，上写"西藏拉萨清真大寺"。清真大寺为三进两院，礼拜殿是其主体建筑。礼拜殿左侧建有一座三层正八角形的邦克楼，塔端层顶有一个绿色穹顶。右侧庭院长有古柏和古槐。第二院落的大门上悬有清咸丰二年（1852年）制刻的"至教永垂"的横匾。

Lhasa Grand Mosque

　　In Lhasa, there stand five mosques. Among them, Lhasa Grand Mosque is the most representative. Its extant buildings were re-constructed in 1959. According to Tibetan historical records, traders from Gansu, Qinghai,

□ 拉萨的清真大寺
Lhasa Grand Mosque

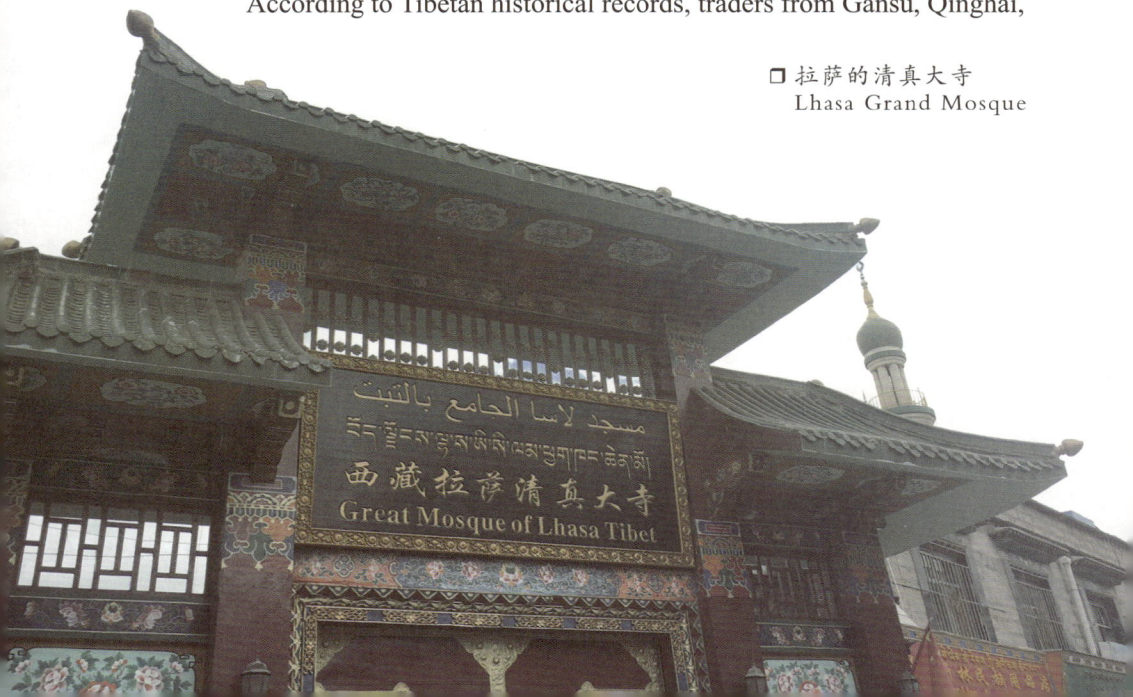

Yunnan, Sichuan and other places came to Lhasa in the early Qing Dynasty, and some Muslims gradually settled down there. With the permission of the local government of Tibet, they collectively donated money for the construction of the Grand Mosque. In 1793, it was maintained and expanded. Now, it occupies an area of over 1,600 square meters. Above the main entrance hangs a horizontal board inscribed with "Qingzhensi" (Mosque). It is composed of two courtyards and a prayer hall is its main building. On its left side is a three-story octagon Minaret with a green dome on its top. Coopers and old Chinese scholar trees are planted in the courtyard on its right side. Above the entrance of the second courtyard hangs a horizontal board with inscriptions of "Teaching Forever" engraved in 1852 (the second year of Qing Emperor Xianfeng's reign).

敦煌石窟

　　敦煌石窟坐落在甘肃河西走廊的西端，是我国和世界珍贵的历史文化遗产。它始建于东晋十六国的前秦时期，经历代的扩建，形成巨大的规模。敦煌石窟南北长 1680 米，高 50 米，洞窟错落有致地分布在鸣沙山多达五层的断崖上。敦煌石窟以精美绝伦的壁画和栩栩如生的塑像闻名遐迩。敦煌石窟共有洞窟 735 个，壁画面积达 4.5 万平方米，泥质彩塑共有 2415 尊。1987 年甘肃敦煌莫高窟被列为世界文化遗产名录，成为世界上现存的规模最大、内容最为丰富的佛教艺术宝库。

Dunhuang Grotto

Dunhuang Grotto is situated in the western end of Hexi Corridor in Gansu Province. As a valuable historical and cultural heritage in China and in the whole world, it was built in the Pre-Qin period (351-394) among sixteen kingdoms of Eastern Jin. After expansions in several dynasties, it formed such a large scale. Dunhuang Grotto is 1, 680 meters long from south to north, and 50 meters high. Caves are distributed well-proportionally on five-layer bluffs of the Singing Sand Mountain. Dunhuang Grotto is famous far and wide for its exquisite murals and lifelike sculptures. It has 735 caves, a mural area forty-five thousand square meters and 2,415 clay painted sculptures. In 1987, Gansu Dunhuang Mogao Grotto was listed on the World Cultural Heritage Directory, becoming the largest extant Buddhist treasure with luxuriant content in the whole world.

莲花生大师

　　莲花生大师（梵文：Padmasambhava）亦称"邬金大师"。他是 8 世纪的一位印度僧人。应吐蕃赞普赤松德赞之邀，他曾入藏传播密法并向藏族弟子传授译经方法。他与另一位印度僧人寂护（梵文：Santaraksita）倡建了桑耶寺，使之成为西藏第一座剃度僧人出家的寺院。桑耶寺的修建对佛教的传播起到了一定的作用。莲花生大师被后世藏传佛教宁玛派尊奉为祖师，是吐蕃王朝"师君三尊"中的轨范师。藏族史诗《格萨尔王传》中称格萨尔是他的化身。每当格萨尔遇到危难时，莲花生大师就会现身为其指引方向，使之逢凶化吉。

Master Padmasambhava

Master Padmasambhava, also known as "Guru Rin-po-che", was an Indian monk in the eighth century. At the invitation of Tubo bTsan-po Khri-srong-lde-btsan, he entered Tibet to preach Tantric Buddhist teachings and impart scripture translation methods to his Tibetan disciples. He and Santaraksita, another Indian monk, advocated the construction of bSam-yas Monastery, the first monastery for people to be tonsured and ordained as monks. The set-up of bSam-yas Monastery played a certain role for the spread of Buddhism. Later on, rNying-ma-pa Sect of Tibetan Buddhism revered him as its forefather. He was also the master among Triad of the Abbot, the Master and the King in the Tubo period. Tibetan epic *King Ge-sar* says that Ge-sar is Padmasambhava's incarnation. Whenever Ge-sar comes up against dangers and difficulties, Padmasambhava will manifest himself, guiding Ge-sar to the correct direction and help him turn calamities into blessings.

六世达赖喇嘛仓央嘉措和《仓央嘉措情歌》

六世达赖喇嘛仓央嘉措（藏文：Tshangs-dbyangs-rgya-mtsho,1683 ～ 1706）是藏传佛教格鲁派大活佛，也是西藏历史上著名的诗人和政治人物。14 岁时，他被认定为五世达赖喇嘛的转世灵童。14 年的乡村生活使他在尘世间的生活经历丰富多彩，也使他对大自然充满了热爱之情。他创作的诗歌数量颇有争议，比较通行的说法为 70 首左右。拉萨藏文木刻版《仓央嘉措

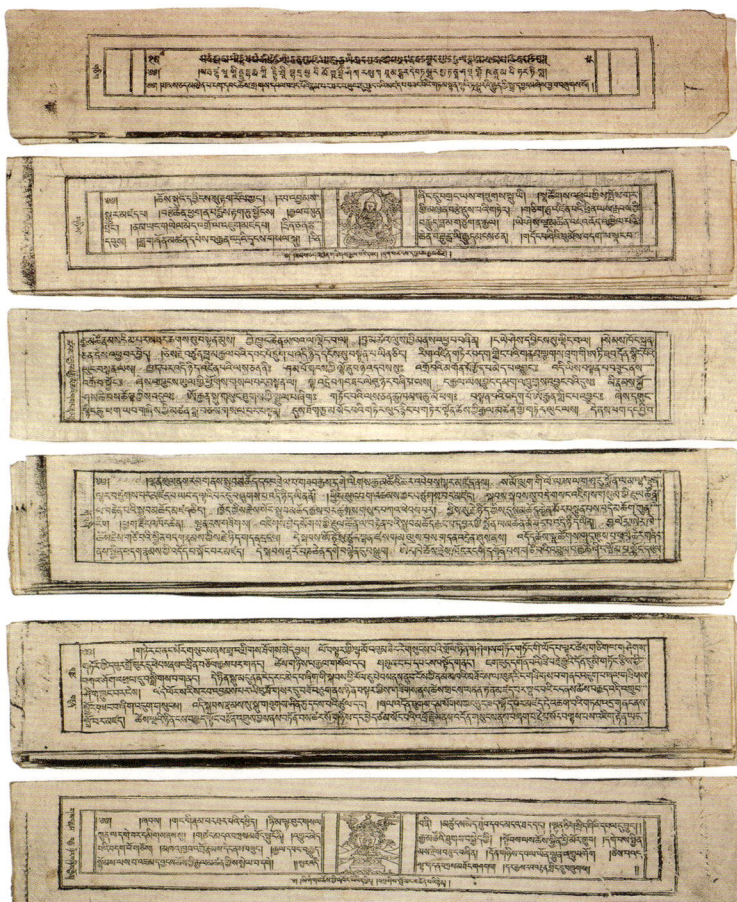

□《仓央嘉措秘传》
Secret Biography by Tshangs-dbyangs-rgya-mtsho

情歌》是他的经典之作。目前流传着多个译本，一些诗歌被谱曲配乐，以歌唱、朗诵甚至舞剧形式广为传播。以《在那东山顶上》和《洁白的仙鹤》为例，第一首被视为情歌，反映出他身为活佛和俗人的双重生活。第二首中有一句是"到理塘转转就回"，这被后人认为是具有暗示性的，因为六世达赖喇嘛的转世灵童恰恰就是在理塘寻访到的。

The Sixth Dalai Lama Tshangs-dbyangs-rgya-mtsho and *Love Songs by Tshangs-dbyangs-rgya-mtsho*

The Sixth Dalai Lama Tshangs-dbyangs-rgya-mtsho (1683~1706) was not only a grand Rin-po-che of the dGe-lugs-pa Sect of Tibetan Buddhism, but also a famous poet and politician in the history of Tibet. At the age of fourteen, he was confirmed as the reincarnated soul boy of the Fifth Dalai Lama. His fourteen years' country life made his secular life experience rich and colorful and enabled him to have deep love for nature. The exact number of poems created by him was very controversial, and the commonly accepted view is that there are about seventy. The woodcut Tibetan version of *Love Songs by Tshangs-dbyangs-rgya-mtsho* in Lhasa is valued as his classic work. Currently, several translated versions are popular, and some poems are set to music or dubbed in background music, and they are also widely circulated in the forms of singing, declaiming, even in dance drama. Taking "From the Top of the Eastern Mountain" and "White Cranes" as examples, the first poem is regarded as a love song, vividly reflecting his double life as a Rin-po-che and a layman. "I'll be back soon from Li-thang", a verse in the second one, is believed as a hint, for his reincarnated soul boy was found just in Li-thang.

龙王潭

　　龙王潭（藏文：rDzong-rgyab-klu-khang）位于布达拉宫后面，是拉萨著名的园林建筑之一。据传，园林中心曾有一片面积较大的潭水。六世达赖喇嘛仓央嘉措从墨竹工卡（藏文：Mal-gro-gung-dkar）迎请了墨竹赛钦（藏文：Mal-gro-gzi-byin）和八条龙，将其供奉在北潭水中，龙王潭由此得名。龙王潭周边的建筑最初形成于六世达赖喇嘛时期，但大水潭形成较早一些，是五世达赖喇嘛时期修建布达拉白宫和第司·桑结嘉措修筑布达拉红宫及经房僧舍时由山脚大量取土形成的。

Dragon-king Pond

Located behind the Potala Palace, Dragon-king Pond (Tib. rDzong-rgyab-klu-khang) is one of the well-known garden architecture in Lhasa. Reportedly, the garden's center used to have a large area of pond water. The Sixth Dalai Lama Tshang-dbyangs-rgya-mtsho once invited Mal-gro Dragon-king (Tib. Mal-gro-gzi-byin) and eight dragons from Mal-gro-gung-dkar and placed them in worship into the water of the northern pond, hence the name Dragon-king Pond. The buildings around it were originally constructed in the reign of the Sixth Dalai Lama, but the big pond came into being a little earlier, when a great amount of earth was taken from the foot of a mountain and used to build Potala Palace's White Palace (the Fifth Dalai Lama's reign), Red Palace (supervised by sDe-srid Sangs-rgyas-rgya-mtsho) as well as halls and monastic premises.

禄东赞

禄东赞（藏文：Blon-stong-btsan，? ~ 667）的全名是噶尔·东赞宇松（藏文：mGar-stong-btsan-yung-zung），简称噶尔东赞（藏文：mGar-stong-btsan）。他是一位吐蕃大相，曾辅佐松赞干布建立吐蕃王朝，协助赞普制定法律及一系列政治制度。640年，他曾赴长安向唐太宗为松赞干布请婚。第二年，他亲赴长安迎请文成公主入吐蕃。珍藏在故宫的唐代著名画家阎立本所绘的《步辇图》描绘的就是唐太宗接见迎婚使者噶尔东赞的历史场面。

Blon-stong-btsan

mGar-stong-btsan-yung-zung (short for mGar-stong-btsan) is the full name of Blon-stong-btsan(?~667). As a major minister of Tubo Kingdom, he once assisted Srong-btsan-sgam-po to establish Tubo Kingdom and make laws and a series of political systems. In 640, he went to Chang'an to ask Tang Emperor Taizong for a marriage on behalf of Srong-btsan-sgam-po. In the following year, he revisited Chang'an to escort Princess Wencheng to enter Tubo. *Chariots Figure* painted by Yan Liben, a well-known painter in the Tang Dynasty, is now preserved in the Palace Museum. It describes the historical scene related to the meeting of Tang Emperor Taizong and Tubo envoy mGar-stong-btsan.

❑ 禄东赞合金像
Blon-stong-
btsan in Alloy

罗布林卡

　　罗布林卡（藏文：Nor-bu-gling-ka）意为宝贝园林。它坐落在西藏拉萨西郊，是西藏最著名的古代建筑之一。据记载，作为达赖喇嘛的夏宫，罗布林卡始建于18世纪中叶，在历代达赖喇嘛和驻藏大臣时期经过几次扩建之后才形成现有的规模。罗布林卡内有大小经堂、辩经台、观戏楼、湖心宫等建筑及大量描绘西藏历史发展的巨幅壁画，是一座融合藏、汉建筑艺术为一体的大型建筑群。逛林卡是颇具藏族特色的一种"郊宴"形式。夏季节日期间，藏族群众身着鲜艳的民族服装全家或邀约亲朋好友到公园游玩。他们在草地上支起白色帐篷，边喝酥油茶和啤酒，边弹琴唱歌跳舞，共享大自然的美景。

Nor-bu-gling-ka

　　Nor-bu-gling-ka means "Jewel Park". Situated in the western suburb of Lhasa, it is one of the most famous ancient buildings in Tibet. It is recorded that it was originally built as Dalai Lama's summer palace in the mid-eighteenth century. Its current size came into being after several expansions in the periods of successive Dalai Lamas and residential officials in Lhasa (Tib. Amban). It is composed of halls of various sizes, Sutra-debating grounds, theatrical stages, mid-lake pavilions and other buildings as well as plenty of extremely huge murals depicting the development of Tibet history. So it is a large-scale building complex integrating Tibetan-Han architectural arts. Going to the park is just like a "barbecue" of Tibetan characteristics. In summer seasons, in their bright-colored ethnic costumes, Tibetans go to parks together with their family members, relatives or friends. They prop up white tents, drink butter tea or beer and sing and dance accompanied by musical instruments, enjoying the beauty of nature.

罗刹女仰卧图

佛教认为罗刹女（梵文：Rakshasi）是个女魔，而西藏恰好位于女魔的身体上。尽管拉萨大昭寺压住了罗刹女的心脏，但还需在其身体的各个部位修建寺院、佛塔和王宫才能令整个雪域得到神佛的庇佑，可以使百姓平安、疆土稳定、佛法兴旺。据藏文史籍的记载，松赞干布和文成公主经过多次商议和缜密推算后，决定在罗刹女身体的头、肩、肘、髋、膝、手、足等部位修造十二座著名寺院，史称"镇魔十二寺"。

Picture Depicting Rakshasi

It is believed in Buddhism that Rakshasi is a she-demon, and Tibet is just lying on her body. Jo-khang Temple was pressed against her heart, but monasteries, pagodas and palaces should be built on different parts of her body. In that case, the entire Snowy Land could get blessings from gods and Buddhas, which would bring safety to common people, stability to the territory and prosperity to Buddhism. According to Tibetan historical books, after several discussions and deliberate calculations, Srong-btsan-sgam-po and Princess Wencheng decided to set up twelve well-known monasteries on her head, shoulders, elbows, hips, knees, hands and feet. In history, they were called "Twelve Suppressing-demon Monasteries".

❑ 罗刹女仰卧图
Picture Depicting Rakshasi

脉轮

　　根据藏医的说法，头、喉、心、脐和私处的交叉脉道形成的辐射圆轮 (梵文 : chakra) 称作脉轮。五大脉轮分指头轮（亦称"大乐轮"）、喉轮（亦称"喜轮"）、心轮（亦称"现象轮"）、脐轮（亦称"生成轮"）和护乐轮（亦称"海底轮"）。不同密宗教派的脉轮略有不同。在许多修习中仅用头轮、喉轮、心轮和脐轮四大脉轮，而在其他修习中亦可观想出七大脉轮。

Channel Wheels

According to Tibetan medicine, radial wheels formed by cross channels at crown, throat, heart, navel and sexual center are called channel wheels. Five major channel wheels (Skt. chakras) include crown chakra (wheel of great bliss), throat chakra (wheel of enjoyment), heart chakra (wheel of phenomena), navel chakra (wheel of emanation) and charkra of preservation of bliss (wheel of sexual center). Channel wheels used by different Tantric Buddhist sects are slightly different. In many Buddhist meditations, only crown, throat, heart and navel chakras are in use, but seven major channel wheels can be visualized in other meditations.

蒙人驭虎图

　　蒙人驭虎图经常绘制在寺院和民宅门廊的墙壁上，寓意祛灾消难、招纳吉祥。图中有一位蒙古勇士，手持铁链牵着一只斑斓猛虎。据称，蒙古勇士、铁链和猛虎分别象征着佛教密宗部三怙主观音菩萨、文殊菩萨和金刚手菩萨。此图是藏传佛教艺术壁画题材和藏族传统吉祥图案之一，有着极为深刻的寓意。人们希望它能带来三怙主的庇护，祛邪引福。民间认为，此图可以防瘟疫，带来吉祥。

Picture Depicting a Mongol Driving a Tiger

　　Picture Depicting a Mongol Driving a Tiger is always painted on walls of monasteries or porches of private residences. The moral of this picture is "eliminating disasters and bringing good luck". In this picture, a Mongol warrior holds an iron chain which ties down a bright-colored tiger. Purportedly, Mongol warrior, iron chain and tiger respectively symbolize Tantric Buddhist Three Masters (Avalokiteshvara, Manjusri and Vajrapani Bodhisattvas). As one of the mural themes in Tibetan Buddhism and one of the traditional Tibetan auspicious patterns, it contains a profound moral. It is hoped that it could bring Three Masters' protection and blessings and to eliminate disasters. This picture is believed to prevent pestilences and bring good luck.

□ 蒙人驭虎图
Picture Depicting a Mongol Driving a Tiger

米拉日巴与《米拉日巴道歌集》

米拉日巴（藏文：Mi-la-ras-pa，1040～1123）是藏传佛教噶举派第二代祖师，著名高僧、宗教宣传家。"道歌"最初属于民歌的范畴，后形成了内容和形式均十分独特的一种诗歌体形式，因此它的形成与藏传佛教教义的宣传密切相关。在成为噶举派宗师后，米拉日巴借鉴藏族民众喜闻乐见的民歌形式，进行诗歌创作，以此宣扬佛教的思想和观点。《米拉日巴道歌集》共分58节，记述了500多首诗歌。据说，有些诗歌是由他本人传唱，被其弟子当场记录下来，有些则是他的弟子或信徒唱的，后流散于民间。尽管该书名为歌集，实际上是诗歌咏唱与散文叙述交织的一部著作。这种创作形式对后世诗歌创作产生了一定的影响，其内容也具有极高的文学欣赏价值。有些学者认为《米拉日巴道歌集》很可能是辑录者桑结嘉措本人创作的。

□ 米拉日巴合金像
Mi-la-ras-pa in Alloy

Mi-la-ras-pa and *Collection of Mi-la-ras-pa's Thousand Songs*

Mi-la-ras-pa (1040~1123) is not only the second forefather of bKav-brgyud-pa Sect of Tibetan Buddhism, but also a well-known eminent monk and a religious advocator. Songs written by great religious masters first fell under the category of folk songs, and then evolved into poetic types of very unique contents and forms. Therefore, its formation had close ties with the dissemination of Tibetan Buddhist doctrines. After he became a great master of bKav-brgyud-pa Sect, Mi-la-ras-pa drew on types of folk songs favored by masses in his poetic creation in an attempt to disseminate Buddhist thoughts and views. *Collection of Mi-la-ras-pa's Thousand Songs* consists of fifty-eight stanzas and featured over 500 poems. As it is said, some poems were sung by Mi-la-ras-pa himself and written down by his disciples on the spot, while others were sung by his disciples or by some Buddhist followers, which were dispersed among people. It enjoys the title of "collection of songs", but actually, it is a book integrating poetry chanting and prose narration. Such a creative style has exerted a certain impact on poetic creation of later generations, and its contents are of great value in literary appreciation. Some scholars believe that *Collection of Mi-la-ras-pa's Thousand Songs* was probably written by its complier Sangs-rgyas-rgya-mtsho himself.

内巡礼道、中巡礼道与外巡礼道

礼道亦称"环形道"。多指环绕坛城或本尊宫殿的道路，共分为内、中、外三层，称作内巡礼道、中巡礼道与外巡礼道。

Inner, Middle and Outer Ring-roads

Ring-roads basically refer to the roads circling around Mandala or Palaces enshrining Yidam statues. They are composed of three layers, known as Inner, Middle and Outer Ring-roads.

热贡艺术

　　热贡（藏文：Reb-gong）指的是现今青海黄南藏族自治州同仁县。热贡艺术始于 15 世纪甚至更久远的年代。热贡艺术是我国藏族佛教艺术的一个重要流派，热贡艺术有着几百年的发展历史。其作品色彩富丽，设色匀净协调，神态刻画逼真，惟妙惟肖，有着独具一格的艺术风格。热贡艺术门类繁多，包括彩绘、泥塑、版画、雕刻、石刻等。它的绘画以壁画为主，以卷轴画为辅，而在金色底上绘制各种金色图案是其独具特色的绘制风格。

Reb-gong Art

　　Reb-gong refers to Tongren County of Huangnan Tibetan Autonomous Prefecture in Qinghai Province. Reb-gong Art originated in the fifteenth century or even earlier. As one of the major Tibetan artistic schools, it has developed for several hundred years. Its gorgeous works are not only painted in uniform colors, but also realistic and vivid in figuring character expressions, which shows its unique artistic style. Because of the diversity of its art, Reb-gong art covers colored drawing, clay sculpting, printmaking, engraving, stonecutting and others. Its paintings take priority to murals over rolled paintings. Drawing various golden patterns on golden backgrounds is its unique painting style.

人体胚胎发育图

人体胚胎发育图是根据《四部医典》绘制的 79 幅唐卡中的一幅。胎儿发育顺序如下：第一周精血相融；第二周开始凝结；第三周胎儿形似凝乳；第四周结成团状；第五周脐带开始形成；第六周命脉形成；第七周眼睛开始形成；第八周头形开始成型；第九周上下躯干开始形成，这一阶段称作鱼期；第十周双肩和双髋开始形成；第十一周感觉器官的九窍开始形成；第十二周五腑开始形成；第十三周六脏开始形成；第十四周双肩和双髋处四肢开始成形；第十五周长出前臂和小腿；第十六周长出手指和脚趾；第十七周连接体内外的脉道开始形成，这一阶段称作龟期，因为胎儿的头和四肢发育起来；第十八周肌肉和脂肪组织开始形成；第十九周韧带和肌腱开始形成；第二十周骨组织和骨髓开始形成；第二十一周外层皮肤发育起来；第二十二周感觉器官的九窍开始张启；第二十三周开始长出头发和指甲；第二十四周脏腑器官发育成熟；第二十五周气开始流动；第二十六周心理回忆清晰；

□ 人体胚胎发育图
Chart of Grouth of the Enbryo and Fetus

第二十七周～第三十周胎儿基本成型；第三十一周～第三十五周胎儿变得更大，这一阶段称作猪期，因为胎儿会消耗不洁之物；第三十六周胎儿产生愤懑之感；第三十七周胎儿极欲翻转；第三十八周胎儿倒转。

Chart of Growth of the Embryo and Fetus

Chart of Growth of the Embryo and Fetus is one of seventy-nine Thang-kas painted on the basis of Four Medical Tantra. The process of fetal development is as follows: first week: semen and blood mingle; second week: clotting begins; third week: the fetus looks like curd; fourth week: it looks rounded; fifth week: umbilical cord starts to form; six week: channel of life forms; seventh week: eyes begin to form; eighth week: shape of the head begins to form; ninth week: shaping of upper and lower parts of the body begins. This is called the period of the fish. Tenth week: shoulders and hips start to form; eleventh week: nine orifices of the sense organs begin to form; twelfth week: five solid viscera start to form; thirteenth week: six hollow viscera start to form; fourteenth week: four limbs from the shoulders and hips begin to take shape; fifteenth week: forearms and lower legs appear; sixteenth week: fingers and toes appear; seventeenth week: channels that connect the outer and inner parts of the body begin to form. This is called the period of the turtle, because the head and limbs of the fetus develop. Eighteenth week: muscle and fat tissue begin to form; nineteenth week: tendons and ligaments begin to form; twentieth week: bone tissue and marrow begin to form; twenty-first week: external skin develops; twenty-second week: nine orifices of the sense organs begin to open; twenty-third week: hair and nails begin to grow; twenty-fourth week: solid and hollow viscera mature; twenty-fifth week: flow of wind originates; twenty-sixth week: mental recollection clarifies; twenty-seventh week: the basic form of the fetus is completed; twenty-eighth to thirtieth weeks: the entire fetus becomes larger; thirty-first to thirty-fifth weeks: this is called the period of the pig, because the fetus consumes unclean substances. Thirty-sixth week: fetus develops a sense of discontent; thirty-seventh week: urge to upside down arises and thirty-eighth week: it turns upside down.

萨班·贡嘎坚赞

萨班·贡嘎坚赞（藏文：Sa-pan Kun-dgav-rgyal-mtshan，1182～1251）是藏传佛教萨迦派第四位祖师，著名宗教活动家、政治家和学者。他学识渊博，通达五明，被佛教界尊称为"萨迦班智达"（藏文：Sa-skya Pandit，意为"萨迦派大学者"）。他亲自撰写的《萨班致蕃人书》对西藏地方纳入元朝的版图发挥了重要的作用。其著述颇多，后世结集为《萨迦全集》，内容涉及宗教、语言、天文、历算、逻辑、医学等，其中颇具深远影响的有《萨迦格言》《智者入门》等。《萨迦格言》不仅在藏地流传甚广，还被译成多种文字，受到国内外学者高度赞赏。

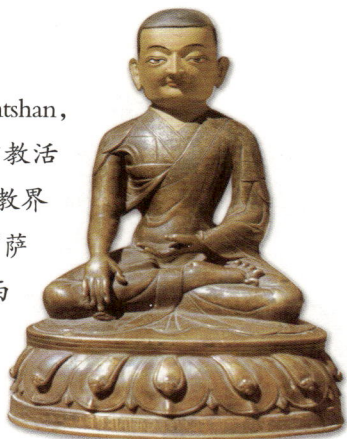

□ 萨班·贡嘎坚赞铜像
Sa-pan Kun-dgav-rgyal-mtshan in Bronze

Sa-pan Kun-dgav-rgyal-mtshan

Sa-pan Kun-dgav-rgyal-mtshan(1182~1251)is not only the fourth forefather of Sa-skya-pa Sect of Tibetan Buddhism, but also a well-known religious activist, politician and scholar. With a thorough insight into Five Kinds of Greater Knowledge, this knowledgeable person was revered as Sa-skya Pandit (a great scholar of Sa-skya-pa Sect). *Letter of Investiture to Zha-lu Monastery by Sa-skya Kun-dgav-rgyal-mtshan* played a significant role in incorporating Tibet into the territory of the Yuan Dynasty. His works are in great numbers, among which, *Completed Works by Sa-skya Kun-dgav-rgyal-mtshan* was edited by later generations. It covers religions, languages, astronomy, calculation, logic, medicine and other fields. Among his works, *Elementary Knowledge for Wise Men* and *Sa-skya Gnomic Verses* are of far-reaching influence. Moreover, *Sa-skya Gnomic Verses* is not only popular in Tibetan-inhabited regions, but also translated into several languages and highly appraised by Chinese and foreign scholars.

《萨迦格言》与《水树格言》

　　《萨迦格言》是由萨迦班智达所著。全书分9章，共有格言诗457首，内容主要包括为政主张、勤学求知和处世哲学等，是藏族文学史上第一部由作家完成的格言诗集。《水树格言》是由贡唐·丹贝准美（藏文：Gung-thang bsTan-pavi-sgron-me）所著。全书包括200多首格言诗，以水和树的各种特性为比喻，阐释藏传佛教的人生哲学和对时政的看法，全部采用四句七言的格律。

Sa-skya Gnomic Verses and Gnomic Verses about Water and Trees

Sa-skya Gnomic Verses written by Sa-skya Pandit contains nine chapters with 457 gnomic verses. Its contents cover political advocates, diligent studies for knowledge and philosophy of life, etc. It is the first collection of gnomic verses compiled by a single writer in the history of Tibetan literature. *Gnomic Verses about Water and Trees* was written

□《萨迦格言》
Sa-skya Gnomic Verses

by Gung-thang bsTan-pavi-sgron-me. With over 200 pieces of gnomic verses, it takes various water and trees' features as analogies to explain Tibetan Buddhist philosophy of life and some political views. All gnomic verses are written in a poetic form of four sentences of seven words.

松赞干布

松赞干布（藏文：Srong-btsan-sgam-po，617～650）是吐蕃第三十三代赞普，也是吐蕃王朝的缔造者。在其在位期间（629～650），他平定吐蕃内乱，确立了吐蕃的政治、军事、经济及法律制度，并从唐朝和天竺引入佛教。为建立和发展与周边部族的睦邻友好关系，他先后迎娶了尼泊尔墀尊（藏文：Khri-btsun）公主和唐朝的文成公主。他对吐蕃政治、经济、文化发展及加强与周边民族的联系做出了重大的贡献。

Srong-btsan-sgam-po

Srong-btsan-sgam-po (617~650) was the thirty-third bTsan-po, also the founder of Tubo Kingdom. During his reign (629~650), he pacified civil strife, regulated Tubo's political, military, economic and legal systems, and introduced Buddhism from the Tang Dynasty and ancient India. In order to establish and develop good-neighborly and friendly relations with surrounding tribal states, he successively married Nepalese Princess Khri-btsun and Tang Princess Wencheng. He made a significant contribution to Tubo's political, economic and cultural development as well as further contacts with neighboring ethnic groups.

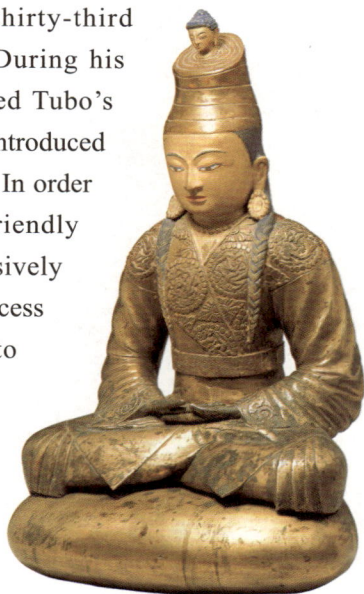

❑ 松赞干布镏金铜像
Srong-btsan-sgam-po
in Gilt Bronze

汤东杰布

汤东杰布（藏文：Thang-stong-rgyal-po，1385 ~ 1464），藏传佛教噶举派僧人，被奉为藏戏和铁器制造的鼻祖。在藏地，他是一位家喻户晓的人物，曾编写过藏戏剧本、修建寺庙、修架铁索桥、研制藏药等。他的众多事迹在藏族民众中代代相传。

Thang-stong-rgyal-po

As a monk of the bKav-brgyud-pa Sect of Tibetan Buddhism, Thang-stong-rgyal-po (1385~1464) is revered as the originator of Tibetan operas and iron manufacturing. He is known to every family in Tibetan-inhabited regions. He wrote screenplays for Tibetan operas, took charge of the construction of monasteries and iron-chained bridges, searched and developed Tibetan medicine and so on. His numerou deeds were passed down from age to age in Tibetan-inhabited regions.

❑ 汤东杰布像
Thang-stong-rgyal-po

唐蕃会盟碑

　　唐蕃会盟碑（藏文：gTsug-lag-khang-rdo-ring）亦称"甥舅和盟碑"。821 年，唐朝和吐蕃派使节先在唐京城长安盟誓，次年又在吐蕃逻些（拉萨）重盟。823 年，盟文以汉藏两种文字镌刻在石碑上，并竖立在拉萨大昭寺门前公主柳下。由于这一事件发生在唐穆宗长庆年间，故该碑亦称"长庆会盟碑"。它是研究唐蕃关系史的重要文物之一，也是千余年汉藏友好关系的一个实证。

Tang-Tubo Peace Pledge Stele

Tang-Tubo Peace Pledge Stele (Tib. gTsug-lag-khang-rdo-ring) is also known as "Uncle-nephew Peace Pledge Stele". In 821, envoys from Tang Court and Tubo Kingdom made a peace pledge in Chang'an, the capital of Tang Dynasty, and in the following year, they made a peace pledge once again in Ra-sa (Lhasa) of Tibet. In 823, the pledge inscriptions were carved in Han-Tibetan scripts on a stele, which was erected under the Princess Willow in front of Jo-khang Temple in Lhasa. This event occurred in Changqing period in Tang Emperor Muzong's reign, so this stele was also called "Changqing Peace Pledge Stele". It is not only a significant cultural relic for the studies on historical relations between Tang Dynasty and Tubo Kingdom, but also a demonstration of Han-Tibetan affiliation with a history of over 1,000 years.

天体日月星辰运行图

　　天体日月星辰运行图是根据《白琉璃》的记载绘制的。该图反映了日、月、水、火、金等星曜在太空中的运行规律。藏族人将土星、木星、水星、火星、金星、地球、月球、地轴上线两端总称为太阳系九大星，将天体分为十二个区域，即十二宫。地面分为十二个部分，即十二地支。根据这些天体星辰的运行规律制定出的藏族历法一直沿用至今。该图中绘有很多星球，一种动物代表一个星球，并按照一定的轨道运行，这反映了藏传佛教及坛城文化的宇宙观。

Chart of the Movement of the Heavenly Body, the Sun, the Moon and Stars

　　The Chart of the Movement of the Heavenly Body, the Sun, the Moon and Stars was drawn on the basis of the records in *White Glaze*. It reflects the movement laws of the sun, the moon, Mercury, Mars, Venus and other stars in the outer space. Tibetans view Saturn, Jupiter, Mercury, Mars, Venus, the globe and two ends of the axis as Nine Stars in the solar system, and divide the heavenly body into twelve sections (Zodiac) and the ground into twelve parts (Twelve Earthly Branches). Tibetan calendar, formulated according to the movement laws of the heavenly body, the sun, the moon and stars, is still in use today. This chart is painted with numerous stars moving in a certain orbit, and each animal represents one star. This reflects the world outlooks of Tibetan Buddhist and Mandala culture.

吞弥桑布扎

吞弥桑布扎（藏文：Thon-mi-sam-bho-ta）是吐蕃赞普松赞干布的大臣。7世纪上半叶，遵松赞干布之命赴印度留学，学习梵文，回国后创制了藏文。据《布顿佛教史》的记载，吞弥桑布扎仿兰扎字创制了藏文印刷体，仿乌尔都字创制了书写体。他一生对藏族语言和文法很有研究，造诣颇深，是一名伟大的语言学家和文学家。他翻译的佛经达21部，其中大部分译典被收入大藏经《甘珠尔》中。

Thon-mi-sam-bho-ṭa

Thon-mi-sam-bho-ṭa was Tubo bTsan-po Srong-btsan-sgam-po's minister. In the first half of the seventh century, by order of Srong-btsan-sgam-po, he went to India to study Sanskrit, and created Tibetan script after his return. It is recorded in *Buston's History of Buddhism* that he copied Lhanda script to create Tibetan print hand and imitated Urdu script to create handwritten form. As a great linguist and writer, he devoted his whole life to Tibetan languages and grammar and gained great attainments. He translated twenty-one volumes of Buddhist scriptures, and most of them were included in *bKav-vgyur of Tripitaka*.

□ 吞弥桑布扎泥塑像
Thon-mi-sam-bho-ṭa
Statue

文成公主

文成公主（？～680）是唐太宗的养女。634年，吐蕃赞普松赞干布派大臣噶尔东赞为请婚使者赴长安请婚。641年，文成公主到达拉萨。此后，她曾主持建造了小昭寺。据传，今大昭寺前的公主柳就是由她亲自所栽。她入藏时携带的释迦牟尼12岁等身佛像现今供奉

□ 文成公主泥塑像
Princess Wencheng Statue

在大昭寺里。据传，她还带去了大批工匠和中原的纺织、造纸等技术，对吐蕃经济、文化的发展和促进唐蕃关系起到了极大的作用，因此，她受到了藏族人民的尊敬和热爱。

Princess Wencheng

Princess Wencheng (? ~680) was an adopted daughter of Tang Emperor Taizong. In 634, Tubo bTsan-po Srong-btsan-sgam-po dispatched his minister mGar-stong-btsan to Chang'an for a marriage. In 641, Princess Wencheng arrived in Lhasa. Afterwards, she advocated the construction of Ra-mo-che Temple. According to legends, she herself planted the Princess Willow in front of Jo-khang Temple. She brought a statue of twelve-year-old Sakyamuni of life size along with her in her entry into Tibet, which is now enshrined in Jo-khang Temple. As it is said, she brought from the Central Plains a large number of craftsmen and weaving, paper-making and other techniques, which not only played a significant role in Tubo's economic and cultural development, but also promoted friendly relations between the Tang Dynasty and Tubo Kingdom. Therefore, she is greatly revered and favored by Tibetan people.

五世达赖喇嘛

五世达赖喇嘛阿旺·罗桑嘉措（藏文：Ngag-dbang Blo-bzang-rgya-mtsho，1617 ~ 1682），藏传佛教格鲁派大活佛，17 世纪西藏地方最著名的佛教领袖、政治家和学者，格鲁派甘丹颇章（藏文：dGav-ldan-pho-brang）政权的缔造者之一。6 岁时，四世班禅喇嘛认定他为四世达赖喇嘛的转世。1652 年，五世达赖喇嘛受清顺治皇帝的邀请，到北京弘法。顺治皇帝颁给他金册、金印，正式册封他为"西天大善自在佛所领天下释教普通瓦赤喇怛喇达赖喇嘛"。1682 年二月二十五日，他在布达拉宫圆寂。在格鲁派掌权、建立西藏地方与清朝中央政府的关系、保持西藏数十年安定和促进西藏社会文化发展等方面，他起到举足轻重的作用，被尊称为"伟大的五世"。

The Fifth Dalai Lama

As a grand Rin-po-che of dGe-lugs-pa Sect of Buddhism, the Fifth Dalai Lama Ngag-dbang Blo-bzang-rgya-mtsho (1617~1682)was not only the most famous Buddhist leading figure, a politician and a scholar of the seventeenth century in Tibet, but also one of the founders of dGav-ldan-pho-brang Regime. At the age of six, he was confirmed as the reincarnation of the Fourth Dalai Lama by the Fourth Panchen Lama. In 1652, he went to Beijing to preach Buddhist doctrines at the invitation of Qing Emperor Shunzhi, who bestowed upon him a gold album and a gold seal, officially conferring upon him the title of "Dalai Lama, Buddha of Great Compassion in the West, Leader of the Buddhist Faith beneath the Sky, Holder of the Vajra". On 25th of the second lunar month of 1682, he passed away in Potala Palace. He played a significant role in helping dGe-lugs-pa Sect wield power, establishing the relations between the local government of Tibet and the Qing Central Government, keeping a steady Tibet for decades and promoting its social and cultural development, so he was revered as "The Great Fifth".

西藏的贵族庄园

　　贵族庄园（豀噶，藏文：sGer-gzhis）指的是旧西藏贵族家族占有并经营的庄园。除了拉萨的罗布林卡外，帕拉（藏文：Pha-lha）庄园和朗色林（藏文：rNam-sras-gling）庄园是保存比较完好的两座贵族庄园。帕拉庄园位于江孜县城西南，始建于 17 世纪 40 年代，是西藏大贵族帕拉家族 37 座庄园中的主庄园，也是目前西藏唯一保存完整的贵族庄园。帕拉庄园占地 5000 多平方米，现存房屋 57 间，主楼高 3 层，内设经堂、会客厅、卧室等。房内雕梁画栋，富丽堂皇。经堂陈设精致考究，还有保存完好的经书和佛龛。朗色林庄园始建于 13 世纪，庄园主楼高达 7 层，会客大厅内矗立着 16 根朱红色立柱，主楼面朝东方，一座经楼毗邻墙体修建，与主楼体相连，浑然一体。其他一些贵族庄园因年久失修已破败不堪，远没有当年的气势与奢华。

Noble Manors in Tibet

　　Noble manors (Tib. sGer-gzhis) refer to manors occupied and managed by noble families in old Tibet. Apart from Nor-bu-gling-ka in Lhasa, Pha-lha Manor and rNam-sras-gling Manor are two well-preserved ones. Built in 1640s and located in the southwest of Gyangtse County, Pha-lha Manor is not only the major one among thirty-seven manors of Pha-lha, the great noble family in Tibet, but also the only perfectly preserved manor. With an area of over 5,000 square meters, it has fifty-seven houses now. A three-story main building, consists of halls, reception halls, bedrooms and so on. The houses with carved beams and painted rafters are richly decorated and magnificent. All the displays in halls are exquisite and elegant, and Buddhist scriptures and shrines are well preserved there. Built in the thirteenth century, rNam-sras-gling Manor has a seven-story main building and a reception hall with sixteen red pillars. Its main building faces east, and its Sutra building was built closely near its wall body. As it is connected with the main building, it looks like part of the main building. Being out of repair for long years, other noble manors are in ruins, falling far short of their momentum and luxury in those days.

□ 面具
Masks

西藏的宗教舞蹈、面具与服饰

　　西藏的宗教舞蹈（羌姆，藏文：vCham）现已成为寺庙古典舞的专有名词。"羌姆"是以身体姿态和步伐节奏并用 12 种伏妖降魔的表情来表现的一种舞蹈，是以舞蹈形式宣传宗教教义，娱神娱人。由于教派不同、寺院规模大小各异，因此羌姆的形式也各有不同。羌姆面具可分为全面具（牛头、狮子头、鹿头等）和半面具（骷髅、死鬼、白老头等）。羌姆中的舞蹈包括"牦牛舞""骷髅舞""仙鹤舞"等，多以"拟兽舞"和"法器舞"混杂而成，内容大多是伏妖降魔、弘扬佛法、因果报应和佛传故事。羌姆最后以焚烧"多玛"（藏文：gTod-ma）结束，满足了寺院和民众祛除邪恶、带来祥和平安的意愿。

Religious Dances in Tibet and Their Masks and Costumes

　　Religious dance (Tib. vCham) has become a proper name for classical dances performed in monasteries. Performers use their bodily postures, pace rhythms and twelve kinds of facial expressions in subduing evil spirits and demons in their dance performance. vCham not only publicizes religious doctrines in a dancing form, but also pleases both deities and ordinary people. Owing to different religious sects and monasteries of different sizes, vCham is performed in different ways. vCham masks can be classified into all-masks (ox-head, lion-head, deer-head masks, etc.) and half-masks (skeleton, evil spirit and white old man masks, etc.) . vCham dances include "Yak Dance", "Skeleton Dance", "Crane Dance" and others, and most of them are integrated with "Animal-imitating Dance" and "Ritual Implement-holding Dance". Their contents cover subduing evil spirits and demons, preaching and expounding Buddhist doctrines, expressing concepts of retribution for good or evil deeds and telling the stories about Sakyamuni's life. vCham performance usually ends with burning ritual cakes (Tib. gTod-ma) so as to satisfy monasteries and ordinary people's desires of eliminating evil spirits and bringing happiness, auspiciousness and safety.

盐井天主教堂

　　盐井天主教堂位于芒康（藏文：sMar-khams）县纳西乡上盐井村，占地面积 6000 多平方米，是西藏唯一的一座天主教堂。它不仅是中西文化交流融合的典范，也是天主教在藏地发展的见证。1865 年天主教传到盐井，后来《圣经》被译成藏文。在盐井，看到藏文版的《圣经》，主尊为耶稣基督的藏式唐卡或带有十字架的念珠及一家信奉两种宗教的现象不足为奇。

Yanjing Catholic Church

　　Yanjing Catholic Church lies in Upper Yanjing Village of Naxi County in sMar-khams. As the only Catholic Church in Tibet, it occupies an area of over 6,000 square meters. It is not only a model of Chinese and Western cultural communication and integration, but also a testimony of the development of Catholicism in Tibet. In 1865, Catholicism was introduced into Yanjing, and later on, the Bible was translated into Tibetan. In Yanjing, it is not at all surprising that there is the Bible of Tibetan edition, Tibetan-style Thang-kas with Jesus Christ as their major images, rosaries with the Cross and different religious adherents in one family.

药师佛与药王宫城唐卡

　　药师佛（门拉，藏文：sMan-bla；梵文：Bhaisajyaguru）是药师佛琉璃光如来的简称。东方琉璃世界是药师佛的净土。据佛经记载，药师佛身色翠蓝，头有顶髻，足现轮圆，右持治病诃子，左持药钵。他曾在药王城内传讲医学，所讲内容后流传到世间，编撰成《四部医典》。药师佛十二大愿中，最令人瞩目的就是"除一切众生病令身心得安乐"。药王宫城唐卡是一幅著名的医学唐卡。唐卡中描绘了善见城（梵文 Sudarshana）、四门方形宫殿、五位隐修圣贤及药师佛对医学的传讲。善见城坐落在盛产各种强效治病药物、四

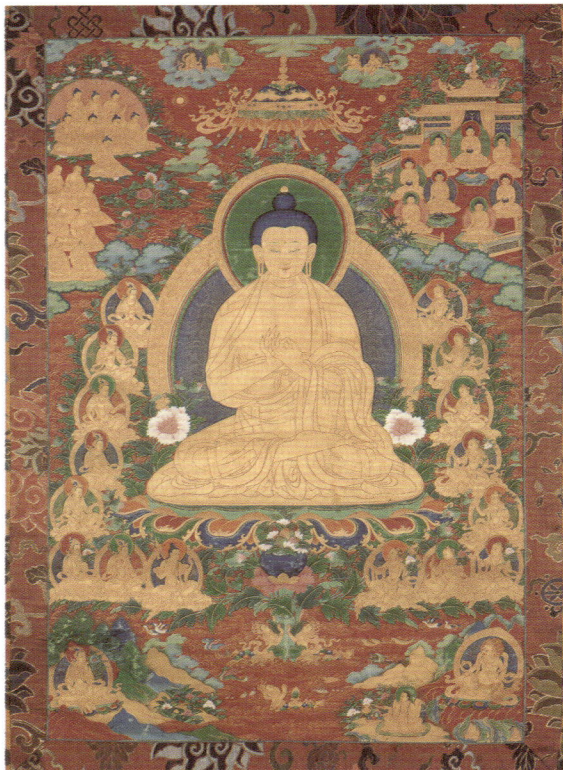

□《药师佛像》唐卡
Medicine Buddha Thang-ka

周环绕丛丛药林的山顶上。在一座四门方形宫殿里，药师佛在向随行的神灵、隐修圣贤、印度教神灵和佛教信徒传讲医学。传讲采用五位隐修圣贤相互问答的方式。

Medicine Buddha and Thang-ka Depicting the Heavenly Abode of Medicine Buddha

Medicine Buddha (Tib. sMan-bla; Skt. Bhaisajyaguru) is a shortened name for Medicine Buddha Bhaisajyaguru. The Eastern Lapis Lazuli World is his pure land. According to Buddhist texts, he has a bright blue body, a topknot on his head and wheel-signs on his feet. He holds a myrobalan fruit and a medicine bowl with his right and left hands. He once explained the science of medicine in the Heavenly Abode of Medicine Buddha. Later on, his explanations were spread to the mortal world, and then compiled into *Four Medical Tantras*. This well-known Thang-ka Depicting the Heavenly Abode of Medicine Buddha describes the City of Sudarshana, a square palace with four gates and five hermit sages as well as the scene where Medicine Buddha explains the science of medicine. The City of Sudarshana is on the summit of a mountain surrounded by forests of medicine, which is endowed with potent and powerful remedies for diseases. In a square palace with four gates, Medicine Buddha explains the science of medicine to the retinues of gods, hermit sages, Hindu divinities and Buddhist adherents. The teaching takes the form of dialogues among five hermit sages.

印章

印章用于文件上以表示鉴定或签署。在西藏历史上有许多重要的印章值得一提。如：白兰王印、敕封班臣额尔德尼之印、灌顶国师之印、西天大善自在佛所领天下释教普通瓦赤喇怛喇达赖喇嘛之印等。

Seals

Seals are used on documents to show identifications or signatures. In the history of Tibet, many important seals are worth mentioning, such as Seal of Prince of Pave-lan, Imperial Seal to Panchen Erdeni, Seal of State Initiation Tutor, Seal of Dalai Lama, Buddha of Great Compassion in the West, Leader of the Buddhist Faith beneath the Sky, Holder of the Vajra, etc.

□ 白兰王印
Seal of Prince of Pave-lan

雍布拉康

雍布拉康（藏文：Yum-bu-bla-sgang），意为"母子宫"，亦称"雍拉寺"，位于西藏山南市乃东区（藏文：sNe-gdong）。相传建于公元前 2 世纪，是西藏历史上的第一座古堡。据传，文成公主进藏后曾居住于此，唐代以后成为佛教寺院。原藏有一些塑像、铜像及大量的文物典籍，因年代久远，现已踪迹全无。

Yum-bu-bla-sgang

Yum-bu-bla-sgang, also known as "Yum-bla Monastery", means "Mother-son Palace". It is situated in sNe-gdong County, Lho-kha of Tibet. The first ancient fortress in the history of Tibet was reported to be built in the second century B.C. According to legends, Princess Wencheng once inhabited there. After the Tang Dynasty, it became a Buddhist monastery. In old days, it kept some sculptures, copper statues and large numbers of cultural relics as well as classic works, but now they are gone because of the old age.

宇妥·云丹贡布与宇妥·萨玛云丹贡布

宇妥·云丹贡布（藏文：g·Yu-thog Yon-tan-mgon-po，729 ~ 853）亦称"老宇妥"。他于八世纪末完成了藏医巨著《四部医典》，为藏医学的最终形成奠定了坚实的基础，因此，他被公认为藏医学体系的鼻祖。宇妥·萨玛云丹贡布（藏文：g·Yu-thog gSar-ma-yon-tan-mgon-po，1126 ~ 1202）是宇妥·云丹贡布的第十三代孙，人称"小宇妥"。他是一位著名的藏医学家，曾撰写了大量的珍贵藏医著作，如《大小八支集要》等。

g·Yu-thog Yon-tan-mgon-po and g·Yu-thog gSar-ma-yon-tan-mgon-po

g·Yu-thog Yon-tan-mgon-po (729~853) is also called "g·Yu-thog Sr.". In the late eighth century, he finished *Four Medical Tantras*, a huge work on Tibetan medicine, which laid a solid foundation for the final formation of Tibetan medicine. Therefore, he is universally acknowledged as initiator of Tibetan medical system. g·Yu-thog gSar-ma-yon-tan-mgon-po, grandson of his thirteenth generation, is known as "g·Yu-thog Jr.". As a well-known Tibetan physician, he wrote large numbers of valuable medical works, such as *Eight Branches of Science of Healing*, etc.

藏传佛教的佛学学位

藏传佛教的佛学学位称作"格西"（藏文：dGe-bshes），意为与佛结缘之人。拉萨三大寺的格西学位分为四等，分别是拉然巴（藏文：Lha-rams-pa）、措然巴（藏文：Tshogs-rams-pa）、林磎赛（藏文：gLing-bsre）和朵然巴（藏文：rDo-rams-pa)。学僧在修习完《般若》《中观》《释量》《戒律》和《俱舍》五部大论后，可以继续深造，然后在法会上以严格的形式进行答辩。法会结束后会揭榜公布结果。

Tibetan Buddhist Doctors of Divinity

Doctor of Divinity in Tibetan Buddhism is known as dGe-bshes. In Tibetan, dGe-bshes means "persons who form ties of affection with Buddhism". In three major monasteries in Lhasa, Doctors of Divinity can be classified into four grades: Lha-rams-pa dGe-bshes, Tshogs-rams-pa dGe-bshes, gLing-bsre dGe-bshes and rDo-rams-pa dGe-bshes. Monk students are able to continue their advanced studies after they finish studying Five Principal Subjects: *Perfection of Wisdom*, *Middle Way School*, *Logic*, *Monastic Discipline and Metaphysics*. And then, they need to defend their dissertations for academic degrees in a very strict form in a prayer ceremony. After the prayer ceremony, a list of successful candidates are openly published.

藏人起源图

猕猴变人的故事在藏族民间广为流传，在古老的经书中也有记载。布达拉宫和罗布林卡的壁画也反映了这一主题。藏人起源图是介绍藏族起源的一幅绘画作品。相传，远古时观音菩萨化身为猕猴，其中一只猕猴入凡世降临泽当（藏文：rTse-thang）。它与一魔女相配，生下六只猕猴，这六只猕猴后又繁衍出数百只，成为藏族人的祖先。人们认为泽当附近贡布（藏文：mGon-po）山上的猕猴洞就是藏族的发源地。

Picture Depicting the Origin of Tibetans

The stories about macaques into men are not only very popular among Tibetans, but also recorded in some ancient Buddhist scriptures. The murals in the Potala Palace and Nor-bu-gling-ka also reflect such a subject. The Picture Depicting the Origin of Tibetans makes an introduction to the origin of Tibetans. Tradition has it that Avalokiteshvara Bodhisattva manifested himself into numerous macaques, and one of them entered this mortal world and descended onto rTse-thang. He had a sexual intercourse with a she-demon, giving birth to six macaques. These six macaques gradually multiplied to several hundreds, who then became Tibetan's ancestors. Therefore, it is believed that the Macaque Cave in Mount mGon-po near rTse-thang is the birthplace of Tibetans.

藏王墓

藏王墓位于西藏山南雅砻（藏文：yar-lung)河谷的琼结（藏文：vPhyongs-rgyas）县境内。藏王墓是7～9世纪吐蕃王朝赞普陵墓群的总称。藏王墓占地约305万平方米，已经发现的墓葬有16座，其中6座可以确定墓主，松赞干布墓和赤德松赞墓是其中最大的墓葬。松赞干布墓的封土层顶部原有一座古庙，内供松赞干布、文成公主、大臣噶尔东赞和吞弥桑布扎等人的塑像及一些佛像。赤德松赞墓前矗立着两通带有石龟碑座的石碑，分别是赤松德赞记功碑和赤德松赞墓铭碑。封土正面有两尊蹲伏式的石狮，是吐蕃时期少量石雕作品的遗存。9世纪中后期发生的奴隶起义，使赞普陵墓均遭捣毁，现有的藏王墓只不过是衣冠冢而已。

Tombs of Tibetan Kings

Located within the territory of vPhyongs-rgyas County in Yar-lung Valley, Lho-kha of Tibet, Tombs of Tibetan Kings are general terms of tombs of Tibetan kings from the seventh century to the ninth century. It occupies an area of about 3.05 million square meters. Sixteen tombs have been found, and among them, six tomb-owners have been identified. Tombs of Srong-btsan-sgam-po and Khri-lde-srong-bstan are the largest ones. There used to be an ancient temple on the top of grave mounds on Srong-btsan-sgam-po's tomb. It once enshrined sculptures of Srong-btsan-sgam-po, Princess Wencheng, mGar-stong-btsan, Thon-mi-sam-bho-ta and others as well as some Buddha statues. Both Stele of the Records of Khri-srong-lde-btsan's Meritorious Service and the Stele with Inscriptions about Khri-lde-srong-btsan have tortoise-shaped bases and stand in front of Khri-srong-lde-bstan's tomb. Two stone lions squat in the frontage of grave ground, which are rare remains of the Tubo period. Several slave uprisings in the middle and later periods of the ninth century destroyed these tombs, so existing tombs are only cenotaphs.

藏玛·藏缘
——藏地行者手卷

藏文

藏文是藏族统一使用的一种书写文字。

藏文创制于 7 世纪，是吐蕃大臣吞弥桑布扎受命于吐蕃赞普松赞干布仿照梵文的一些文字体系而创制的。藏文是由构成藏文音节主体的基字、前加字、上加字、下加字和再后加字及元音组成，但并非所有的藏文都必须有这些要素。加在基字前面的前加字共有 5 个，分别是ག་ད་བ་འ。加在基字上面的上加字共有三个，分别是ར་ལ་ས。加在基字下面的下加字共有 4 个，分别是ཡ་ར་ལ་ས。加在基字后面的后加字共有 10 个，分别是ག་ད་ན་བ་མ་འ་ར་ལ་ས。加在后加字后面的再后加字只有 1 个ས。4 个元音分别是ྀ ེ ོ，它们无法单独使用，必须与辅音拼合。

藏文 – 拉丁文转写表

辅音

ཀ ka	ཁ kha	ག ga	ང nga	ཅ ca	ཆ cha	ཇ ja	ཉ nya
ཏ ta	ཐ tha	ད da	ན na	པ pa	ཕ pha	བ ba	མ ma
ཙ tsa	ཚ tsha	ཛ dza	ཝ wa	ཞ zha	ཟ za	འ va	ཡ ya
ར ra	ལ la	ཤ sha	ས sa	ཧ ha	ཨ a		

元音

ྀ i   ུ u   ེ e   ོ o

Tibetan Script

Tibetan script is a kind of unified writing script used by Tibetans. By order of Tubo bTsan-po Srong-btsan-sgam-po, Minister Thon-mi-sam-bho-ṭa imitated Sanskrit writing system to create it in the seventh century. It is composed of base letter (main part of syllables), prefixed letter, upper letter, lower letter, suffixed letter and re-suffixed letter. However, a single Tibetan word is unnecessary to contain all these elements. Five prefixed letters (ག་ད་བ་མ་འ) are added before base letters; three upper letters (ར་ལ་ས) above base letters; four lower letters (ཡ་ར་ལ་ཝ) beneath base letters; suffixed letters (ག་ང་ད་ན་བ་མ་འ་ར་ལ་ས) after base letters. There is only one re-suffixed letter (ས) after suffixed letters. Four vowels(ི ུ ེ ོ) can not be used alone, instead, they must be used together with consonants.

藏文《大藏经》

　　《大藏经》是藏传佛教经、律、论的汇编，分《甘珠尔》（藏文：bKav-vgyur, 佛语部）和《丹珠尔》（藏文：bsTan-vgyur, 论疏）两部。后世有多个版本，如《永乐版大藏经》（刻印于 1410 年）、《万历版大藏经》（刻印于 1594 ~ 1605 年）、《理塘版大藏经》（刻印于 1609 年）、《北京版大藏经》（刻印于 1683 年）、《明藏》（刻印于明代）、《卓尼版大藏经》（刻印于 1721 ~ 1731 年，1928 年毁于大火）、《德格版大藏经》（刻印于 1729 年）、《那塘版大藏经》（始刻于六世达赖喇嘛时期，《甘珠尔》部分于 1732 年完成，《丹珠尔》于 1742 年完成）、《拉萨版大藏经》（刻印于 1916 ~ 1931 年）、《布达拉版大藏经》（刻印于 1926 ~ 1936 年）、《昌都版大藏经》（刻印于 20 世纪 30 年代）等。

Tibetan *Tripitaka*

Tripitaka is a canonical collection of Buddhist scriptures. It consists of *bKav-vgyur* (Buddhist Treatises) and *bsTan-vgyur* (Commentary Works). Many editions emerged in later generations, including *Tripitaka of Yongle Edition* (engraved and printed in 1410), *Tripitaka of Wanli Edition* (engraved and printed from 1594 to 1605), *Tripitaka of Li-thang Edition* (engraved and printed in 1609), *Tripitaka of Peking Edition* (engraved and printed in 1683), *Ming Tripitaka* (engraved in the Ming Dynasty), *Tripitaka of Co-ne Edition* (engraved and printed from 1721 to 1731, but destroyed by fire in 1928), *Tripitaka of sDe-dge Edition* (engraved and printed in 1729), *Tripitaka of sNar-thang Edition* (engraved and printed in the reign of the Sixth Dalai Lama. bKav-vgyur finished in 1732, and *bsTan-vgyur* finished in 1742), *Tripitaka of Lhasa Edition* (engraved and printed from 1916 to 1931), Tripitaka of Potala Edition (engraved and printed from 1926 to 1936) and *Tripitaka of Chab-mdo Edition* (engraved and printed in 1930s).

藏药

藏药是在广泛吸收融合中医药学、印度草医学和大食（藏文：sTag-gzig）医药学等理论的基础上，通过长期实践形成的十分独特的一种医药体系。藏药距今已有上千年的历史，是我国民族医药宝库中较为完整、颇有影响的医药之一。以珍珠七十九（藏文：Mu-tig-bdun-bcu）和仁青常觉（藏文：Rin-chen-grang-sbyor）为例，珍珠七十九主治中风、瘫痪、半身不遂、脑出血等重症，仁青常觉主治泌尿系统、神经系统和妇科类疾病。据说藏地的冬虫夏草治疗肝腹水的效果十分显著。

Tibetan Medicine

Tibetan medicine formed a set of very unique medical system after it absorbed and integrated various theories of Chinese medicine, Indian Ayurvedic medicine, sTag-gzig medicine and long-term practice. With a history of over 1,000 years, Tibetan medicine is one of the comparatively complete and great influential medicine sciences in China's ethnic medicine treasury. Take Mu-tig-bdun-bcu and Rin-chen-grang-sbyor as examples. Mu-tig-bdun-bcu mainly treats apoplexy, paralysis, hemiplegia, cerebral hemorrhage and other serious diseases. And Rin-chen-grang-sbyor mainly treats urinary and nervous system diseases as well as gynecological diseases. Caterpillar fungus from Tibetan-inhabited regions is said to be very effective in treating liver ascites.

藏医、《四部医典》和《蓝琉璃》

　　藏医学是中国传统医学的一个重要组成部分。它有着自己完整的理论体系和丰富的临床经验。《四部医典》是藏医学中最重要的经典著作，全书共分156章，分为《根本医典》《论述医典》《秘诀医典》和《后续医典》。原作者为藏医医圣宇妥·云丹贡布，成书于8世纪末。今天的版本是经宇妥·云丹贡布的十三代孙宇妥·萨玛云丹贡布修改、补充、诠释而成。《蓝琉璃》为第司·桑结嘉措所著，成书于17世纪中叶。它对《四部医典》从词意到内容进行了全面详细的诠释。

Tibetan Medicine, *Four Medical Tantras* and *Blue Glaze*

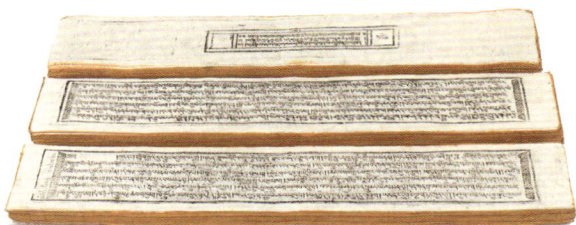

□《四部医典》
Four Medical Tantras

Tibetan medicine is an important component of Chinese traditional medicine. It has its own complete ideological system and rich clinical experience. As the most important classic work, *Four Medical* Tantras contains 156 chapters and consists of *Fundamental Medical Tantra, Commentary Medical Tantra, Secret Medical Tantra* and *Subsequent Medical Tantra*. It was written by g·Yu-thog Yon-tan-dgon-po, a medical sage of Tibetan medicine and completed in the late eighth century. g·Yu-thog gSar-ma-yon-tan-dgon-po (grandson of his thirteenth generation) modified, added and annotated the current version. *Blue Glaze* written by sDe-srid Sangs-rgyas-rgya-mtsho was completed in the mid-seventeenth century. It gives full and detailed explanations to each meaning of vocabularies and contents mentioned in *Four Medical Tantras*.

藏族的文房用品

　　藏族人常用的文房用品包括铜墨水瓶、铁笔、墨盒、粉简（藏文：Sam-ṭa）、文具盒、木尺、书套等。其中，粉简用木片或象牙片制成，代替纸张使用。一般用粉简书写临时的、不必保留的书信。书套是盛放藏式活页经书的长箧。根据藏俗，书套常用竹木薄板制成，外用布、缎包裹，既便于人们开阅又便于行时携带。

Tibetan Stationary Articles

　　Copper ink bottles, iron pens, ink containers, writing boards (Tib. Sam-ṭa), writing cases, wooden rulers, book-holders and others are stationary articles frequently used by Tibetans. Among them, instead of paper, writing boards made of wood or ivory are used when writing down temporary letters unnecessary to save. Book-holders are long boxes used to contain Tibetan-type unbound pages. According to Tibetan customs, book-holders made of thin bamboo slices and wrapped with cloth or satin are convenient for people to read scriptures and to carry in their trips.

□ 木文具盒、木尺和竹笔
Wooden Writing Case, Ruler and Bamboo Pens

造像量度与《佛说造像量度经》

造像通常用泥、石头、木头、金属等材料制成。造像量度是藏传佛教造型艺术造像尺寸的名称。佛造像是有严格的尺寸、比例和规矩的，不能随意而为。古人为了使塑造的佛像更为标准和统一，造像时用手指量度佛像的各个部位。《佛说造像量度经》的作者是舍利弗（梵文：Sariputra）。《佛说造像量度经》原为梵文著作，于1742年被译成汉文。它是藏传佛教造型艺术注疏名著之一，也是一部关于佛教造像度量标准的经典著作。它对传统的造像量度经典进行了系统的注疏，归纳出佛像的量度分类，并对护法造像的量度、仪轨、造型等有关内容做了系统的阐述，提出佛陀造像应符合三十二大相。

Statue Iconography and *Buddha Saying Iconography of Buddhist Statues*

Statues are usually made of clay, stone, wood, metal or other materials. Statue iconography is a title of standard size of Tibetan Buddhist modeling art. Buddha statue-making needs to strictly, not casually, follow the sizes, proportions and standards. In order to make sculpted Buddha statues more standard and unified, the ancients measured each part of Buddha statue with their fingers. *Buddha Saying Iconography of Buddhist Statues* was written by Sariputra. Its original version is in Sanskrit, and in 1742, it was translated into Chinese. It is not only one of the commentary masterpieces on Tibetan Buddhist modeling art, but also a classic work about standards of Buddha statue iconography. It makes systematic comments on traditional statue iconography, sums up the classification of Buddha statues and systematically expounds iconography of protective statues, rituals, modeling and other contents, for example, statue of Buddha Sakyamuni must accord to the Thirty-two Marks.

宗喀巴大师

宗喀巴（藏文：Tsong-kha-pa, 1357 ~ 1419）生于青海宗喀地方（现今青海西宁市湟中区）。他不仅是中世纪伟大的佛教思想家、宗教改革家，也是藏传佛教格鲁派的创始人。他大力推进宗教改革，倡导僧人要严守戒律。他一生积极著书立传，为格鲁派创立了坚实的理论基础。他对中观哲学做了极为独到的解说和阐述，对藏传佛教思想史产生了极大的影响。《菩提道次第广论》是他的主要哲学著作。他还承担了大昭寺的维修工程，首创了拉萨祈愿大法会并倡建了甘丹寺。

Master Tsong-kha-pa

Tsong-kha-pa (1357~1419) was born in Tsong-ka (present-day Huangzhong) of Qinghai Province. He is not only a great Buddhist thinker of the Middle Ages, but also a religious reformer and the founder of dGe-lugs-pa Sect of Tibetan Buddhism. He greatly promoted religious reform and encouraged monks to follow strictly monastic precepts and disciplines. In addition, he actively engaged in writing in his whole life, which laid a solid theoretical foundation for the set-up of the dGe-lugs-pa Sect. He made a very original explanation and exposition of the Middle Way philosophy, which exerted a great impact on the thinking history of Tibetan Buddhism. *The Great Exposition on the Stages of the Path to Enlightenment* is his major work on philosophy. He also took charge of the maintenance project of Jo-khang Temple, initiated the Grand Prayer Ceremony in Lhasa and advocated the construction of dGav-ldan Monastery.

图书在版编目（CIP）数据

藏源·藏缘：藏地行者手卷：汉英对照 ／ 向红笳
著. -- 北京：朝华出版社，2023.6
ISBN 978-7-5054-4852-0

Ⅰ. ①藏… Ⅱ. ①向… Ⅲ. ①旅游指南－西藏－汉、
英 Ⅳ. ①K928.975

中国版本图书馆CIP数据核字(2021)第227745号

藏源·藏缘——藏地行者手卷

作　　者	向红笳	
出　版　人	汪　涛	
责任编辑	张　璇	
执行编辑	范佳铖　沈羿臻	
责任印制	陆竞赢　崔　航	
封面设计	微言视觉｜乔　东	
排版制作	青桃涵文化	

出版发行　朝华出版社

社　　址	北京市西城区百万庄大街 24 号	邮政编码	100037
订购电话	（010）68996522		
传　　真	（010）88415258（发行部）		
联系版权	zhbq@cicg.org.cn		
网　　址	http://zhcb.cipg.org.cn		
印　　刷	北京印刷集团有限责任公司		
经　　销	全国新华书店		
开　　本	710mm×1000mm　1/16	字　　数	400 千字
印　　张	20.25		
版　　次	2023 年 6 月第 1 版　2023 年 6 月第 1 次印刷		
装　　别	平		
书　　号	ISBN 978-7-5054-4852-0		
定　　价	89.00 元		

版权所有　翻印必究·印装有误　负责调换

First Edition in June 2023, First Printing in June 2023

Tibetan Sources & Predestination with Tibet: A Pocket Book for Travelers in Tibetan-inhabited Regions

Written by Xiang Hongjia

Published by Blossom Press

Address: No. 24 Baiwanzhuang Street, Xicheng District, Beijing 100037, China

Telephone: (010) 68996522

Fax: (010) 88415258 (Sales Department)

Printed by Beijing Printing Group Co., Ltd.

ISBN 978-7-5054-4852-0

Printed in the People's Republic of China

ISBN 978-7-5054-4852-0

定价：89.00 元